WINNING AT
MATCHPOINTS

BILL TREBLE

Master Point Press • Toronto, Canada

Master Point Press
214 Merton St. Suite 205
Toronto, Ontario, Canada
M4S 1A6 (647)956-4933
info@masterpointpress.com

Websites: www.masterpointpress.com
               www.teachbridge.com
               www.bridgeblogging.com
               www.ebooksbridge.com

Library and Archives Canada Cataloguing in Publication

Title: Winning at matchpoints / Bill Treble.
Names: Treble, Bill, author.
Identifiers: Canadiana (print) 20200272004 | Canadiana (ebook) 20200272101 | ISBN 9781771400589
   (softcover) | ISBN 9781771405522 (PDF) | ISBN 9781554946990 (HTML)
| ISBN 9781771408981 (Kindle)
Subjects: LCSH: Contract bridge.

Classification: LCC GV1282.3 .T74 2020 | DDC 795.41/5—dc23

Funded by the Government of Canada
Financé par le gouvernement du Canada | Canada

Editor   Ray Lee
Copy editor/interior format   Sally Sparrow
Cover and interior design   Olena S. Sullivan/New Mediatrix

1 2 3 4 5 6 7   23 22 21 20

Foreword

In writing this book, I'm treading in the footsteps of several renowned players. The most well-known of them are Marshall Miles, author of *How to Win at Duplicate Bridge*, and Kit Woolsey. Woolsey, like Miles, has won several major pairs events and divulged the secrets of his success in *Matchpoints*.

Since Woolsey's fine treatise on the subject was first published, however, the typical pairs game has undergone many changes. Rather than Standard, 2/1 has become by far the most popular bidding system. In contrast to the 1980s, when strong notrumps were used by a healthy majority of players, nowadays you'll likely see weak notrumps just as often. Moreover, the tactic of getting in the opponents' faces with preemptive action is growing by leaps and bounds. Several of the chapters in this book focus on those trends.

Partnerships at all levels have more specific agreements nowadays, so they aren't flying by the seat of their pants so much. Even in a local club game, the scores will not be all over the place as they might have been in the past. In higher-level events, there is even greater uniformity in the results.

Once I have covered the various aspects of pairs strategy, I'll conclude with a chapter of problems focusing on matchpoint decisions. All the deals are from real life — club games, sectionals and regionals. They will be presented in groups of three, as you'd encounter them in a nine-round pairs game. Each troika will be presented in a quiz format, followed by the analysis of bidding and play.

I'd like to thank my editor, Ray Lee, my ever-supportive wife Sue, and several players who helped me select the deals for this book — most notably Keith Balcombe of Whitby, Ontario and Andy Anderson of Saskatoon, Saskatchewan. Keith has represented Canada in international competition on several occasions, and they both played in the finals of their respective events at Canada Bridge Week 2019 (Keith in the Canadian National Teams Championships, Andy in the Canadian Mixed Teams Championships).

Bill Treble
January 2020

Contents

1

Is Pairs a Whole Different Ball Game?

During my forty-plus years of playing bridge, I've often heard duplicate pairs spoken of in less than glowing terms. It's random, people say. There's too much luck involved. It rewards unsound bidding and play. Well, it may occasionally seem that way, but it's a very rich and fascinating variation of the game. It's very much a test of skill, mettle and character.

In rubber or social bridge, of course, everything is decided at your table since there are just the four people involved. In a team game, you and your partner will have to match or exceed the results of your opponents at the other table to claim victory. At matchpoints, a large number of pairs hold the same hands you and your partner do. In bridge parlance, your opposition in a pairs game is referred to as 'the field'. You might know some of those players very well, and have a passing acquaintance with others, while there may be a few that you've never run into before. What are they going to do on your cards?

A widely-held assumption is that, in this form of the game, you need to be bolder and take more chances, both in the bidding and the play. In general, that is true in declarer play and competitive bidding, but not so much in defense and constructive bidding.

Let's start by examining some of the decisions that you might be faced with in a typical matchpoint session. We're going to look at eight deals from actual play, identifying the key decision points, and seeing what the results of different actions turned out to be. Declarer play will take center stage on the first two.

$$
\begin{array}{l}
\spadesuit \text{ Q 10 8 5 3} \\
\heartsuit \text{ A Q 7} \\
\diamondsuit \text{ K 3} \\
\clubsuit \text{ K 10 9}
\end{array}
$$

$$
\begin{array}{l}
\spadesuit \text{ A 9} \\
\heartsuit \text{ 8 6 3} \\
\diamondsuit \text{ Q J 7} \\
\clubsuit \text{ A Q J 8 6}
\end{array}
$$

Contract: 3NT by South   Opening Lead: ♡4

The play to the first trick here hinges on the form of the game. Playing match-points, with nine easy tricks and a lot of potential for extra winners in both pointed suits, declarer should aim for multiple overtricks and put in dummy's ♡Q. There is a good chance that it will hold, and now he can work on either diamonds or, more likely, spades.

At teams, a farsighted declarer will think before playing to the first trick and consider how the contract might possibly go down. The worst-case scenario would be if he finessed the queen and lost to the king on his right. Now, if hearts are 5-2 with LHO also having the ◇A, the defense will have five tricks before he has nine. The way to a virtually guaranteed nine tricks is to play low from dummy at Trick 1. RHO will surely win the trick, but he can't do anything damaging and two diamond winners can be established for the game-going tricks.

In a pairs game, though, declarer can't afford the super-safe line of play; he should have loftier ambitions than just nine tricks, as 3NT is a normal contract that will be bid at almost every table. He'll want to score more tricks than other declarers and will duly call for the queen at Trick 1. On this deal, the queen holds, as the entire layout is:

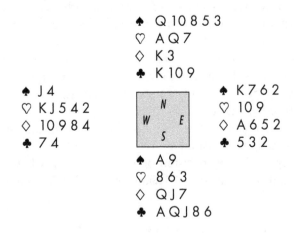

Let's look at the other results from the board to see how the various Souths fared:

North-South	+660	7 pairs
	+630	3 pairs
	+620	2 pairs
	+170	1 pair*

Save for the three pairs that landed in a spade contract, everyone got to 3NT. The declarers who finessed in hearts at Trick 1 ended up with eleven tricks, likely playing on spades at Trick 2 and developing four winners in that suit. While ducking the first trick is the right play at IMPs, it costs big-time here, as South will lose a diamond and spade in addition to a heart, and get a paltry 3 out of 12 matchpoints.

Taking the first-round finesse seemed like a natural thing to do on this deal, but in our next example, the stakes are much higher:

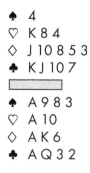

Contract: 3NT by South   Opening lead: ♣6

It was a quick auction with a 2NT opening being raised to game. Since the opponents are playing fourth-best leads and there are lower spades out, West could well have led from a five-card or longer suit.

Compare this to the first deal. This time you already have enough winners on top to make the contract. However, as in the previous example, there is the potential for additional tricks, here in the diamond suit. If the queen is doubleton in either hand, the diamonds will produce five tricks. Alternatively, you can cross to dummy and run the jack, finessing East for the queen.

There are a fascinating number of variables on this deal, of which the play in the diamond suit is only one. For example, you'll notice that 6♣ is a very good contract here. Will there be any pairs in the minor-suit slam? That will depend on what opening bid South chooses. In a club game, you can expect 2NT to be the norm although some players will upgrade the hand

---

* Sometimes in this book I report the scores from when the deal was actually played. Since the examples were gathered from many different events, there are varying numbers of results depending on the exact table count.

because of the wealth of aces and kings and opt for 2♣ followed by 2NT. Responder is not going to try for a marginal slam opposite a 2NT opening, but might look for one after a strong 2♣. Even then, however, he might take the low road.

You, though, are in 3NT. You cannot outscore anyone who bids 6♣ (assuming they make it), so your real opponents are those who like you are in the notrump game. How is that contract going to be played by the other declarers? How many times will they hold off on taking the ♠A? How will they play the diamond suit? One option is to try for overtricks by finessing RHO for the queen, although that risks going down. The other is to plunk down the ace and king, which will result in nine tricks most of the time as the missing honor is unlikely to fall. If it does, though, you'll have five winners in the diamond suit.

Although it goes against the grain of what you've been taught to do in books on play of the hand, you should only duck one round of spades regardless of what you intend to do in diamonds. Whichever line of play you subsequently choose, the diamond finesse or cashing your winners, twelve tricks could be available if the cards lie favorably.

The entire layout is:

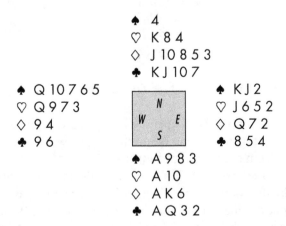

In this case, you'd have twelve tricks by finessing in diamonds, but if you switched East's queen with West's nine, that honor would drop upon the play of the two top honors and you would be losing overtricks by ducking a second round of spades. This is another example of matchpoints requiring a different kind of thinking than teams.

Here is the list of scores for the deal:

North-South	+690	6 pairs
	+660	2 pairs
	+600	3 pairs

You'll notice that all the North-South scores were +690 (the intrepid declarers who crossed to dummy and finessed in diamonds), +600 (those Souths who were unwilling to take the risk and simply cashed out), and +660.

I can tell you what might have happened with the declarers who made eleven tricks instead of twelve. They ducked both the first and second spades, winning the third round. They intended to plunk down the ◇AK and take whatever number of tricks were available. However, the West hand, after following to one high diamond, pitched his second card in the suit on the run of the clubs. This was enough to convince South to change horses in midstream and take the diamond finesse after all.

The opening leader may have felt it was necessary to keep all his spades and at least three hearts. However, it's never a good idea to discard from a worthless holding in a suit dummy has length and strength in, because it gives declarer more information than he is entitled to. Here, it turned a near-top (-600) into an average result.

For our next exhibit, you're faced with a decision on whether to try for slam. As East, you've picked up:

♠ A K 10 9 6 3　♡ 7　◇ A Q 8 2　♣ 8 5

The auction so far has gone:

West	North	East	South
			pass
1♠	2♡	4♡*	pass
4♠	pass	?	

After making the splinter raise of 4♡, should you respect partner's sign-off or make one further attempt?

We can assume that opener has a minimum hand and/or wasted values in our singleton. However, that does not preclude East-West from having a slam. What would West have done with one of these hands?

♠ Q x x x x ♡ J x x ◇ K x ♣ A K x
♠ J x x x x ♡ Q x x ◇ K x ♣ A K x
♠ J x x x x ♡ K 10 x ◇ K J x ♣ A x
♠ Q x x x x ♡ K J x x ◇ K x ♣ A x

With the first example, there's an argument to be made for cuebidding over 4♡, even with the minimum point-count. Opener might not cooperate with the second hand because of the weak spade suit, as partner could easily have just four of his spades rather than wonderful six-card support. Neither of the final two hands would encourage opener to think seriously of bigger things.

It's quite reasonable, therefore, for East to continue with 5◇ and find out if opener is willing to cooperate, as he should with any of the above hands. Also, you don't expect a five-level contract to be in any jeopardy.

Over a 5◇ cuebid, opener actually bids 5♡, at which point responder can't go any further than 5♠ without a club control. Opener passes, and they've nicely investigated for slam and stopped at the brink, as the entire deal is:

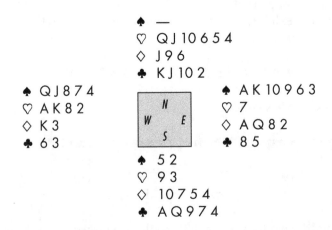

North, however, has been paying attention to the bidding and knows by now why the other side hasn't taken the plunge. He leads a club against 5♠ and they cash the first two tricks, after which declarer has the rest.

If the contract had been 4♠, North might have just led a top heart, even with partner not having doubled East's 4♡. A minor-suit lead could be more productive, but it's tough to know which one and a club might easily be giving away a trick.

Once again, let's look at the various scores for the deal:

East-West	+980	2 pairs
	+510	2 pairs
	+480	4 pairs
	+450	3 pairs
	–50	1 pair

All the 450s were East-West pairs who stopped in 5♠ on the auction described above. I'm sure that a few Easts just blasted into slam, making twice on a heart lead and going down the other time. At the other tables, 4♠ was the final spot and the ♡Q would have been the lead. Now declarer had twelve tricks and at a couple of tables made all thirteen when South carelessly threw a diamond away.

In discussing the deal afterwards, one East said that once West didn't cuebid over 4♡, he really couldn't have the ◇K and the ♣AK as well. He did realize there could still be a play for slam, but took the pessimistic view and passed 4♠. It's a close decision, and this is reflected in the scores, as six pairs quit in 4♠ and six others went higher.

It may seem unfair that if you bid the hand accurately to 5♠ you get a poor result, but it's fairly typical of matchpoints in a way. In this case, the slow approach carried a price because the defense learned where East-West lacked a control, and led that suit. By contrast, it's quite likely that with the three pairs that bid slam, East just asked for keycards and only one of the Norths decided to put a club on the table.

The next problem features a choice of strain for opener, as he is in the West chair and holds these cards:

♠ Q J 8 5   ♡ K J   ◇ A J 6 3   ♣ A 9 2

The auction thus far has gone:

West	North	East	South
1NT	pass	2◇*	pass
2♡	pass	3◇	pass
?			

Over a 1NT opening, a transfer followed by a new suit creates a game force in the vast majority of partnerships. That is all we know at this point. Responder has two suits and could either be interested in slam or merely looking for the best game. He is almost certain to have shortness in one of the black suits.

If opener were to bid some number of hearts, partner would expect at least three of them. West's immediate decision, then, is whether to bid 3NT or support partner's diamonds. He can do the latter either by raising to 4◊ or showing the first-round club control with 4♣.

West's hand has some useful cards if slam is what responder has in mind. The heart honors are excellent, the diamond support is good, and he also has the ♣A. However, the ♠QJ are probably not going to be all that relevant.

As for 3NT, that contract will depend on which black suit East is short in. If it's spades, West has enough strength there to cope with that lead. However, if East's shortness is in clubs, notrump may not be a picnic if the defenders lead that suit.

Some players holding these cards supported diamonds and then passed when responder bid 4♡, effectively denying a spade control. At teams, that would be the ideal contract as the combined hands are:

♠ QJ85		♠ 64
♡ KJ		♡ AQ1074
◊ AJ63		◊ Q9874
♣ A92		♣ J

Here, 3NT may go down on a club lead if the diamond suit isn't friendly, and the same goes for a 5◊ contract. However, 4♡ is essentially cold no matter where the ◊K is, since it's almost certain that the only losers are two spades and a diamond.

Unfortunately, virtue was not rewarded in this case as the entire deal was:

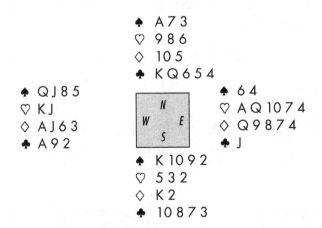

Since the diamonds were 2-2 with the king onside, the same eleven tricks were available in both hearts and notrump. Looking at the results after the session was even more frustrating:

East-West	+490	4 pairs
	+460	3 pairs
	+450	2 pairs
	+400	1 pair
	+200	1 pair
	–50	1 pair

One could expect to lose out to the 460s that some of the 3NT bidders scored, but four of them raked in *twelve* tricks! That was because the North hand not unreasonably led a small club against 3NT rather than a top honor, and was chagrined to see the lonely jack come down on table. Eleven tricks in hearts isn't a total zero, as one pair missed game, another got to 5♢ and yet a third went minus. Still, there's not a lot of company in 4♡ and +450 is a below-average result.

You can't always predict what the rest of the field is going to bid, but your thinking here should go along these lines. Most pairs are going to avoid a minor-suit game like the plague unless they feel the West hand is good enough to try for slam. At the same time, they would not fancy a 5-2 heart fit. So a fair number of West players would bid 3NT over 3♢, albeit somewhat reluctantly.

In a team game, players often bid more aggressively, especially if they might reap a game bonus. In a pairs event, they tend to be fixated on main-taining a plus score. The next hand is a classic example of the differences in strategy. You are not vulnerable against vulnerable opponents:

♠ 10 5 3 ♡ K J 10 6 2 ♢ K 10 8 ♣ 9 4

Partner has opened 1♡ and RHO passes. How vigorously do you raise?

You have a ten-card or better fit, and the chances are the opponents have a good fit of their own, let's say nine cards on average. According to the Law of Total Tricks, there would be nineteen total trumps in each side's best fit and an equivalent number of tricks. A sizable contingent of players might bid 4♡ on these cards for two reasons. One is that ten tricks might be available, and the other is to make it difficult for the other side to locate their fit. At teams the successes would usually compensate for the failures.

At pairs, though, the holder of these cards should be analyzing the possi-bilities in a different way. He expects that, without any singletons or voids in responder's hand, 4♡ is more likely to go down than to make. Unless partner has extra values, the points will be evenly split between the two sides. Also, since responder is not particularly short in spades, the opponents might not even have a fit in the unbid major. The objective in matchpoints should be to go plus or, at the very least, incur the smallest minus result. Rather than the majestic leap to 4♡, the constructive bump to the two-level (or a Bergen raise if you play them) may work out better.

The two combined hands are:

Partner
♠ A K 9
♡ Q 7 5 4 3
◇ 4 3 2
♣ A 7

You
♠ 10 5 3
♡ K J 10 6 2
◇ K 10 8
♣ 9 4

You will lose at least five tricks playing in hearts; one each in spades, hearts and clubs plus two or perhaps even three diamonds. The remaining high cards are split evenly between the opponents, so they might not even come into the auction. If they do, you can push on to 3♡ and go down one for -50 against their making three-level contract. An immediate 4♡ buys the contract but goes down two. Looking at the traveler, we see there are a variety of results on the hand, the most common being:

- +110 or +140 for a heart partscore declared by your side
- +100, the opponents going down in their contract
- –50 for 3♡ going down a trick
- –100 or –300, 4♡ going down two tricks, sometimes doubled

One of the major battlegrounds of pairs games is the competitive auction, and we'll now turn our attention to a couple of examples. In the first one, you're in the West chair having been dealt these cards with both sides vulnerable:

♠ K 10 7 ♡ 9 8 7 5 3 ◇ A Q J ♣ K 7

Of course, with your 13 HCP and a five-card suit, you'd open 1♡. However, you don't have that luxury as RHO gets the ball rolling with 1♠ and the question now is whether you venture a 2♡ overcall. Should you?

One plus in this situation is that your high cards are sitting behind the opening bidder, which means they are likely tricks, but only *if* you can reach partner's hand enough times. The 'major' negative (forgive the pun) is that your long suit is putrid, and you could be going for a number if two passes are followed by a reopening double and LHO is loaded in your suit.

That said, you still have sound opening values. If your side belongs in the auction, you'll likely have to get involved at some point. Suppose you pass initially, maybe intending to come in later. Here are two ways the bidding might continue:

West	North	East	South
			1♠
pass	2♠	pass	pass
?			

West	North	East	South
			1♠
pass	1NT	pass	2♣
?			

In the first case, you'd either have to pass or bid the same ratty suit at the three-level. In the second auction, the opponents may not have an eight-card fit and could easily just stop off to double you instead of bidding on if you come in now. Some hands are well-suited for delayed action or balancing if the opponents grind to a halt in the bidding, but this is not one of them. Even if your long suit is of suspect quality, the best time to compete is on the first round, rather than later, after the opponents have told each other their story. If you catch a fit in partner's hand, you might either buy the contract and go plus or jostle the opponents to a level where you have a chance of defeating them.

Well, enough of the suspense about what might happen, as the four hands are:

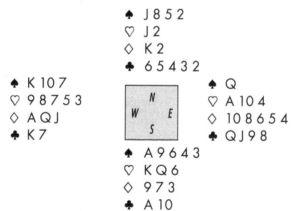

```
                    ♠ J 8 5 2
                    ♡ J 2
                    ◊ K 2
                    ♣ 6 5 4 3 2
    ♠ K 10 7                        ♠ Q
    ♡ 9 8 7 5 3          N          ♡ A 10 4
    ◊ A Q J         W       E       ◊ 10 8 6 5 4
    ♣ K 7               S          ♣ Q J 9 8
                    ♠ A 9 6 4 3
                    ♡ K Q 6
                    ◊ 9 7 3
                    ♣ A 10
```

If West overcalls in hearts, both North and East will raise, and now is when it gets quite interesting. An aggressive South might double 3♡, but he'll likely pass as he can't count on two trump tricks out of his KQx, and with seven losers opposite a single raise, he won't take the push to 3♠. However, North might go on, even with his meager five-count, if he subscribes to the Law of Total Tricks.

What can each side make? Double-dummy, the ♡J lead will beat 3♡ two tricks, as North-South can then prevent the spade ruff in dummy and hold up the ♣A for one round. However, North will probably choose one of two other leads, in which case the worst-case scenario for East-West is down one undoubled, which is a good result since 2♠ can make eight or nine tricks. If the lead is a spade to South's ace, he will need to shift to a diamond to ensure his side's trick in that suit, otherwise two of West's diamonds might go away on dummy's clubs.

It would seem as if 3♠ can indeed make, since it appears that declarer has just four losers, one in each suit, as the spades are friendly. If West finds the ♣K lead, though, he will defeat the contract as he can reach partner's hand with the ♡A later to get a club ruff and score his ♠10.

The bottom line is that North-South can get their best result by doubling 3♡ and beating it one or two tricks, but that is easier said than done.

Now we can look at the actual results. On competitive deals, there is usually quite a variety of them, and this is no exception:

North-South	+140	5 pairs
	+110	2 pairs
	+100	2 pairs
	−100	2 pairs
	−140	1 pair

North-South played 2♠ or 3♠ at more than half the tables, making either eight or nine tricks. Indeed, four declarers were held to eight tricks, which means that West did lead the ♣K at several tables. Since he has a sure winner in the trump suit and three trumps, it's a reasonable shot. Also, half of the declarers were in 3♠, which means they were either pushed there or went to that level on their own, perhaps via a Bergen preemptive raise by North.

On three occasions, North-South defended a 3♡ contract, which accounts for the two +100s along with the -140. How did East-West make 3♡? The answer would be that North played hero with the ◇K lead from his doubleton. This did not strike fear into the heart of declarer, who now had nine tricks. Because North only has two hearts and no sure entry in the trump suit, it's a far riskier lead than the ♣K from the West hand against a spade contract.

As we'll see many times later in the book, a simple variance by one player in the bidding will drastically affect the result. Here is one such instance:

Both sides vulnerable again, you have this collection of assets:

♠7 ♡A K Q J 9 8 2 ◇Q 4 ♣5 3 2

Partner passes and RHO opens 1NT. What are your thoughts?

While a few players might try to be clever and pass, most would bid some number of hearts, with some doing it at the two-level and others jumping to 3♡, which prevents LHO from mentioning spades cheaply.

However, if partner were to open a weak two-bid in spades and RHO now bid 2NT, all thoughts of bidding would vanish. You may not be able to make 3♡ your way, but you do have a quick seven tricks to run off against their notrump contract and, best of all, they are vulnerable so that would be at least +200.

The whole story here is:

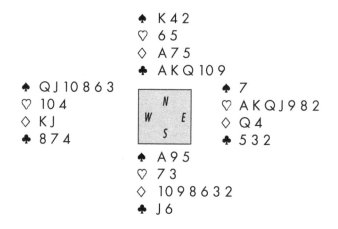

```
              ♠ K 4 2
              ♡ 6 5
              ◇ A 7 5
              ♣ A K Q 10 9
♠ Q J 10 8 6 3              ♠ 7
♡ 10 4          N          ♡ A K Q J 9 8 2
◇ K J        W   E         ◇ Q 4
♣ 8 7 4          S          ♣ 5 3 2
              ♠ A 9 5
              ♡ 7 3
              ◇ 10 9 8 6 3 2
              ♣ J 6
```

I'm sure that the West hand would open 2♠ at most tables at favorable colors or if neither side were vulnerable. However, it's more of a toss-up whether to do the same under these vulnerability conditions, since the point-count is minimum and the suit lacks two of the top three honors. Many years ago a well-known player told me that 'vulnerability is for accountants', thus implying that real bridge players shouldn't be concerned with such trivialities. I can't for the life of me remember who it was, but the Wests who opted for preemptive action on this hand were kindred spirits.

If North gets to open 1NT, his side will go plus regardless of whether East passes or bids some number of hearts. Responder will either place the contract in 3◇ or sell out to hearts at the three-level or higher. After a 2♠ opener by West, North has a perfectly sound 2NT overcall but is doomed to failure. Most partnerships still use Stayman and transfers in that situation, so South will either have to pass or commit his side to the four-level.

The tally of results for this deal is:

North-South		
	+110	3 pairs
	+100	3 pairs
	−100	1 pair
	−110	1 pair
	−200	4 pairs

You can pretty much tell from the scores what happened at the respective tables. The +200s for East-West occurred when West opened 2♠ and North overcalled 2NT. Otherwise, North got to open 1NT and usually either his side played 3◊ or East got to 3♡, going down.

All the deals so far have been examples of bidding and declarer play. Now we'll put you in the East chair, on defense against a 3NT contract. You've been dealt:

♠A K Q 7 3 2   ♡A 7 2   ◊9 5   ♣10 6

Of course, you were hoping at the onset to buy the contract in some number of spades, but the bidding has gone:

West	North	East	South
		1♠	pass
pass	2◊	pass	2NT
pass	3NT	all pass	

Your partner leads the ♣6 and dummy appears on your right:

♠ 10
♡ K 8
◊ A K Q 10 6
♣ K 8 7 4 3

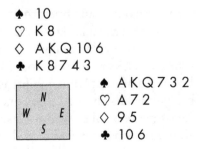

♠ A K Q 7 3 2
♡ A 7 2
◊ 9 5
♣ 10 6

Not surprisingly, partner shows out on the third round of spades, marking declarer with ♠J9xx as he tosses a heart and a club from dummy. For South to have anywhere near the values for his 2NT bid, he'll be in possession of both the ♣A and the ♡Q. The choice facing you now is whether to give up on beating the contract and cash the ♡A, or play another spade and hope partner has enough to prevent dummy's other five-card suit from running.

In a team game, it's a no-brainer, as you're willing to concede an overtrick if the contract can be defeated. However, in a pairs game, surrendering that extra trick could mean the difference between an average-minus and close to a zero. If you assume that declarer has in the neighborhood of 10 HCP for his invite, he is a favorite to hold the ♣Q in addition to the ace and you should therefore take your heart winner.

Taking your side ace here will hold declarer to nine tricks, as the four hands are:

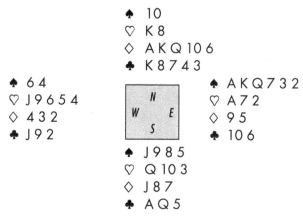

```
              ♠ 10
              ♡ K 8
              ◇ A K Q 10 6
              ♣ K 8 7 4 3
  ♠ 6 4                        ♠ A K Q 7 3 2
  ♡ J 9 6 5 4      N           ♡ A 7 2
  ◇ 4 3 2      W       E       ◇ 9 5
  ♣ J 9 2          S           ♣ 10 6
              ♠ J 9 8 5
              ♡ Q 10 3
              ◇ J 8 7
              ♣ A Q 5
```

South indeed has both top club honors and will take the rest if you persist with another spade. Yes, partner might have had ♣Q9x while declarer's rounded suit holdings were QJx and AJx, in which case 3NT could be defeated. But then again, South's 2NT could also have been based on 11 or even 12 HCP, leaving virtually nothing for the West hand.

One more to conclude our presentation for this chapter. The West hand is:

♠ A 10 6 3   ♡ 8 6 2   ◇ K 6 5   ♣ K 6 5

The auction commences with:

West	North	East	South
		1◇	pass
1♠	pass	3◇	pass
?			

With opener's jump rebid, showing 16-18 points and at least a six-card diamond suit, your side belongs in game. But which one? Diamonds or notrump?

If West's red king were in hearts, he'd automatically bid 3NT. But with the actual hand, what if opener has shortness opposite his three rags? The opponents would lead and possibly take many tricks in that suit. That is the pessimist's view of the world. Those who have a sunnier disposition would reason that partner, having shown a very good hand, could easily have enough values in hearts for 3NT to make.

Is it right to be a notrump hog this time? Well, let's see all four hands:

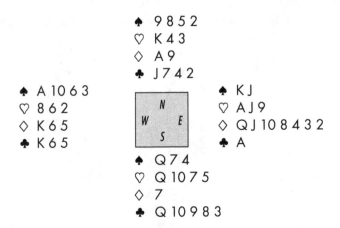

A heart is indeed the best lead for North-South, but 3NT will still make ten tricks. Declarer can hold off until the third round, somewhat disappointed that the ♡AJ9 did not provide a second stopper. Then he knocks out the ◊A and North is out of hearts.

But would North actually lead a heart from Kxx or a club from Jxxx? An argument could be made for either suit. Let's look at the scores to find out what the rest of the East-West pairs were doing:

East-West		
	+690	5 pairs
	+660	1 pair
	+630	1 pair
	+620	3 pairs
	+600	3 pairs
	+150	3 pairs

We can see from the traveler that seven pairs were in notrump, six played game in diamonds, and three responders chickened out entirely and left opener in 3◊.

In the deals we've examined to this point, I've included the actual scores so that the reader can get an idea of what the other pairs are doing. As we move along, I'll do so intermittently but not for every example. The primary focus will be on the decisions you have to make over the course of a session.

As we'll find out on many deals over the course of the book, the outcome may not hinge solely on what one player elects to do. On some of them, such as this last one, the onus will fall on one player, after which the dominoes fall neatly into place. In an earlier example, West has to choose between overcalling and passing over a 1♠ opening. If he makes the overcall, then North-South in turn are faced with the choice of defending or bidding on to the three-level in their suit.

As lead-in to what comes next, I'll make some general comments and observations about duplicate pairs based on the years of experience I've had:

- Some people think there's a huge difference in the strategy at match-points as compared to rubber bridge or teams, and that's a false assumption in my opinion. There are differences to be sure, but they are subtle ones. It's still bridge.

- You shouldn't get overly fixated on what the rest of the field is going to do on each deal. For one thing, except on the most obvious ones, it's going to be tough to predict. Your prediction will inevitably be based on your own value system, which may not be the same as that of the other pairs in the event, many of whom you don't even know. Moreover, it's okay to go against the field at times, although you don't want to do it consistently and wildly. If your partnership has a bidding gadget that provides you with an edge in a given situation, you should take full advantage of it. Also, if you know that your evaluation of a hand may not be the same as other people in your chair but *emphatically* feel that your view is superior, you can go ahead and back your judgment.

- A pairs event shouldn't automatically transform you into a madman. The successful players at this form of the game will often be quite bold in some ways and somewhat cautious in others. To list them one by one:

  » They will take some risks in declarer play, attempting to gain extra tricks even if it means occasionally jeopardizing the contract.

  » On the flip side, they'll want to avoid giving away tricks on defense. In teams, you want to defeat the contract and may have to make an aggressive lead to do so. At pairs, however, the consensus is that you don't want to give away free overtricks and ought to be more cautious in your approach. We'll examine the validity of this in a later chapter.

» When it comes to bidding, they will avoid stretching for paper-thin games and slams. The reason for that degree of caution is that you want to have lots of company if you go down.

» Whenever the two sides have the same approximate values, each of them becomes much fiercer in their bidding if they have a playable trump suit. If you can't buy the contract, you'll at least want to push the opponents to a level where you have a chance of beating them.

- Mental toughness and determination to weather the setbacks is an absolute must at pairs. In the get-togethers with my fellow players after the game, there's often some moaning about bad luck and getting fixed by the opponents. I've done some of it myself on occasion. Sometimes you will have to endure that fate — luck will indeed have prevented your partnership from winning.

- However, if you take a good hard look at your scorecard, whether you've come out on top of the heap, in the middle of the pack, or near the bottom, you'll *always* find about 4-6 percentage points that you've left on the table. Those miscues will typically arise out of not giving sufficient thought to a decision, or having your mind on a previous board rather than the current one. That's going to happen at some point; it's hard to maintain your focus and proper rhythm for twenty-six or so deals. One of my friends once told me that his objective was, if he could not play a perfect round of bridge, then to limit his obvious mistakes to one. That was good and sensible advice. You're likely to goof up at least once, so don't beat yourself up when it happens, just keep looking ahead so you can get your mojo back.

Anyway, that's my pep talk. Let's move on now to cover more specific aspects of the pairs game.

2

The Changing Landscape of Bridge

Kit Woolsey's landmark book *Matchpoints* was first published in 1982, almost forty years ago. A second edition with some additions and updates came out in 2015. When you compare bridge nowadays to what was happening in the early- to mid-1980s, there are not only a greater number of conventions in use, but the bidding style in general is more enterprising, notably with preempts but in all competitive situations.

Before I go any further, I'd like to stress that this chapter is *not* a promo for adding lots of gadgets to your bidding repertoire. It's mostly an information session in which you can gain a degree of familiarity with what and how your opponents bid in the current bridge environment.

What are the differences in today's landscape from the days of yore? Well, here is a list of the most significant changes:

1) The split between strong (15-17) and weak (normally 12-14) notrumps is getting close to equal nowadays. At the time of Woolsey's first edition, strong notrumpers were in a sizable majority.

2) People used to yield to a strong notrump and refrain from interfering. That is no longer the case. With many conventions available to show two-suited hands, the opponents will step into the fray more often.

Here is an example of the trend in favor of competing when you have an unbalanced hand. In the East chair with no one vulnerable, you hold:

♠ K 9 7 5 4   ♡ K 10 7 5   ◇ 6 5 4   ♣ A

RHO has opened 1NT. Back when overcalls were natural, you'd be taking your life into your hands by overcalling 2♠ on such a moth-eaten suit. Even if you have a way of showing both majors, this hand is not exactly a prize, with your ace being in your short suit. Maybe a quarter-century ago, the passers would outnumber the bidders on this hand. That is no longer true: in a high-level game, most Easts would compete on the theory that they want to get North-South out of the highest-paying contract of notrump. Even in a club pairs event, close to half of the players would be inclined to take a bid on these cards.

So, in the end, will bravery or caution be rewarded? Here are all four hands:

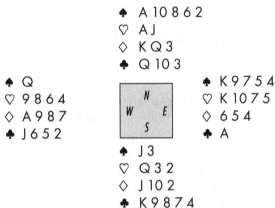

```
                        ♠ A 10 8 6 2
                        ♡ A J
                        ◇ K Q 3
                        ♣ Q 10 3
   ♠ Q                                    ♠ K 9 7 5 4
   ♡ 9 8 6 4          N                   ♡ K 10 7 5
   ◇ A 9 8 7      W       E               ◇ 6 5 4
   ♣ J 6 5 2          S                   ♣ A
                        ♠ J 3
                        ♡ Q 3 2
                        ◇ J 10 2
                        ♣ K 9 8 7 4
```

First off, you'll see that North has opened 1NT with a five-card major. There is still a divergence of opinion on that tendency, but the pendulum has moved in favor of showing the balanced 15-17 points right away. I'll touch upon the subject briefly in the next chapter.

In this case, declarer in 1NT will get a favorable lead, as East will start out with his long suit. Upon winning the first spade, North will likely tackle clubs and do quite well when the ace pops on the first round of the suit.

If East competes, he ought to show both majors if he can do so rather than bid spades. Now his side will locate a 4-4 heart fit. South is in an uncomfortable situation if 2♡ gets passed around to him. He would have gladly passed 1NT, but with the opponents competing, he faces a difficult choice. Passing cannot yield a good result, as he expected to make 1NT, and +50 against their heart contract will pale in comparison to +90 or +120. A double would likely be interpreted as takeout rather than penalty, and means taking a huge chance in any event. Bidding 2NT is also somewhat dicey, so most players would now try 3♣.

It will be touch and go whether South makes that contract if West leads the singleton ♠Q. A heart turns out slightly better, but declarer might go down even on a spade lead. The main thing, irrespective of the outcome, is that North-South have been jostled out of 1NT and because of that, will likely end up with a below-average result no matter what the final contract turns out to be.

3) A related development is that a partnership may elect to use different competing methods against strong and weak notrumps. An example would be DONT or Meckwell versus strong, and HELLO or Cappelletti (Hamilton) over weak notrumps. There are many more

methods, however, which can be found on either the BridgeGuys or David Stevenson's 1NT Defenses websites.

While it might be a good idea to vary your conventional agreements depending on the strength of their 1NT opening, making that choice has the pitfall of the occasional memory lapse. When that happens, not only will the opponents be peeved, the director will not be all that sympathetic concerning any mix-ups.

4) 'Up-the-line' bidding in responding to a 1♣ bid has virtually disappeared. The fashion is to show a major unless you have a game-forcing hand, and diamonds are often bypassed.

5) Three-card raises of responder's major suit used to be common but aren't so frequent any more. In a bygone era, opener might have elected to raise hearts after 1◇ – 1♡ if his hand was something like:

♠ A 8 4   ♡ K J 4   ◇ A J 9 7 6   ♣ 7 2

He'd be a trifle worried about the worthless doubleton club for notrump purposes, and among the alternatives of 1NT, 2◇ and 2♡ might opt for the immediate supporting gesture even though partner might only have four of his major suit.

This hand is no longer that much of a headache and most openers would now rebid 1NT. The reason is that a lot of partnerships have some checkback mechanism in their arsenal, and responder can always use that convention if he has a five-card major and invitational or better strength.

Where the three-card raise might still occur is if opener has a minimum unbalanced hand. Suppose the bidding has gone 1◇ – 1♠ and he's looking at:

♠ A 9 3   ♡ A 9 3 2   ◇ K Q 10 8 4   ♣ 6

Opener isn't strong enough for a 2♡ reverse, so he has to decide between a 2◇ rebid and the three-card raise to 2♠. Although I'm perfectly all right with supporting the major here, my expert friends seem to disagree. Even in this scenario, they tend to shy away from raising unless they have four-card support.

6) Weak two-bids are trotted out with a greater degree of frequency as there are no longer stringent requirements as to suit quality. Any of these hands might be opened 2♡ at favorable colors:

♠3 ♡AJ9652 ◇J108 ♣765
♠95 ♡KQ10754 ◇A8 ♣962
♠A3 ♡Q98743 ◇QJ2 ♣74

Because of this widening of the scope of weak two-bids, the traditional feature-ask of 2NT has been overtaken in popularity by some form of Ogust, where 2NT asks for both range and suit quality. The weak two-bidder answers thus:

3♣	minimum hand, poor suit
3◇	minimum hand, good suit
3♡	maximum hand, poor suit
3♠	maximum hand, good suit
3NT	maximum hand, AKQ or better in the long suit.

The last of these replies seldom comes up as many people feel that a six-card or longer suit headed by the AKQ is too good a hand for a weak two-bid. But just so you know...

Here is a case study of how Ogust enables the partnership to stop on the brink. The opponents are vulnerable and you're not, as you see a 2♠ bid from partner. You've been dealt this collection:

♠AJ ♡Q973 ◇Q865 ♣AK8

You make the 2NT inquiry, and get a response of 3♣, showing a weak hand and a weak suit. While he might have an outside card, there now rate to be four losers; discretion is the better part of valor here and a sign-off in 3♠ seems to be the right course to take.

The four hands are:

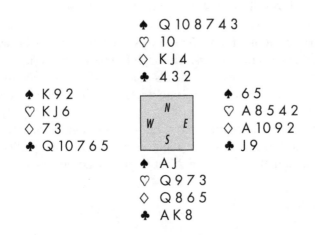

```
              ♠ Q 10 8 7 4 3
              ♡ 10
              ◇ K J 4
              ♣ 4 3 2
♠ K 9 2          N          ♠ 6 5
♡ K J 6                     ♡ A 8 5 4 2
◇ 7 3        W       E      ◇ A 10 9 2
♣ Q 10 7 6 5     S          ♣ J 9
              ♠ A J
              ♡ Q 9 7 3
              ◇ Q 8 6 5
              ♣ A K 8
```

East won't try either of his aces on opening lead, so he'll begin with a trump or the ♣J. Regardless of which black suit he goes with, the contract will go down.

If North-South had been using 2NT as a feature ask, North might have shown his diamond card and responder would then be far more likely to bid game, expecting partner's suit to be more robust. If opener just has the ♠K rather than the ♠Q, 4♠ would have a decent play.

Here is another opportunity to get the information you need when partner opens a weak two-bid. Your hand this time is:

♠ A 7 4   ♡ K 10 2   ◇ A Q 6 4 2   ♣ A J

Over partner's 2♡, you ask with 2NT and he replies with 3◇, showing a minimum hand with a good suit. This is a case of good news-bad news, as he won't have anything much outside of hearts. The bad news is that 4♡ will probably need the diamond finesse to make. If the king of that suit is offside, the contract likely goes down. On the flip side, the good news is that 3NT is going to be a claimer, with six hearts plus three outside aces, and could make with overtricks. As South, you can take the sure thing and bid the game in notrump rather than hearts.

The layout here is:

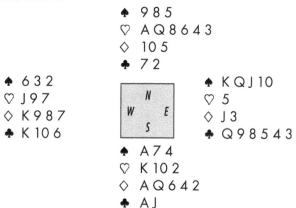

<pre>
                    ♠ 9 8 5
                    ♡ A Q 8 6 4 3
                    ◇ 10 5
                    ♣ 7 2
   ♠ 6 3 2   ♠ K Q J 10
   ♡ J 9 7   N   ♡ 5
   ◇ K 9 8 7   W   E   ◇ J 3
   ♣ K 10 6   S   ♣ Q 9 8 5 4 3
                    ♠ A 7 4
                    ♡ K 10 2
                    ◇ A Q 6 4 2
                    ♣ A J
</pre>

Here, 4♡ likely goes down as East has a natural lead of the ♠K. North wins and draws trumps, and then finesses in diamonds. It loses, the defense cashes two spades and then switches to a club. With diamonds splitting 4-2, the contract goes down one.

With hearts dividing 3-1, 3NT by South is ironclad. A bonus for declarer is that West in all likelihood leads a low diamond, in which case there are now ten tricks.

What has the field done on this particular hand? Here are the results:

North-South	+630	1 pair
	+620	1 pair
	+600	1 pair
	+140	2 pairs
	−100	4 pairs

As we can see from the traveler, a couple of North-South pairs languished in a partscore. This might have been due to North passing in first seat rather than opening a vulnerable weak two-bid. Alternatively, South might have taken a dim view of the world. Five Souths auto-reflexed a jump to 4♡, and that contract went down four times. Two responders made the inquiry as to the quality of the 2♡ bidder's hand, and parked the contract in 3NT. One West led a diamond, resulting in the 630 score, and the other would have led the unbid major, whereupon declarer had just the nine tricks.

7) What you'll also see is three-level preempts being made on hands that would have opened a very sound weak two-bid in the past. Not vulnerable against vulnerable opponents, I've had experts tell me they'd open 3♡ on a hand like: •

♠ 7 3   ♡ K Q J 10 8 7   ◇ 8 5   ♣ Q 8 7

8) Low-level penalty doubles are gradually fading into extinction. To show how the times they are a-changing, look at the following auctions:

West	North	East	South
	1◇	pass	1♠
2♣	dbl		

This double by opener would have been 'Gotcha!' for most partnerships some twenty-five to thirty years ago. Nowadays, it would be a support double (three cards in responder's major) or extra values but not necessarily a trump stack.

West	North	East	South
	1♠	pass	1NT*
2◇	dbl		

Here, responder has bid a forcing notrump instead of a suit and the next player has overcalled. Again, the double by opener used to be pure penalty but most experts would now play it as takeout, with a likely hand being:

♠ A Q 8 7 4 ♡ K Q 3 ◇ 6 ♣ A 8 7 2

If North were to bid 3♣ here, responder might expect 5-5 distribution or at least much better clubs. If the double is agreed upon as takeout, aside from clubs the partnership could play a major suit at the two-level or even 2◇ doubled if that is responder's long suit.

West	North	East	South
	1♣	1♠	dbl
2♠	dbl		

The double by opener in this situation would in the distant past show a balanced or semi-balanced good hand with no clear action. However, it is more takeout-oriented in this day and age, with North having something like:

♠ 7 ♡ K 10 4 ◇ A K 9 3 ♣ K J 7 5 2

Partner will have the unbid major for his negative double but while he could have diamond length as well, it's not an absolute guarantee. Having the double as takeout here keeps the road open to all possible contracts.

The one exception where a low-level double is strictly for penalty is when the opponents are in some number of notrump, as witness this troika of auctions:

West	North	East	South
1◇	dbl	1NT	dbl

West	North	East	South
1♡	1NT	dbl	

West	North	East	South
1♣	1♡	pass	1NT
dbl			

In all these examples, the double is for penalty. The opponents haven't established a fit and the doubler is announcing that his side has the balance of power.

By contrast:

West	North	East	South
1♡	2♣	2♡	pass
pass	dbl		

North has overcalled in his long suit, but the subsequent double is intended as takeout, with decent support for either of the remaining suits. Either of these hands would qualify:

$$♠KJ4 \quad ♡9 \quad ◇AQ53 \quad ♣KQ986$$
$$♠A83 \quad ♡9 \quad ◇AQJ \quad ♣A107542$$

On the second hand, you don't want to be putting all your eggs in one basket with 3♣ when your side might have an adequate fit in either pointed suit.

On the topic of negative doubles, the level at which they are used has become progressively higher. By decade, we can see how much things have changed:

50s/60s	Negative doubles through 1♠, penalty at the two-level and beyond
70s	Negative doubles through 2♠, sometimes even higher
80s/90s	Negative doubles through 3♡/3♠
2000s	Negative doubles through 4◇/4♡

9) There are more ways of showing two-suited hands in the bidding than had previously existed. They come in three main variants:

   a) Leaping Michaels. This is a convention that partnerships some-times decide to use over a weak two-bid by the opponents. Let's say RHO starts out with 2♠ and you have any of these three hands:

$$♠42 \quad ♡AK \quad ◇AKJ10865 \quad ♣K3$$
$$♠7 \quad ♡KQJ94 \quad ◇A8 \quad ♣AKJ42$$
$$♠— \quad ♡QJ10973 \quad ◇AQJ84 \quad ♣KJ$$

The first hand is too strong for a mere 3◇ overcall, and doesn't have enough heart support for a double. Because you'd like to be in 3NT if partner has a high card in the enemy suit, you'd like to address that issue quickly.

In the next two examples, you have enough playing strength to go to the four-level, and it would be nice to identify both your suits in one fell swoop so that partner will be in the know in case the opponents have a fit and bid on.

Since a jump to four of a minor over a weak two-bid is practically non-existent as a natural bid (never preempt over a preempt), the following is a common treatment:

- A 3♠ cuebid shows the first of our hands and asks partner to bid 3NT with a stopper in the opponents' suit.
- A jump to four of a minor is Leaping Michaels, showing 5-5 or better distribution with that suit and the unbid major.

b) Fit-showing jumps (or FSJ for short). These take two forms:

Responder, having passed originally, jumps in a new suit opposite a third- or fourth-seat opener with no interference by the opponents. This shows the bid suit and excellent support, with a hand that counting distribution has revalued to a full opening. Ergo, after pass by you and 1♠ by partner, you'd jump to 3♣ with the likes of:

♠Q 1076 ♡4 ♢K 65 ♣A J 983

There has been an opening bid by partner followed by a double or overcall by RHO. Now a jump by responder may not be as strong in high cards, but again shows that suit, at least four-card support for partner and values concentrated in those suits. So, for example, after 1♡ – 1♠, you could jump to 3♢ on:

♠6 ♡K 1075 ♢K Q 942 ♣874

Having done that, if the opponents bid some number of spades, responder won't have to take further action as he's fully described what he has and can leave the final decision to partner.

c) Sandwich Notrump

Direct 1NT overcalls after an opening bid typically show the same values as a 1NT opening along with a high card in the opponents' suit. To do the same when LHO has opened and RHO has also bid is treading in dangerous waters, as partner rarely has enough for game or even a safe haven at the two-level, and you may well run into a double from the bad guys. A more frequently occurring hand type is one with 5-5 distribution in the remaining suits and moderate high-card strength. The 1NT bid here would suggest that hand. A side benefit is that you're now able to use the cuebid of either suit as a natural action, showing a suit of length and quality that is willing to play in that strain.

To illustrate, suppose the auction has gone, with you sitting South:

West	North	East	South
1◇	pass	1♠	?

♠ 8 2　♡ K J 7 6　◇ A 5 4　♣ A Q 9 3

Here you'd make a takeout double, willing to compete in the longer of partner's rounded suits.

♠ 5　♡ K 10 7 6 5　◇ A 9　♣ Q 9 8 7 3

This hand contains fewer high-card points, but with 5-5 shape the chances of having an eight-card or better fit are improved and the way to distinguish between the two hand types is with the sandwich 1NT.

♠ A J 3　♡ 9　◇ K Q 10 8 6 3　♣ K 10 8
♠ K J 9 8 7 6　♡ 7 4　◇ A 5 4　♣ A 10

In each of these cases, you might have a playable contract in your long suit despite its having been bid by the opponents. More important, however, is that you'd like to get partner to lead that suit rather than the heart he will probably shoot out if you remain silent. If you are using the sandwich notrump approach, then 2◇ and 2♠ can be used as natural bids.

I will hasten to add that none of these two-suited treatments is universal amongst bridge players today. That said, these methods have gained a significant following.

10) Other forms of signaling, such as upside-down count and attitude, and various discarding methods, have been adopted by many players in place of traditional 'standard' carding.

It is not my intent to devote a lot of time to this subject, since carding agreements are a matter of choice. There is, however, one defensive convention that I'd like to touch upon because it has some definite value, particularly at matchpoints, and that is the Smith echo. The gist of it is that when declarer first plays a suit and giving count is not a vital consideration, then both defenders can give attitude towards the suit that was led. Opening leader will convey the message as to whether he has strength in addition to his length. Meanwhile, his partner, who normally has had to play a high card to the first trick, can indicate whether he has any more honors in that suit.

How does it work? When declarer plays his suit, a high card shows enthusiasm for the suit led, while a low card suggests relative weakness. The following deal illustrates the concept:

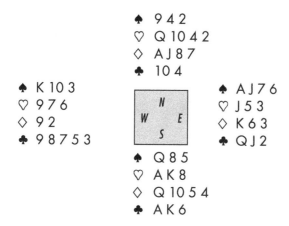

```
              ♠ 9 4 2
              ♡ Q 10 4 2
              ◇ A J 8 7
              ♣ 10 4
♠ K 10 3                      ♠ A J 7 6
♡ 9 7 6          N           ♡ J 5 3
◇ 9 2        W      E        ◇ K 6 3
♣ 9 8 7 5 3      S           ♣ Q J 2
              ♠ Q 8 5
              ♡ A K 8
              ◇ Q 10 5 4
              ♣ A K 6
```

South has opened 1◇ and then jumped in notrump, showing 18-19 HCP. Responder had a coin-toss on whether to pass or carry on to game, but elected to take the plunge because of his good holding in partner's suit.

At the table, West led his fourth-best club and East played the jack, the lower of his touching honors. Declarer won the first trick with the ace, hiding his king, a matter of good technique. He then played the ◇10 from hand and ran it. East took his king and played another club, at which point South was home free with nine tricks; four hearts, three diamonds and two clubs. There was some gnashing of teeth by the defenders, who realized after the fact that they could have taken four spade tricks and beaten the contract.

Although East thinks his side is off to a good start with the club lead, West should have his doubts after the play to the first trick. South must have a second honor in the suit, as he would have otherwise ducked his ace at least once.

If East-West have agreed to use the Smith echo, they have a decent chance of finding the spade shift. On the first round of diamonds, West can try and get the message across that he has nothing much in the suit he's led by playing the ◇2. From East's point of view, this means declarer has a second club stopper, and he therefore plays a low spade back when he wins the ◇K. South's queen is trapped and no matter what he does, the defenders will be able to take four spade tricks.

You'll notice on the ACBL convention card that there are boxes for the Smith echo. There is a variation of it called reverse Smith, whereby a *low* card in declarer's suit says you're gung-ho about the led suit and a high card suggests a distaste for it. What you'll see most often at the table is that standard carders would use the basic Smith echo, while the upside-downers prefer reverse Smith.

Bob Hamman in his book *At the Table*, from which I'll be quoting several times, mentions one of his pet peeves about the Smith echo, which is that he's encountered opponents who haven't made their plays in tempo. That is a legitimate concern. It's a good tool, but you need to have thought the matter out beforehand and avoid hesitating on your turn to play.

QUIZ HANDS

Your regular partner canceled out on you, so you're playing with a pickup partner. This is someone you know is good, but who has also suggested in filling out your card that you play Ogust and Smith echo along with leaping Michaels, fit-showing jumps, etc. You will be West in each case.

1. East dealer, E-W vulnerable.

♠ K 9 6   ♡ A 8 2   ◇ K 5 4 3   ♣ A J 5

Partner opens 2♠ and you ask with 2NT. He now bids 3♡, showing a good hand and a weak suit. What should you do at this point?

2. East dealer, E-W vulnerable.

♠ 8 5   ♡ J 6 3   ◇ A 7 6   ♣ K 10 5 3 2

The bidding so far has gone:

West	North	East	South
		1◇	pass
1NT	2♠	pass	pass
?			

What's your pleasure? Pass or bid? If the latter, how do you proceed?

3. East dealer, neither vulnerable.

♠ A Q 10 9 8   ♡ 7   ◇ A K J 8 7 6   ♣ 4

Partner passes and RHO opens 2♡. What is your choice here?

4. For this one you'll be on defense. You are West and the auction has gone:

West	North	East	South
	1NT	pass	2♣
pass	2♠	pass	3NT
all pass			

Partner leads the ♣5. This is your hand and what you see in dummy:

♠ 9 8 7 2
♡ J 10 6 4 2
◇ 9 7
♣ Q 8

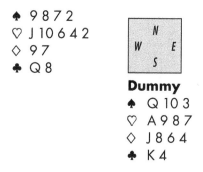

Dummy
♠ Q 10 3
♡ A 9 8 7
◇ J 8 6 4
♣ K 4

Declarer flies with the ♣K at Trick 1 and you play the ♣8. He then calls for the ♠10 to start the next trick. Which spade do you play?

5. East dealer, both sides vulnerable.

♠ A J 9 4 3   ♡ 10 9   ◇ 6   ♣ Q 10 9 8 5

Partner opens 1♣ and RHO overcalls 1♡. What action do you take?

6. Now you find yourself on lead. Not vulnerable against vulnerable opponents, this has been the auction:

West	North	East	South
		2♡	3◇
pass	3♠	pass	3NT
all pass			

Your hand consists of:

♠ A 8 7 2   ♡ 7 4   ◇ Q   ♣ Q 10 9 7 6 5

So which suit do you lead – partner's hearts or your clubs?

1.   E-W vulnerable

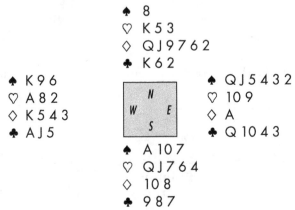

```
            ♠ 8
            ♡ K 5 3
            ◇ Q J 9 7 6 2
            ♣ K 6 2
♠ K 9 6                        ♠ Q J 5 4 3 2
♡ A 8 2          N             ♡ 10 9
◇ K 5 4 3    W       E         ◇ A
♣ A J 5          S             ♣ Q 10 4 3
            ♠ A 10 7
            ♡ Q J 7 6 4
            ◇ 10 8
            ♣ 9 8 7
```

To recap the bidding, partner has opened 2♠, you bid an Ogust 2NT and he answered 3♡, showing a good hand and bad suit. While 3NT is certainly an option because of the 4-3-3-3 shape, there will be a hole in your side's long suit and you might have to give up a trick in it. If the opponents lead a red suit, they may be able to defeat a notrump game as you just have the one stopper. So 4♠ could be the better spot as partner will have some outside strength if his spades are not that great.

Here, North will lead a diamond against 3NT, which spells the end of any chance you have of making it despite having two stoppers in the suit. The entry to partner's spades has been taken out and South will duck two rounds of the suit. Dummy's winners will be stranded.

As an aside, South should play the ◇10 at Trick 1 as he expects partner to have a broken sequence of QJ9 for his lead of the queen.

The results for this deal were:

East-West	+650	1 pair
	+620	1 pair
	+200	2 pairs
	+170	1 pair
	+140	1 pair
	+50	1 pair
	−100	2 pairs

Four pairs bid game here, and four did not. The 4♠ bidders were successful, while the -100s were 3NT going down. North-South bought the contract in diamonds at one table, going down a trick.

2.   E-W vulnerable

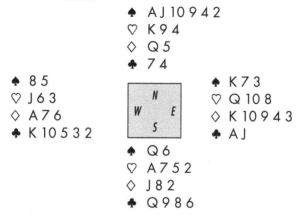

```
                        ♠ A J 10 9 4 2
                        ♡ K 9 4
                        ◇ Q 5
                        ♣ 7 4
    ♠ 8 5                              ♠ K 7 3
    ♡ J 6 3           ┌─────────┐      ♡ Q 10 8
    ◇ A 7 6           │    N    │      ◇ K 10 9 4 3
    ♣ K 10 5 3 2      │ W     E │      ♣ A J
                      │    S    │
                      └─────────┘
                        ♠ Q 6
                        ♡ A 7 5 2
                        ◇ J 8 2
                        ♣ Q 9 8 6
```

West	North	East	South
		1◇	pass
1NT	2♠	pass	pass
?			

North's 2♠ was not a super-sound overcall, but with a decent six-card suit, most players would get in there at favorable colors.

West has the decision to make here, being mid-range for his 1NT response. Since he has denied length in either major already, he can double, showing a willingness to compete, but a hand that lacks any clear direction. East doesn't have quite enough to leave the double in, so he will rebid diamonds, his five-card suit. That contract will make, losing only a spade, two hearts and a trump.

Note that if West bids clubs, that contract will go down as the tally of losers will be a spade, two hearts, a diamond and a club. The double by responder as takeout-oriented works nicely here, as the trump suit for the partnership can end up being either clubs or one of the red suits. Also, if East leaves in the double, his side rates to go plus.

3.   Neither vulnerable

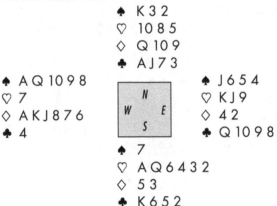

```
                    ♠ K 3 2
                    ♡ 10 8 5
                    ◇ Q 10 9
                    ♣ A J 7 3
  ♠ A Q 10 9 8                      ♠ J 6 5 4
  ♡ 7              N                ♡ K J 9
  ◇ A K J 8 7 6   W   E             ◇ 4 2
  ♣ 4                 S             ♣ Q 10 9 8
                    ♠ 7
                    ♡ A Q 6 4 3 2
                    ◇ 5 3
                    ♣ K 6 5 2
```

On this deal, South opens 2♡ and it's now West's turn at bat. Should he over-call one of his suits and hope he then gets a chance to show the other one? Using regular Michaels, he could bid 3♡, which is spades and a minor, but if North jams the auction with some number of hearts, East is under pressure: he has a decent spade fit but the rest of his hand is of questionable value.

Fortunately, this three-loser hand can be shown immediately in Leaping Michaels, as West jumps to 4◇, showing that suit and at least five spades as well. His side winds up in 4♠, which makes since the only losers are the two rounded aces and the ♠K. If North persists with 5♡, East doubles as he has nothing of consequence in partner's other suit and some trick-taking poten-tial in hearts and clubs. Having shown the precise nature of his hand with 4◇, West can now pass in good conscience.

4.

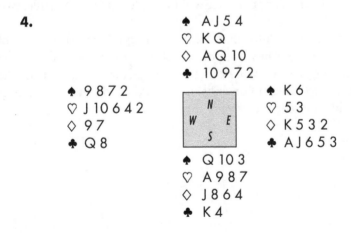

```
                    ♠ A J 5 4
                    ♡ K Q
                    ◇ A Q 10
                    ♣ 10 9 7 2
  ♠ 9 8 7 2                         ♠ K 6
  ♡ J 10 6 4 2     N                ♡ 5 3
  ◇ 9 7           W   E             ◇ K 5 3 2
  ♣ Q 8               S             ♣ A J 6 5 3
                    ♠ Q 10 3
                    ♡ A 9 8 7
                    ◇ J 8 6 4
                    ♣ K 4
```

As you'll recall, North-South got to 3NT after a Stayman auction and East led the ♣5. Declarer rose with the king and then tested the spade suit, running the ♠10. East's problem on the hand once he gets in is that he doesn't know who has the ♣Q, as declarer would have made the same play at Trick 1 if he had Qxx(x) of clubs, to preserve his own honor as a possible second stopper.

Playing the Smith echo, West can give his partner a helping hand at the second trick by playing the ♠9. This implies he has a high card in partner's suit, as he would have played a low spade otherwise. Now East can underlead his remaining clubs with some confidence, and later get in with a diamond to defeat the contract.

5.   Both vulnerable

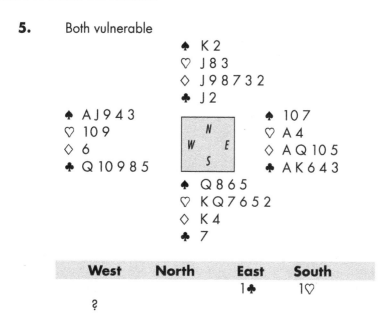

	♠ K 2	
	♡ J 8 3	
	◇ J 9 8 7 3 2	
	♣ J 2	

West	East
♠ A J 9 4 3	♠ 10 7
♡ 10 9	♡ A 4
◇ 6	◇ A Q 10 5
♣ Q 10 9 8 5	♣ A K 6 4 3

	♠ Q 8 6 5	
	♡ K Q 7 6 5 2	
	◇ K 4	
	♣ 7	

West	North	East	South
		1♣	1♡
?			

By definition, a fit-showing jump when the opponents have competed does not have to be a fistful of high-card points. A 2♠ bid by responder here would simply promise nine or ten black cards with whatever points he has located in the black suits. This hand qualifies for that action, although West could have slightly more in the way of high cards.

Sometimes the FSJ enables the partnership to uncover a double fit. That's not the case here, but it does provide opener with some vital information. First off, there aren't going to be any problems in the club suit. Moving over to the red suits, if responder has a maximum of three cards in them, East's losers can easily be ruffed, and he won't lose more than one trick in hearts and diamonds. Finally, partner rates to have enough high-card strength in spades to cover one or both of those losers. Adding it all up, eleven tricks figure to be a breeze in a 5♣ contract.

Like many two-suited bids, fit-showing jumps can be a double-edged sword, as the opponents also gain information. However, the pluses generally outweigh the minuses and give the opener (or overcaller) an easier time of it in deciding how high to go in higher-level auctions.

6. N-S vulnerable

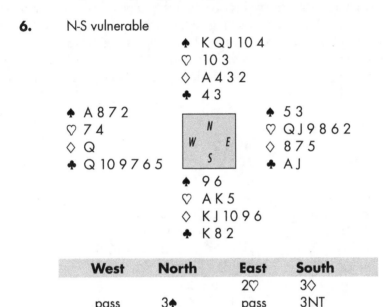

♠ K Q J 10 4
♡ 10 3
◊ A 4 3 2
♣ 4 3

♠ A 8 7 2
♡ 7 4
◊ Q
♣ Q 10 9 7 6 5

♠ 5 3
♡ Q J 9 8 6 2
◊ 8 7 5
♣ A J

♠ 9 6
♡ A K 5
◊ K J 10 9 6
♣ K 8 2

West	North	East	South
		2♡	3◊
pass	3♠	pass	3NT
all pass			

Frankly, this opening lead is a coin-toss where there is no right answer. A club probably has the best chance of defeating the contract but may give up a pivotal overtrick, while leading partner's known six-card suit is not as likely to cost.

There are two factors that might lean you in the direction of a club lead. As I mentioned earlier in the chapter, there is no guarantee of excellent suit quality with the weak two-bids of the present day. Also, when the opponents don't have a known fit that will be a good source of tricks, they like to have the enemy suit well stopped.

Here, if West goes with the club, he will defeat 3NT as declarer only has eight tricks. That's not to say that a club lead is clearly the best by far, since it may not be. However, with the variety of hands that a weak two-bid can be made on today, opening leads are not as straightforward as they used to be.

3

Notrump Issues

In the previous chapter, I talked about how the bridge world has evolved in the last twenty-five to thirty years. That has also occurred with notrump openings in many aspects. It's no longer a given that the range will be 15-17, a pair is just as apt to be playing a lower range. At the same time, bidding over a 1NT opening bid has become much more commonplace. Your partnership therefore needs to have effective ways of dealing with situations where the opponents have decided to compete.

Without going into great depth, I'll touch upon several of these issues in the pages ahead.

Off-Shape 1NT Openings

Before you get the wrong idea about this, I'd like to stress that I do not mean opening 1NT with hands that contain a singleton. Although the ACBL has softened the restrictions on doing so, that's a matter of personal choice; bridge teachers and writers strongly advise against it.

By 'off-shape', I mean some hands that contain two doubletons instead of the normal one or none. There are two hands of this type where people might consider opening 1NT rather than the longest suit:

1) Opener has 15-17 points and 5-4-2-2 distribution where the long suit is a minor. If the five-card suit is a major, he will open the major even if he is in the prescribed notrump range.

There have always been some hands that pose a rebid problem if you don't open 1NT. For example, suppose you have:

♠K4 ♡Q973 ◇AJ654 ♣AQ

The general feeling would be that this hand is not good enough to reverse into 2♡ if you open 1◇ and partner responds 1♠. Consequently, players of all levels, past and present, often go with 1NT as their opening salvo, to describe the approximate nature of the hand and, more importantly, to avoid any rebid headaches.

It is in regard to the following hand where opinions in the expert community have changed:

♠ Q 9 7 3 ♡ A 4 ◇ K 8 ♣ A K 6 5 2

There are no rebid problems whatsoever if this hand is opened 1♣, as the major suit can then be introduced at the one-level if partner responds in a red suit. At the time of Woolsey's book, most players would indeed have begun the auction with the minor-suit opening. In the present day, however, a sizable contingent of experts would go with 1NT here. Their reasoning is that you can show basically what you have in one bid, rather than take three calls to describe your shape and values fully, giving the opponents a lot of information to work with along the way.

2) Opener has 15-17 points and 6-3-2-2 distribution with the long suit being a minor. There is a sharper divide on this type of hand, with more players refraining from a 1NT opening as you can always open and jump in the minor. Here is an example:

♠ A 6 ♡ Q 10 2 ◇ K 3 ♣ A K 10 8 3 2

The player holding these cards wanted to protect his ◇K and opened 1NT. Partner bid 2♣, Stayman, and opener responded 2◇ to deny a four-card major. This was followed by three passes, whereupon a spade was led and partner laid down this dummy:

♠ J 8 3 2 ♡ K 9 8 7 ◇ 10 7 5 4 ♣ 6

The 4-2 diamond fit was not a success, especially with LHO holding five to the ace-jack.

This was an instance of 'crawling' Stayman, where responder wanted desperately to get out of 1NT and was willing to pass any of opener's replies, including 2◇. You can hardly blame him for doing so, as he will have improved the contract most of the time.

It's debatable whether opener should get any sympathy for his poor result, though. If he opens 1♣ and partner knows that you shouldn't respond on a measly 4 HCP, his side will end up with a plus instead of a minus, whether he declares a club partscore or the opponents compete beyond that.

There is the very occasional time, however, where a 1NT opening on 6-3-2-2 shape could be the best option. Suppose you have:

♠A74 ♡AJ ◇A87532 ♣K7

The long minor isn't nearly as robust as on the previous hand. You wouldn't feel that great about opening 1◇ and then jumping to 3◇ next time around. All in all, a 1NT opening here would certainly be more understandable. Suppose partner's hand this time is:

♠K86 ♡Q9743 ◇64 ♣J106

After 1NT, your side will land in 2♡, with fair chances of making eight or nine tricks. If the bidding goes 1◇ – 1♡; 3◇, that contract will go down more often than not.

Opening 1NT with a Five-card Major

At one point, there was a spirited debate as to whether you should open 1NT when holding a five-card major. However, it's pretty much a dead issue now as players of all levels will do it routinely.

In researching examples for this book, I expected the gain/loss for opening 1NT with a five-card major to be negligible either way, and that indeed turned out to be the case. The disadvantage, obviously, is that you could miss a 5-3 major fit. What you gain back is some measure of preemption, where the opponents might have competed over a suit opening but might be less inclined to do so over your 1NT. Partner will also know immediately what your exact range is, as opposed to having to wait to find out if you had opened the major suit.

Here are a few examples:

	♠ J 10 7 5 3		♠ K 8
	♡ 6 2	N	♡ A J 8 5 3
	◇ Q 3	W E	◇ K J 7
	♣ J 10 9 7	S	♣ K 8 2

If East were to begin with 1♡, either it would be passed out or the opponents would compete and find their eight-card diamond fit. After a 1NT opening, however, it doesn't matter whether North-South pass or compete, as the West hand will put the contract in 2♠, which has decent chances.

In this next deal, North-South miss an eight-card fit but that isn't such a bad thing. Here are all four hands:

E-W vulnerable

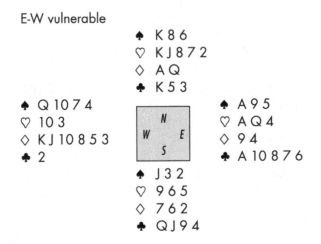

```
                    ♠ K 8 6
                    ♡ K J 8 7 2
                    ◇ A Q
                    ♣ K 5 3
    ♠ Q 10 7 4                         ♠ A 9 5
    ♡ 10 3              N              ♡ A Q 4
    ◇ K J 10 8 5 3   W     E          ◇ 9 4
    ♣ 2                  S             ♣ A 10 8 7 6
                    ♠ J 3 2
                    ♡ 9 6 5
                    ◇ 7 6 2
                    ♣ Q J 9 4
```

If North opens 1♡, East-West will get to diamonds in one of two ways. East could get in there with a risky 2♣ overcall, and West then would bid his long suit twice. Suppose instead that East and South pass. West goes by the matchpoint tenet, 'Thou shalt never let the opponents play at the one-level' and balances with 2◇. Partner will try for game, but then respect a 3◇ sign-off, and that contract will make.

After a 1NT opening bid, it's even more dangerous to overcall in clubs, so East might pass. West's perspective changes somewhat knowing there is a 15-17 hand on his left so the balancing action is no longer so automatic.

If North declares 1NT, he will get the favorable lead of a club and play one back at the second trick. East will hold off and declarer can use the entry to go after hearts. He winds up getting two clubs, three hearts, the ◇A and quite possibly an extra trick in one of the pointed suits, making seven tricks.

It's not all sunshine and roses, however, as the next example will show:

```
    ♠ 10 9 3                          ♠ A 5 4 2
    ♡ A Q 6 4 3         N             ♡ J 8 5
    ◇ A Q 8          W     E          ◇ J 9 7 6
    ♣ Q J                  S          ♣ 3 2
```

West opened 1NT and played it there. The defense took the first five clubs, switched to a spade and later got two spades and the ♡K for down two. A heart contract would have made eight tricks.

The results for these three hands show a gain on the first deal, a probable gain on the second, and a loss on the third. The bottom line is that opening

1NT with a five-card major isn't going to lead to a string of bad results and, since most of the bridge crowd goes that route, you might as well do the same.

Some players are under the impression that having opened 1NT, you can eventually show the five-card major later if you get the chance. The concise reply to that is, 'Sometimes, but not always'. Here is another case study. You are East and the auction has gone:

West	East
	1NT
2♣	2♡
2NT	?

What you've been dealt is:

♠A 7 4   ♡K J 8 6 3   ◇A 3   ♣K 9 6

If your fifth heart were a minor-suit card, this would be a no-brainer as you'd pass, being on the low end of your 15-17 point range. That's what you should also do on the actual hand. In a form of the game where getting the most plus scores you can is of vital importance, you simply cannot afford to bid the major again in the hope of getting to a 5-3 fit. If you do bid 3♡ in this case, partner will carry on to 3NT, as his hand is:

♠K J 10 3   ♡A 2   ◇J 7 5 2   ♣8 5 4

Yes, 3NT might come home some days, but the opponents are going to lead a minor and you'll need plenty of good fortune for the contract to make. Most of the time, eight tricks will be the limit of the hand, and your side goes minus when you could have had +120.

For opener to show his five-card major in this sequence, he also needs a *maximum* hand, so the partnership can settle in either four of the major or 3NT, depending on how many hearts responder has.

Strong notrumpers aren't overly troubled about missing a possible 5-3 fit in a major suit, because:

- There may be no trick difference between the major suit and notrump;
- Even if the major suit plays better, you'll have lots of company in a notrump contract, and...
- You'll gain back an advantage with the stronger hand always declaring in notrump.

For players who use the weak notrump, however, it's more of a concern. The following hand came up in a team game:

```
        ♠ A Q 3              ┌──────────┐        ♠ K J 7 5 2
        ♡ J 9                │    N     │        ♡ 10 7 6
        ◇ Q 10 8             │ W     E  │        ◇ A J 7
        ♣ K 9 7 6 3          │    S     │        ♣ A 10
                             └──────────┘
```

East opened a 12-14 1NT and got raised to game, whereupon the opponents led a heart and took the first five tricks in the suit. Meanwhile, 4♠ makes easily and there will even be an overtrick if the diamond finesse is successful. That contract was reached at the other table, where the East-West pair were using strong notrumps and opened the East hand 1♠. It was a double-digit swing in a team game, but would also be a poor result at matchpoints since more than half the field will be using strong notrumps and also open the major suit.

To avoid this kind of setback, aside from regular Stayman, weak notrumpers may set aside a 3♣ response as Puppet Stayman, asking for a four- or five-card major.

When the Opponents Bid 2◇ or Higher Over Your 1NT

As I've mentioned earlier, the opponents these days are far more likely to compete against your 1NT opening no matter what the range is. The question facing your partnership, then, is whether to try to maintain your structure despite the interference. There are really two distinct situations, and the first one we'll deal with is when their action goes past 2♣.

Although some pairs elect to play 'stolen bid' (sometimes known as 'system on', call it what you will), most established partnerships choose not to do this but rely on natural bidding when the opponents have taken away a fair amount of room. To illustrate why, we'll put you in the South chair after the auction has gone:

West	North	East	South
	1NT	2♡	?

Here is a pair of hands that you are equally likely to have:

♠ Q 10 7 6 5 ♡ 8   ◇ J 8 4 3 ♣ A 9 5
♠ Q 10 7 6   ♡ 8 7 ◇ J 8 4 3 ♣ A J 5

If you play 'system on' as responder, you can double as a transfer to make partner the declarer in a spade contract on the first example. The second hand, though, leaves you grasping for straws as you'd like to compete but are unable to double for takeout.

However, if you elect to play 'system off' except over a double or 2♣, now you're in good shape with either hand. Holding the first one, you'd bid 2♠, natural and non-forcing. On the second holding, you can announce values and support for the other suits with a takeout double.

For weak notrumpers, takeout doubles after the opponents bid is a matter of necessity. We'll now show a full deal with the auctions that would occur with both a strong and weak notrump partnership:

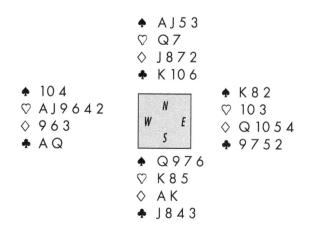

```
              ♠ A J 5 3
              ♡ Q 7
              ◇ J 8 7 2
              ♣ K 10 6
♠ 10 4                        ♠ K 8 2
♡ A J 9 6 4 2      N          ♡ 10 3
◇ 9 6 3        W      E       ◇ Q 10 5 4
♣ A Q             S           ♣ 9 7 5 2
              ♠ Q 9 7 6
              ♡ K 8 5
              ◇ A K
              ♣ J 8 4 3
```

Strong Notrumpers

West	North	East	South
			1♣
1♡	dbl	pass	1♠
pass	2♠	all pass	

Weak Notrumpers

West	North	East	South
			1NT
2♡	?		

In a strong notrump environment, South lacks the values for 1NT, so he opens 1♣. LHO overcalls in hearts and responder makes a negative double. Opener then bids spades and North will then either raise or pass, depending on whether he gives full value to his ♡Qx.

After a weak notrump by South, West still overcalls his six-card suit. Responder again would like to compete, but is in a tough spot unless the partnership has agreed upon takeout doubles. If they have, North-South will be well-placed to get to their eight-card spade fit and 'keep up' with the strong notrumpers.

If the choice of notrump range is 15-17 and the auction begins similarly, it's not quite unanimous, but again the majority of partnerships would use takeout doubles. Here's a new auction and pair of hands:

West	North	East	South
1NT	2♠	?	

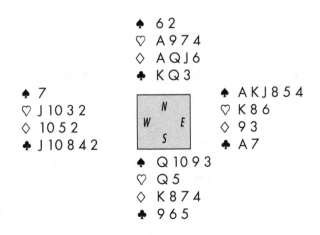

♠ A 6 3
♡ K Q 8 4
◇ J 10 3
♣ A J 8

♠ 9 4
♡ J 9 7 2
◇ A 8 7 6
♣ K 9 7

Since responder has the values to compete but no five-card or longer suit, he makes a takeout double and partner bids 3♡, ending the auction. If opener's ◇J were the ◇K, he would jump to 4♡, as responder should have 8-9 points at least to support bidding to the three-level.

If responder has length in the opponents' suit along with some high cards, he can't double as that would be takeout. With insufficient points to bid game, he should pass in the hope that partner will reopen with a double; then he can decide whether to leave it in or pull. If a strong notrumper has a maximum and a doubleton in the opponent's suit, he will likely reopen. As for weak notrumpers, it's more dangerous since partner could be relatively broke, but some of those partnerships will act in a similar manner.

As usual, a picture is worth a thousand words:

♠ 6 2
♡ A 9 7 4
◇ A Q J 6
♣ K Q 3

♠ 7
♡ J 10 3 2
◇ 10 5 2
♣ J 10 8 4 2

♠ A K J 8 5 4
♡ K 8 6
◇ 9 3
♣ A 7

♠ Q 10 9 3
♡ Q 5
◇ K 8 7 4
♣ 9 6 5

West	North	East	South
	1NT	2♠	pass
pass	dbl	all pass	

There's nothing wrong with East's 2♠ overcall, but this time he catches partner with virtually nothing along with shortness in his long suit. Unable to double, as that would be for takeout, South passes and North has just enough to reopen. The result is +300, which rates to be a good score for North-South.

When the Opponents Double or Bid 2♣ Over Your 1NT

If the other side competes with a double or 2♣, it's now more feasible for the partnership to use 'system on'. Before rushing to do so, however, you should consider the usual meanings of these actions by the opponents, which will probably depend on what the range of your 1NT opening is.

If you're using 15-17 notrumps, their double will in all likelihood be conventional, showing either any one-suiter (DONT) or some kind of two-suiter (other defenses to 1NT). A 2♣ bid could be just about anything, but in DONT it would be clubs and another suit. What a partnership is apt to do here is to keep 'system on' with Stayman and transfers, and use the redouble as showing the balance of power and seeking to penalize the opponents in their eventual contract.

The meanings change if your side plays 12-14 notrumps. Now their double will almost certainly be for penalties, in which case you need to have a system of runouts. There are many available, and you can either do a web search on the topic or refer to Andy Stark's book *The Weak Notrump*. Meanwhile, their 2♣ bid will likely be artificial. For example, in Cappelletti, it shows any one-suited hand and in HELLO, it shows either diamonds or a major-minor two-suiter. While 'system on' is an option for weak notrumpers here (i.e. double is Stayman), many of them use the double of 2♣ by responder as again showing the balance of power.

Once responder has made a 'balance of power' double or redouble, the premise is that wherever the opponents go, their contract will never be passed out. Your side has to either double or bid on. To avoid mix-ups, though, you need to have an understanding on what subsequent doubles by either partner will be. Are they going to be takeout or penalty-oriented?

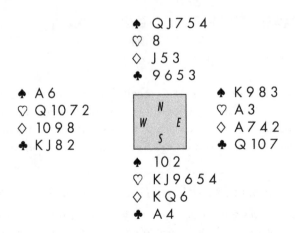

♠ QJ754
♡ 8
◇ J53
♣ 9653

♠ A6　　　　　　　　　　　♠ K983
♡ Q1072　　　　　　　　♡ A3
◇ 1098　　　　　　　　　◇ A742
♣ KJ82　　　　　　　　　♣ Q107

♠ 102
♡ KJ9654
◇ KQ6
♣ A4

East-West are playing weak notrumps, and the auction begins with:

West	North	East	South
		1NT	2♣*
dbl	pass	pass	2♡
?			

South's 2♣ was any one-suited hand, and West's double is 'balance of power' indicating 10+ HCP. This comes back around to South, who bids 2♡.

The key now is whether later doubles by either player are for takeout or for blood. If penalty doubles are agreed upon, that's what West does and opener passes. If the partnership has opted for takeout doubles, then West passes. No need to worry that it will end the auction, as East will have to bid or make a takeout double at his turn. East doubles and West leaves it in, with the same result, down two or three.

This sounds like quite a bit of work, but you need to be prepared for the opponents to interfere over your 1NT opening as they will frequently do so. After all, DONT is an acronym for 'Disturbing the Opponents' NoTrump', and if you've gone over these issues with your partner, you'll be able to overcome the roadblocks they throw in your path.

Should You Invite Game with Borderline Hands?

When your side can have as many as 26 HCP, you should always be inviting or bidding game. You'll therefore make the try if you have 9 HCP opposite a strong notrump, or 12 HCP when partner has opened a 12-14 notrump.

The gray area is when the maximum number of points your side can have is 25. That total can sometimes make game, but not always. Should responder invite with 8 points when partner opens a strong notrump? How about 11 points when he starts with a weak notrump?

My gut feeling based on a fair amount of experience was that you shouldn't invite with most 8-counts opposite 15-17, but that it might work out better to look for game with 11 points when partner has shown a balanced 12-14. As I collected about a year's worth of hand records, I had more than enough to test my theory.

Let's first consider the 8 HCP opposite 15-17 scenario. Who comes out ahead more often, the players who invite or those who pass? Well, let's take a look:

♠ A 5 4		♠ K Q 2
♡ 7 5 4 3	N	♡ A K Q
◇ Q 9 2	W E	◇ 8 7 6 3
♣ Q 9 3	S	♣ J 7 6

The West hand has a couple of nines, but it's 4-3-3-3 with no high-card strength in the longest suit. Inviting with this 8-count will result in a minus, as North leads his five-card club suit.

♠ 8 4		♠ A 10 3 2
♡ 9 6 3	N	♡ A Q 8 7
◇ K Q 7 2	W E	◇ A 8 5
♣ Q J 10 3	S	♣ K 2

On the plus side here, responder has his points in the long suits and the ♣10 as a kicker. That turns out to be an extra trick. West is worth an invite with HCP of good quality, and opener will accept.

♠ A K J 5		♠ 7 4
♡ A 3	N	♡ Q 5 4 2
◇ K 9 7 5	W E	◇ Q 8 6 4 3
♣ 8 6 5	S	♣ A 7

Most people would invite with this 8-point hand, and justifiably so because responder has 4-5 in the red suits. Opener will decline and the defense will lead clubs, but it turns out diamonds are friendly enough for declarer to make eight tricks in all.

♠ 10 9		♠ K 7 4 3
♡ K 10 7	N	♡ Q 9 5
◇ A J 2	W E	◇ 6 3
♣ A Q J 7 5	S	♣ K 10 4 3

An invite seems acceptable on this East hand, and opener will likely pass, although the good five-card suit is a temptation. Alas, on a diamond lead, West has just seven tricks available, as the defense get four diamonds and two aces.

♠ K 8 4		♠ A Q 7
♡ A J 2	N	♡ Q 6 5 4
◇ J 5 3	W E	◇ 10 6 4
♣ A Q 7 2	S	♣ 9 8 6

Responder has 4-3-3-3 shape, but the high cards are concentrated in the long suits. It looks to be worth an invite, which opener declines. Yet once again, even with a favorable club lead, declarer will only have seven tricks. When this deal was played, four Easts passed while six invited.

♠ A K Q		♠ J 8 7 5
♡ A 4 3	N	♡ K J 9 6
◇ Q 7 3	W E	◇ 6 4 2
♣ Q 7 4 2	S	♣ K 6

This time responder has 4-4 in the majors, and there could be an eight-card fit in either suit. With 17 HCP, opener will accept an invite. But once again, 3NT has little play and with the heart finesse offside, goes down two. The ratio of actions taken is similar to that of the last hand, as three Easts passed and eight invited.

♠ Q 10 9 7		♠ K 6 5 2
♡ A K Q 10	N	♡ J 6 2
◇ A 7 3	W E	◇ K J 10
♣ Q 5	S	♣ 9 6 2

A ho-hum 8-count for responder here. If he invites, the partnership will get to 4♠, which is makeable but only if declarer guesses the trump suit correctly. Against 1NT, North will probably start out with a low club from his AKxx, and West will end up making eight or nine tricks.

Sometimes responder's first action is clear-cut, such as a transfer bid. His decision on whether to invite will come on the next turn. Here is our next pair of hands:

```
♠ 8 6 3                            ♠ K 7 5
♡ A 10 9 7 4        N              ♡ K 5 3
♢ 8 5           W       E          ♢ A K 3
♣ A 6 5             S              ♣ K 4 3 2
```

If West invites with 2NT after the transfer, opener is smack-dab in the middle of his range. As it turns out, both hearts and notrump make eight tricks so his only winning action is to pass. Both possible games and a 3♡ contract will fail.

```
♠ Q 7 6 4                          ♠ A 9 8
♡ Q 6              N               ♡ A 10 4 2
♢ A 7 3        W       E           ♢ K Q 9
♣ 9 7 6 5          S               ♣ A 4 2
```

This West hand isn't as appealing as some of the others, so you would think responder might pass. However, only three of the twelve pairs did. Naturally, opener carried on to game with his 17 HCP. He got a favorable spade lead and dummy's ♡Q scored because the king was onside. However, even with the good fortune in the major suits, declarer only had eight tricks.

```
♠ Q 10                             ♠ K 8 7 6
♡ A 6 3 2          N               ♡ Q J 9 5
♢ 8 4          W       E           ♢ A 7 2
♣ Q 10 7 5 3       S               ♣ A J
```

Inviting with these West cards has two ways to win. If opener has four hearts, there could well be a game in that suit, but even if there isn't a major-suit fit, the five-card suit might enable a 3NT contract to make.

```
♠ K Q 9 2                          ♠ J 8 7
♡ Q 5              N               ♡ A 9 8 7
♢ K Q 8        W       E           ♢ 10 6 4 3
♣ A 9 5 2          S               ♣ K 3
```

East's 8 HCP look quite decent and seems to justify inviting game. If he does so, opener has the final decision to make with his 16-count. In 3NT, declarer will have some good luck on the actual layout, with the spades 3-3 and the ♢A on his right. However, the ♡K is offside, so he might well be held to eight tricks.

What we've seen, then, is that poor 8-counts will seldom produce game even if partner is maximum for his 1NT opening. Not only that, but even reasonable looking 8-point hands will often not suffice. It seems as if the only hands of this type that are worth the invite are:

- Those that have a little extra in the way of distribution, such as 5-4 shape.
- Hands that have points concentrated in the long suits and good spot cards to boot.

What we've also seen is that the two-level might not even be safe if opener declines the invite. On at least a third of the examples we've looked at, partner can only make seven tricks in a 1NT contract.

The moral of the story so far, then, is that unless responder has an 8-point hand that he's super-excited about, he should pass 1NT if he is relatively balanced and doesn't have a five-card major.

Does the same trend apply when our side has opened a weak notrump and the other hand contains exactly 11 HCP? The only way to find out is to go through another bunch of examples:

♠ K J 10 4		♠ Q 7 6
♡ K J 8		♡ 10 7 4
◇ Q 7 2		◇ A J 6 5
♣ Q 8 4		♣ A 7 5

Over partner's 12-14 notrump, East decides to invite based on his 11 HCP with two aces. Opener declines, but won't have any problems getting to eight tricks in his contract. In fact, North has ♣K109x and will probably lead that suit, allowing declarer to score his queen.

♠ K 5		♠ Q 9 6 4
♡ A Q 6 4	N	♡ J 7
◇ J 9 7	W E	◇ K Q 5 4
♣ J 9 8 2	S	♣ A 5 4

East is the weak notrumper this time, and responder has a coin-toss on whether to invite. I wouldn't criticize either a pass or an invite from West. The auction grinds to a halt in 2NT, and South leads a diamond, his five-card suit. That is one more trick for declarer and he goes after the club suit, eventually developing another one and staggering home with eight tricks.

```
♠ A 10 9 7              ♠ 8 4
♡ Q 7 2          N      ♡ K 9 8 6 3
◇ A 9 8      W       E  ◇ K J 10
♣ Q J 5          S      ♣ A 7 4
```

This combination of hands will produce a weak notrump by West, and a transfer to hearts followed by 2NT from East. Opener now could either pass, bid 3NT, sign off in 3♡ or bid game in partner's major. The partscore contracts and 3NT will all make; 4♡ is not quite so good, but also can be made as the cards lie.

```
♠ K 5 4 2               ♠ A 8 7 6
♡ 6 3 2          N      ♡ A Q J 8
◇ K Q 5 2    W       E  ◇ 10 9 3
♣ A Q           S       ♣ 7 5
```

East has a nice-looking 11 HCP and makes a Stayman inquiry, after which 4♠ is reached. North has a singleton diamond and leads it to get a ruff. There is still a trump to be lost as South started with ♠J109. However, both the heart and club kings are onside, so the contract will stumble home.

```
♠ 10 9 3                ♠ A K Q 4
♡ A Q J 4        N      ♡ 10 3 2
◇ Q 7 6 4    W       E  ◇ A 5
♣ Q 8           S       ♣ J 9 4 3
```

Again, responder (West) has a borderline hand for inviting, but does so based on the quality of his heart suit. Opener carries on to game. The heart finesse loses, but the spades come home for four tricks and declarer can develop his ninth trick in either minor suit.

```
♠ A 8                   ♠ Q 10 2
♡ J 5 4 2        N      ♡ Q 9
◇ A J 10 8 6  W       E  ◇ K 9 3 2
♣ K 4           S       ♣ A 10 9 8
```

East has a wealth of tens and nines as part of his 11-count, so this hand is a comfortable invite. North leads a spade but between the two hands declarer has a second stopper. If the contract is 3NT, it will make if the diamonds come in for five tricks.

```
♠ K J 5 2                    ♠ A Q 7
♡ Q 9 2          N           ♡ 10 8 4 3
◊ Q 8 4 2    W       E       ◊ 10 3
♣ A 6            S           ♣ K Q 8 7
```

If East tries for game over partner's weak notrump, the final contract will
be 2NT. Whichever red suit the defense leads and continues will provide declarer with his eighth trick.

```
♠ K Q 9 4 3                  ♠ 10 8 6
♡ K 6 2          N           ♡ A 8 3
◊ J 7        W       E       ◊ A Q 5 3
♣ Q 6 5          S           ♣ K 8 3
```

In this case, West will transfer and then decide whether to pass or invite.
With none of the high cards outside spades having supporting honors or spot
cards, he might not want to be too ambitious here. The partnership can make
eight or nine tricks in notrump and nine in spades, so if responder does take
the optimistic view, his side may prevail in their final contract.

```
♠ Q 3                        ♠ 9 7
♡ A 6 5 3        N           ♡ Q 8
◊ J 9 2      W       E       ◊ K Q 6 5
♣ K Q 4 2        S           ♣ A 8 7 5 3
```

When partner opens a weak notrump, East has three routes to choose from.
He can pass, invite or try to play in a minor suit. With only four cards in the
majors and his ♡Q being of dubious value, this hand would seem to fall short
of a game invite.

```
♠ K 10 8 7                   ♠ Q J 9 4
♡ A J 3          N           ♡ K Q 4 2
◊ Q 4        W       E       ◊ K 8
♣ J 10 9 2       S           ♣ K 8 7
```

With good spot cards in the black suits, West tries for game beginning with a
Stayman ask. He then raises spades and opener bids the major-suit game. It's
a reasonable one to be in and will succeed if the ♣Q is onside. On this deal,
it was in the right place.

What we've seen over the course of the last several pages is that raising
a strong notrump with 8 HCP works out well only if responder has a great-
looking hand. Even a halfway decent 8-count isn't going to cut it. Conversely,

if you have 11 HCP opposite a weak notrump, you won't often jeopardize a plus by inviting unless the hand is downright unappealing in its quality.

Why is that?

The explanation relates to flexibility in declarer's line of play. When there is a marked disparity in strength between opener and responder, there won't be a lot of dummy entries that can be used to lead towards your hand. Moreover, if the opponents go with fourth-best from longest and strongest with their lead, it will usually be a productive endeavor. However, if the two hands are roughly equal, declarer will be able to access dummy more readily, giving him additional options in the play. A side benefit is that he might get a more favorable lead, where starting out with their long suit may cost the defenders a trick.

Of course, the proof is always in the hand records, which you can browse through after each of your games and decide whether my views on the matter are valid.

QUIZ

1. Vulnerable against not and sitting East, you hold:

♠ 7 4   ♡ K 10 8 2   ♢ 10 9 3   ♣ K Q 8 2

Partner opens a strong notrump and RHO overcalls 2♠. You've agreed to play takeout doubles over interference. So...

　　a) Do you pass or make the takeout double?
　　b) If you double, what should you do if partner bids diamonds?

2. Neither vulnerable, you're now in the South chair with this hand:

♠ 10 4   ♡ K Q 6 5   ♢ K 10 9 8 3   ♣ 8 7

Partner again opens with a strong notrump and you have the 8-point decision.

　　a) Is this hand attractive enough to invite?
　　b) If you bid 2♣, the auction proceeds:

West	North	East	South
	1NT	pass	2♣
2♠	2NT	3♠	?

The opponents have seen fit to rain on your parade. You assume that for partner's 2NT bid, he'll have a double stopper in the enemy suit. How do you continue?

3. Both sides vulnerable, you pick up as South:

$$\spadesuit J\,5\,2 \quad \heartsuit K\,Q\,6\,3 \quad \diamondsuit A\,5\,4 \quad \clubsuit J\,4\,3$$

Partner opens 1NT (12-14). Should you try for game or pass?

4. Not vulnerable against vulnerable opponents, you're in the West position with this hand:

$$\spadesuit A\,5 \quad \heartsuit Q\,10\,9\,5\,2 \quad \diamondsuit A\,K\,3 \quad \clubsuit K\,9\,3$$

The auction starts with three passes and you open 1NT (15-17). Partner bids 2♣, Stayman, and then 2NT after your 2♡ reply. Should you pass or show the fifth heart, offering a choice of games?

QUIZ DISCUSSION

1.   E-W vulnerable

                          ♠ K Q J 10 5
                          ♡ A 4
                          ◇ K 8 4 2
                          ♣ 4 3
    ♠ A 6 2   ♠ 7 4
    ♡ 6 5   ┌─────────┐   ♡ K 10 8 2
    ◇ A Q J 7 6   │   N   │   ◇ 10 9 3
    ♣ A 9 5   │ W   E │   ♣ K Q 8 2
                       │   S   │
                       └─────────┘
                          ♠ 9 8 3
                          ♡ Q J 9 7 3
                          ◇ 5
                          ♣ J 10 7 6

West	North	East	South
1NT	2♠	dbl	pass
3◇	all pass		

To answer the first part of the question, East should compete over 2♠ and the only real option is a takeout double. Without a five-card suit, responder would just be guessing if he bid one of the rounded suits or 2NT.

Once West bids diamonds, responder will have to sigh and respect partner's choice, even though he only has three of them. Opener hasn't bid hearts or clubs, nor has he left the double in as he would have if he had spade length. He could easily have a five-card suit so you shouldn't be all that nervous.

That's exactly what partner holds here, five good diamonds. So 3◊ will play rather well, always making at least nine tricks with fair chances for a tenth.

Amusingly enough, with full opening values and an excellent five-card suit, North would have done better by passing 1NT and leading a top spade, holding declarer to seven tricks. Bridge is an always fascinating and sometimes maddening game.

2.   Neither vulnerable

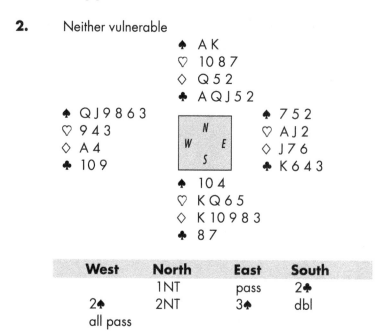

	♠ A K	
	♡ 10 8 7	
	◊ Q 5 2	
	♣ A Q J 5 2	

West	North	East	South
	1NT	pass	2♣
2♠	2NT	3♠	dbl
all pass			

Again this was a two-part question. Yes, with good diamond spots and his points concentrated in the long suits, responder has a good enough hand to try for game and asks for a four-card major with 2♣.

West desperately wants a spade lead and bids 2♠, offering his head up on a platter.

North's 2NT is reasonable, with a double stopper in the opponent's suit and a source of tricks with his long clubs.

East's 3♠ was a case of not paying enough attention to the bidding. South should have invitational values and the 1NT opener has shown extras by taking another bid in direct position. That means partner has a very skimpy overcall. At this point in time, East can go plus if he holds his tongue and obediently leads partner's suit.

South, however, has a better idea of what is happening. Even if partner has a maximum for his 1NT opening, the defense will get a head start by leading one of responder's short suits. It would take the ♡A and two diamond honors in opener's hand for the notrump game to have a play, and those are long odds. Better to double and take whatever plus is available. Opener will realize the double is values rather than penalty as their suit has been bid and raised.

Here, 3♠ doubled goes down two tricks, losing two tricks in each major suit plus a club and a diamond.

North-South may end up with a below-average score, as not many Wests stick in the overcall against a strong notrump on his left. But it's still better to go plus rather than minus, as responder would have if he had gone on to 3NT after the opponents bid spades.

3. Both vulnerable

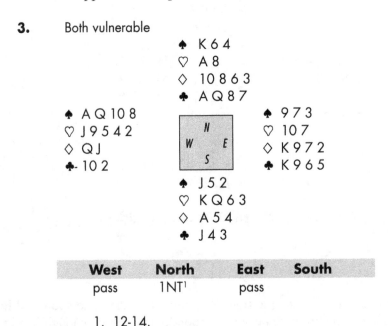

      ♠ K 6 4
      ♡ A 8
      ◇ 10 8 6 3
      ♣ A Q 8 7

♠ A Q 10 8   ♠ 9 7 3
♡ J 9 5 4 2   ♡ 10 7
◇ Q J   ◇ K 9 7 2
♣ 10 2   ♣ K 9 6 5

      ♠ J 5 2
      ♡ K Q 6 3
      ◇ A 5 4
      ♣ J 4 3

West	North	East	South
pass	1NT[1]	pass	

1. 12-14.

South has 11 HCP, but the 4-3-3-3 distribution is a negative, as are the two unsupported jacks. Experienced players at matchpoints know that it's better to tally up a plus score than try for what is going to be a very borderline game.

The East hand is interesting from a lead perspective. Does he lead from one of his kings or try a major suit instead, on the premise that responder hasn't looked for a heart or spade contract? A spade is best on this hand, but declarer only has seven tricks on anything but a club lead.

4.   N-S vulnerable

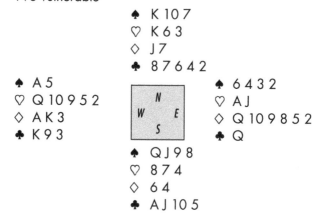

	♠ K 10 7	
	♡ K 6 3	
	◊ J 7	
	♣ 8 7 6 4 2	

♠ A 5		♠ 6 4 3 2
♡ Q 10 9 5 2		♡ A J
◊ A K 3		◊ Q 10 9 8 5 2
♣ K 9 3		♣ Q

	♠ Q J 9 8	
	♡ 8 7 4	
	◊ 6 4	
	♣ A J 10 5	

West	North	East	South
	pass	pass	pass
1NT	pass	2♣	pass
2♡	pass	2NT	pass
3♡	pass	3NT	all pass

With 16 HCP mostly in aces and kings plus his five-card heart suit, opener has enough to accept the invite and bids 3♡, offering a choice of games. East then puts the contract in 3NT.

North's lead at the table was a high spot card in clubs, won by partner's ace. The jack was returned and declarer held up until the third round. After cashing a top diamond from hand, West has nine sure tricks, six in diamonds plus a club and the two major-suit aces. Should he take the heart finesse and try for overtricks?

This is a close one. It's not a given that all pairs will be in 3NT. Some might languish in a partscore, but others will be in 5◊ or perhaps even 4♡. Those who play game in hearts will usually manage ten tricks. To beat those pairs, you'd have to take the finesse. However, +400 will probably be slightly above average. As Clint Eastwood famously said in the movie *Dirty Harry*, 'Do you feel lucky, punk?' Of course, we'd never behave that churlishly in a bridge game. Right?

4

Direct versus Balancing Action

An important skill at matchpoints is being able to compete effectively when one of the opponents has got in the first bid. Regardless of how little or how much bridge you've played, knowing when and how to make your entry into the auction can sometimes be more than a little baffling.

In the world of bridge, there will always be a contingent that favors immediate action, even if the hand isn't the most robust, and those who prefer to have more solid takeout doubles and overcalls, with the option of balancing later when it seems appropriate. There have been some interesting developments in that area. Light overcalls, especially at the one-level, have become somewhat more prevalent. However, four-card overcalls, which were fairly popular in the wake of Mike Lawrence's *The Complete Book on Overcalls at Contract Bridge*, have waned in their usage. The players whom I've consulted in the writing of this book now generally refrain from that type of overcall, electing to pass at the outset and then consider balancing later on.

Throughout the duration of this chapter, I'll touch upon the various ways to compete and the current state of expert opinion on those matters, adding some of my own comments and observations.

Overcalling

As Lawrence in his book and most teachers of the game will explain, there are three purposes for making an overcall. They are to buy the contract, to take away the opponents' bidding room, and to give partner some useful information if he winds up on lead. In a pairs game, when a one-level overcall is made on considerably less than opening values, it should at least promise a suit of good quality. For example, if the opening bid is 1◇ and the next player is not vulnerable, a 1♡ overcall could easily be made on a hand such as:

♠75 ♡KQ1096 ◇KJ6 ♣954

or even

♠J8 ♡KQJ87 ◇96 ♣10865

The reason for making such an aggressive bid, of course, is that hearts is the only suit that you have a strong desire for partner to lead. In a form of the game where even one extra trick for your side may be crucial, risky actions like this are often taken. Even if your side is vulnerable, you might still bid 1♡ with the first hand, and at least think about it with the second hand.

Here is a hand where the long suit is not as good but on which some players would once more stick in an overcall at favorable vulnerability after a 1♣ opening on their right:

♠73 ♡A 10 8 6 3 ◇Q J 10 7 ♣6 2

I personally would not bid 1♡ on these cards, but the hand does contain two suits, each of which is at least halfway decent.

Angling for a certain lead can be overdone, though, and the suit RHO has bid may increase or decrease the chances of partner being on lead. To explain further, here are two scenarios that may appear to be identical on the face of it, but in actuality have subtle differences:

- RHO has opened the bidding in a minor suit. Now your LHO is more apt to be the declarer in a major-suit contract, while either opponent might be declarer in notrump. Ergo, the lead-directing aspect of the overcall is quite important, and it would not be a shock if you saw someone bid 1♠ over 1♣ at any vulnerability with:

♠K J 9 7 6 ♡8 5 ◇7 6 4 2 ♣A 4

Besides having lead-directing value, the overcall also takes the entire one-level away from responder.

- If RHO has opened in a major suit, it's not quite the same. If LHO has a fit he'll agree that suit as trumps and you are going to be on lead. As a matter of fact, even if they have a fit in the other major, you'll still be on lead most of the time after an auction like 1♠ – 1NT; 2♡. Because of the forcing notrump response, it's more likely that LHO will declare the notrump contracts, but if they have no fit, you're treading on more dangerous ground. Also, you'll probably need to go to the two-level in making your overcall. Since you'll be on lead a greater amount of the time when they open 1♡ or 1♠, the main reason for overcalling will be an attempt to buy the contract, based on high-card values and/or attractive distribution.

Sometimes what they open will not make one speck of difference in whether you decide to overcall. Suppose your hand is:

♠ 9 7   ♡ K 9 5 2   ◇ A Q 10 8 7 2   ♣ J

If RHO opens 1♣, you'd gladly bid 1◇. Even if he were to open 1♠, you still have enough distribution to bid diamonds at the two-level, as your loser count is six.

On the next hand, you are not vulnerable against vulnerable opponents:

♠ Q 6   ♡ K Q 9 7 5   ◇ A 4   ♣ 8 7 5 2

If RHO has opened 1◇, you have a clear-cut 1♡ overcall. Your suit is pretty good and one you'd want partner to lead. Since you don't have to increase the level, you have a reasonable margin of safety.

However, if the bid on your right is 1♠, there is a greater degree of risk in overcalling. The loser count is seven, which makes venturing to the two-level a marginal proposition. Two of your high-card points consist of the dubious holding of Qx in the opponents' suit. Also, if they have a fit in opener's suit, you'll be the one on lead, so that purpose for overcalling has gone by the wayside. Even if responder declares a notrump contract, you don't really mind either a diamond or club lead from partner.

This might well be the entire deal:

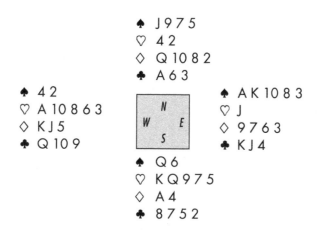

After 1♠ – 2♡, it would go two passes followed by a double from opener. Yes, the East hand is minimum, but in this age of negative doubles, he is expected to cater to the trap pass and reopen if he has the normal complement of defensive tricks as he does here. Looking at the traveler for this board, we have:

North-South	+100	3 pairs
	−120	1 pair
	−140	1 pair
	−150	1 pair
	−300	3 pairs
	−500	2 pairs

For our next hand, you are vulnerable against non-vulnerable opponents. You've been dealt this collection:

♠ Q 9 5   ♡ —   ◇ K J 6 2   ♣ Q J 9 7 5 4

RHO opens 1♡. With 9 HCP, do you pass or overcall in your long suit?

The pluses in favor of bidding are that the distribution is attractive and it's a six-loser hand. As one of my consultants for this book has remarked, a void (especially in the opponents' suit) is a 'wild card' that can have a huge impact on who can make what.

The main strike against overcalling is that you'll feel slightly uncomfortable in sitting for any high-level penalty doubles that partner makes. In a pairs game, there would be some passers and some 2♣ bidders.

The entire deal is:

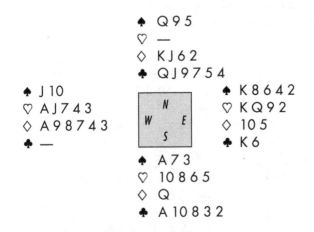

```
                    ♠ Q 9 5
                    ♡ —
                    ◇ K J 6 2
                    ♣ Q J 9 7 5 4
   ♠ J 10                              ♠ K 8 6 4 2
   ♡ A J 7 4 3          N              ♡ K Q 9 2
   ◇ A 9 8 7 4 3    W        E         ◇ 10 5
   ♣ —                  S              ♣ K 6
                    ♠ A 7 3
                    ♡ 10 8 6 5
                    ◇ Q
                    ♣ A 10 8 3 2
```

West	North	East	South
1♡	2♣	4♡	5♣
5♡	pass	pass	6♣
pass	pass	dbl	all pass

As you can see, East-West can make ten tricks in hearts and only the 4-0 trump split prevents them from making eleven. Meanwhile, North-South are cold for eleven tricks in their club fit and can make twelve if declarer finesses in the trump suit.

Although this rather famous deal was actually played in a team game, North also has an important decision to make with that hand at matchpoints. This example demonstrates that having extra length in your suit and an un-balanced hand can be more important than high-card strength.

I've discovered in the course of my research for this book that many ex-pert players are loath to make four-card overcalls at matchpoints. Since there are a lot of competitive auctions in a pairs game, they'd rather be secure in the knowledge of whether there is an eight-card fit. That doesn't mean, though, that you should shy away from overcalling a decent four-card suit if there isn't a convenient way to enter the bidding later. The following two hands will serve to illustrate.

First, you are vulnerable against not, looking at these cards:

♠ Q J 5   ♡ A K 8 4   ◇ 10 9   ♣ A 8 4 3

RHO has opened 1♣. While you have a good hand, no direct bid is ideal. You lack the diamond support for a takeout double, and the four-card heart suit doesn't have enough texture. This is one of the three hand types that is well-suited to balancing later if the opponents grind to a halt.

For our second example, both sides are vulnerable and your hand consists of:

♠ A K 10 8   ♡ 9 2   ◇ 8 6 4   ♣ A 8 3 2

Another 1♣ opening on your right, so do you dip your toes into the water with 1♠? I asked two experts – one passed, and the other bid 1♠. In contrast to the last example, it will be difficult to enter the fray later with this hand, because of the minimal point-count and lack of support for the red suits.

The pluses for overcalling are that you do want a spade lead, you are taking away the opponents' bidding space, and you may be able to win the contract since you have the master suit. The main disadvantages, of course, are that you don't have a fifth spade and are vulnerable.

All right, then, recognizing that it's just one example, what's the verdict when we see all four hands in this case? Here they are:

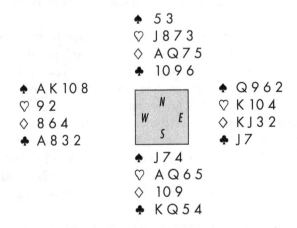

```
                    ♠  5 3
                    ♡  J 8 7 3
                    ◇  A Q 7 5
                    ♣  10 9 6
♠ A K 10 8                              ♠ Q 9 6 2
♡ 9 2                 N                 ♡ K 10 4
◇ 8 6 4           W       E             ◇ K J 3 2
♣ A 8 3 2             S                 ♣ J 7
                    ♠  J 7 4
                    ♡  A Q 6 5
                    ◇  10 9
                    ♣  K Q 5 4
```

Assuming West overcalls 1♠, then regardless of whether North makes a negative double, East will compete to 2♠. At this point, North-South will go down one or two tricks if they push on to 3♡.

If West passes 1♣, responder will bid 1♡ and get raised. Now it's very dicey for either East or West to act at the two-level.

Takeout Doubles

You'll often have a decision to make between an overcall and a takeout double. More experienced players will generally lean in favor of the double as it caters to more possibilities for the trump suit. Here are a few examples.

The auction starts with 1♠ on your right, and you have:

♠7 ♡Q 10 7 6 ◇A Q 7 5 3 ♣K 9 2

Yes, there is a five-card diamond suit, but also four-card support for the unbid major and a respectable club holding to boot. A fair number of players would go for the takeout double instead of the overcall. It leads to the best result for your side on this occasion as partner has:

♠Q 9 8 6 ♡A J 5 ◇6 ♣J 10 7 6 3

The eight-card fit happens to be in clubs, not in either of the red suits. After a 2◇ overcall, partner may be less than enthused, but will have to pass as he has neither the values nor the suit for either 2NT or 3♣.

In our next one, both the double and overcall have a flaw:

♠ A Q 4   ♡ 6   ◇ A 9 6 5 3   ♣ K 10 8 6

RHO has opened 1♡. Unlike the previous hand, you don't have four cards in the unbid major. At the same time, however, the quality of the five-card suit is not great. Since there are a couple of honors in the three-card spade holding, the takeout double seems to offer more flexibility than a 2◇ bid.

Sometimes, though, it's best to go with the overcall even if you have shortness in the enemy suit. When RHO opens 1♠ and you have:

♠ 5   ♡ J 9 7   ◇ A Q J 10 6   ♣ A K 4 2

Here, 2◇ is the most descriptive initial salvo. Also, with 15 HCP, you have enough values to take a further call if the auction continues:

LHO	Partner	RHO	You
		1♠	2◇
2♠	pass	pass	?

At that point, you could either bid 3♣ or double, which is for takeout and usually will be 1=3=6=3 or 1=3=5=4 shape, as you haven't made a takeout double in the first place.

If the hand is in the ballpark for a takeout double, you might want to take that route even if there is a slight distributional flaw. The next two hands are cases in point.

Everyone vulnerable, you hold:

♠ A 9 6 2   ♡ K J 9   ◇ Q 9 8 4   ♣ J 6

RHO has opened 1♣ after two passes. You have 11 HCP, with the ♣J probably a wasted value. But the hand has too many queens and jacks for a later entry into the bidding. If you intend to compete at some point, now would be the best time to do it, when the auction is still at a convenient level. The three-card heart holding is good enough to play as the trump suit if partner bids them.

Neither side is vulnerable for the next hand:

♠ K 10 7 6   ♡ A Q J 9   ◇ A 4   ♣ 8 6 3

The auction starts with 1♣ again by the player on your right. You'd like to have a third diamond, but you should still double. If partner bids a major, you'll be in clover. And if he bids 1◊? You can't do anything other than pass since if you now bid a major suit or 1NT, he will expect a better hand. You'll have to pass and hope that's the best strain. Advancer may well have five or more of the suit to bid diamonds rather than a major or notrump. Besides, the auction is unlikely to die at the one-level.

Balancing

Balancing has always been part of the game, yet it seems counter-intuitive to pass originally and then compete later when the opponents have been able to describe their respective hands to each other. But there is indeed a method to the madness. There are both advantages and pitfalls to biding your time before choosing whether to enter the bidding. Here is the rationale behind the waiting game in a nutshell:

- If you bid immediately, one of the opponents hasn't yet been heard from, and if he has a medium to strong hand, you could be in serious trouble. Also, the information you convey will be a two-way street, possibly of more use to the other side than it is to partner.

  If the opponents have exchanged a bid or two and then settled in a partscore, there is less chance of running into a buzz-saw as they're known to have a limited amount of high-card points. Now, rather than partner maybe being close to broke, you have the assurance that he'll have at least a smattering of values.

- The nature of the opponents' bidding may have increased the chances of your side having a decent fit. Suppose, for example, that you have three or even four cards in their suit, in an auction like:

LHO	RHO
1◊	1♡
2♡	pass

Without giving you the entire deal, all you need to know is that you have 10-11 HCP and three relatively nondescript hearts. Since they presumably have an eight- or nine-card fit in hearts, that will be partner's shortness and there is now a greater degree of safety in competing. Also, one of the precepts of winning at matchpoints is never to sell out at the two-level if there is any justification whatsoever for bidding. As we'll see in a later chapter, the three-level is an entirely different matter.

- The payback for competing later rather than earlier is the time you've given the opponents to divulge the nature of their hands. That is why, if you are thinking of balancing, you should have either:

  a) A distributional hand where it was not feasible to take immediate action, and/or

  b) A more balanced hand that is near opening strength with the high cards being aces and kings. A plethora of queens and jacks is not going to cut it when you're competing this late in the auction.

Anyway, that's enough of the lead-in for this discussion; let's now examine the three hand types on which you should come into the auction belatedly.

Sometimes you'll be coming in with a takeout double, your strength being limited by the fact that you haven't done so on your previous turn. Your side is vulnerable and the opponents are not as the auction has gone:

West	North (you)	East	South
		1♦	pass
1♠	pass	2♠	pass
pass	?		

You're looking at these cards:

♠ A J 7 2   ♡ K 9 7 3   ♢ 4   ♣ Q 10 8 6

At adverse vulnerability, without a lot of points or body in the red suits, you sensibly passed at your first turn. When LHO has supported responder's suit and the auction has died in a partscore, you now have two key pieces of information that should tilt you in favor of competing. Since they have a likely eight-card or better fit, partner is marked for extreme shortness. He will also have roughly 7-10 points of his own since they haven't tried for game. Barring a lot of diamonds in his hand, your side will also have a playable fit in a rounded suit. Taking all this into consideration, you can make a takeout double and be on reasonably safe ground. It turns out partner's hand is:

♠ 4   ♡ Q 10 4   ♢ Q 10 6 3   ♣ K 9 4 3 2

Trumps divide 2-2, so you make 3♣ easily, losing a club, a diamond and one or two hearts. If the opponents soldier on to 3♠, that contract will go down. As you see here, partner is on the low end of his assumed 7-10 points, although he does have a fifth club.

On some occasions, you'll find yourself balancing with a delayed overcall, usually for similar reasons as on the last example. On the next deal, both sides are not vulnerable and you have:

♠A 9 2   ♡J 10 8 7 5 4   ◇K J 3   ♣6

The bidding so far is:

West	North	East	South (you)
1♣	pass	1♠	pass
2♠	pass	pass	?

Your decision not to make an immediate overcall was due to the limited number of points but also the mediocre quality of your long suit. With the king-jack of the other unbid suit, you didn't necessarily want to suggest a heart lead.

When the opponents then stop in 2♠, though, you should now reevaluate the situation. Once again, partner can't have a lot of spades, one or two at the most. He will also have around 7-10 points. And while he might not have length in hearts, you would expect him to have two or three. Finally, you do have some chance of beating 3♠ if you lead your singleton club. There is enough justification, then, to bid 3♡, as you could either make it or push the opponents a level higher and beyond their depth.

This time, you hit the jackpot in a big way, as the entire deal is:

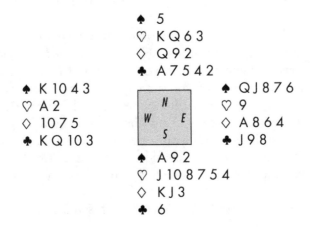

♠ 5
♡ K Q 6 3
◇ Q 9 2
♣ A 7 5 4 2

♠ K 10 4 3   ♠ Q J 8 7 6
♡ A 2   ♡ 9
◇ 10 7 5   ◇ A 8 6 4
♣ K Q 10 3   ♣ J 9 8

♠ A 9 2
♡ J 10 8 7 5 4
◇ K J 3
♣ 6

Although a veteran player knows not to 'hang' partner for balancing, North felt this hand was an exception and raised to game. As you can see, despite his 11-count, he never had a convenient action to take. Over 4♡, East made what we call a 'spite' double ('How dare you!') and the result was making five, for +690.

The third hand-type is one that is richer in high cards but didn't shout out for a direct bid. We touched upon it briefly in the discussion about four-card overcalls. You were vulnerable against non-vulnerable opponents and had been dealt:

♠QJ5 ♡AK84 ◊109 ♣A843

RHO had opened 1♣ and you were caught in no-man's land. The only half-way reasonable action was 1♡ and you didn't have a five-card suit, so for the time being you passed. The auction continued:

West	North (you)	East	South
1♣	pass	1◊	pass
1NT	pass	2◊	pass
pass	?		

The difference between this and the earlier sequences is that opener has not supported responder's suit. That said, West has shown a balanced hand and his partner has shown extra diamond length. Partner may be a shade weaker this time, but so might East as he's shown no inclination to leave opener in 1NT, the highest-paying contract.

It's right to balance here because your hand is mostly aces and kings, and your major-suit holdings are rather good. Also, the shortness in the opponents' diamonds could be useful if your side declares the eventual contract. Since you're prepared for whichever of the majors South bids, you can make a takeout double here.

This time, you don't have an eight-card fit, but will manage to go plus anyway, as partner has:

♠K873 ♡J103 ◊Q73 ♣QJ2

As it turns out, everything is friendly with the spades 3-3 and both the ♡Q and ♣K onside. But even if one of the outstanding cards were wrong, you'd have made eight tricks as opposed to defeating their contract two tricks and only chalking up +100. Incidentally, if South had passed your double (which is a very risky option), that would have yielded a top board for your side.

Pre-balancing

I'll just touch briefly on this subject. Pre-balancing is when the player in direct seat has slightly less than full values for a takeout double or overcall, but knows from his holdings that the other hand won't have the distribution to reopen. Consequently, he takes upon himself the onus of competing, with the understanding that partner should give him some leeway. This will typically occur in a bid-and-raise auction by the opponents.

Suppose, with North-South vulnerable, the auction goes:

West	North	East (you)	South
			1♡
pass	2♡	?	

You're in possession of this middling hand:

♠K Q 4   ♡4   ◇A 8 7 5 3   ♣J 9 5 3

First off, you can tell from your shortness in hearts that if you pass, West is unlikely to balance, as he will have some length in hearts, a flattish hand and not that many points. So if your side is going to buy the contract or nudge the opponents to the three-level, it will have to be you who takes action. Bidding 3◇ seems too unilateral and could be very wrong, so that leaves a takeout double. In fact, partner has a void in diamonds and length in both black suits, so either 2♠ or 3♣ are playable contracts.

Free Bids

I was looking on the internet for an adequate definition of the term 'free bid' and nothing seemed to quite get to the heart of the matter. So here is my attempt. The situation is that you've taken an earlier bid during the auction:

1) RHO has bid or overcalled.

2) Since you're in direct seat, partner can keep the bidding alive if you pass.

3) Ergo, an immediate action by you ought to show better than a minimum hand.

In the distant past, *any* such bid was deemed to show extra values, and that still holds true if the 'free bid' is made at the three-level. That principle does not hold so much at the two-level, as you might have to establish a fit in a major suit or advertise extra length.

Two more quickies for you. On the first one, North-South are vulnerable and you're sitting West. The auction has begun with:

West (you)	North	East	South
1◊	1♡	dbl	2♡
?			

Your hand is:

♠ Q 9 7 5   ♡ A 9 6   ◊ A Q 8 7   ♣ 8 2

Since partner has made a negative double, you're fine bidding 2♠ here to confirm the fit, as you are not increasing the level of the contract.

Sometimes you could take another bid at the two-level even though there might not be a fit. With both sides vulnerable, the bidding unfolds as follows:

West (you)	North	East	South
1♠	pass	1NT*	2◊
?			

We'll look at two similar hands for opener here. One is:

♠ A Q 9 6 3   ♡ A Q 6 2   ◊ 2   ♣ J 4 3

You would have bid 2♡ over partner's forcing notrump response. Does RHO's interference change things? Although your side is never going to lose a spade fit, it could miss out on a heart contract if you pass and LHO raises diamonds. Therefore, you should bid 2♡ here.

♠ A Q 9 6 3   ♡ A Q 6 2   ◊ 8 2   ♣ 4 3

The only difference here, aside from having a point fewer, is that you're 2-2 in the minors instead of having shortness in their suit. Now it's just as likely that the player on your left will pass, in which case responder still has a say. A case can be made for passing with this minimum hand, although no one would fault a 2♡ bid here either. When this deal was played, it turned out that East had the same nine cards in the minors that you had in the majors, so your best result was defending their 2◊ contract.

QUIZ

1. North-South vulnerable, you are sitting East with:

$$♠A872 \quad ♡10654 \quad ◇K10 \quad ♣AK10$$

The auction so far is:

West	North	East (you)	South
			1◇
pass	1♡	?	

You have 14 HCP in prime values, although the ◇K could be badly placed. Do you pass or venture a takeout double?

2. North-South vulnerable again, you are in the South chair with this hand:

$$♠AQ1075 \quad ♡63 \quad ◇93 \quad ♣AKJ6$$

There's been a fair amount of bidding prior to your turn:

West	North	East	South (you)
1NT¹	pass	2◇*	?

1. 15-17.

After RHO's transfer to hearts, should you get in those spades now or pass, expecting to have the chance to balance at the two-level at your next opportunity?

3. Neither side vulnerable this time, you pick up a slightly better than average hand pointwise:

$$♠98 \quad ♡KQJ8 \quad ◇J972 \quad ♣A32$$

The auction gets underway with:

West	North	East	South (you)
pass	pass	1◇	?

Is this a good time for a four-card overcall?

4. For this one, North-South are vulnerable and you as West have:

♠ Q J 10 7 5   ♡ J 10 2   ◇ A 4   ♣ J 10 5

RHO deals and opens 1♡. You can mention your suit at the one-level here. Should you?

5. Both sides vulnerable, this 12-count is your lot in life:

♠ K Q 9 4   ♡ K 5 3   ◇ Q 9   ♣ Q 8 6 2

After two passes, East on your right opens 1◇. Do you pass for now or go with a takeout double?
    This is a two-parter. Suppose you pass and the auction continues with:

West	North	East	South (you)
pass	pass	1◇	pass
1NT	pass	pass	?

Is it time for you to balance?

6. East-West vulnerable, you're in the West seat holding these cards:

♠ A 9 8   ♡ J   ◇ J 10 6 3   ♣ A Q 9 7 5

After two passes, RHO opens 1♡. What's your choice – a 2♣ overcall or a takeout double?

1.   N-S vulnerable

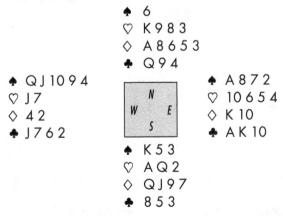

                    ♠ 6
                    ♡ K 9 8 3
                    ◇ A 8 6 5 3
                    ♣ Q 9 4

♠ Q J 10 9 4   ♠ A 8 7 2
♡ J 7   ♡ 10 6 5 4
◇ 4 2   ◇ K 10
♣ J 7 6 2   ♣ A K 10

                    ♠ K 5 3
                    ♡ A Q 2
                    ◇ Q J 9 7
                    ♣ 8 5 3

West	North	East	South
			1◇
pass	1♡	dbl	pass
1♠	2◇	pass	pass
2♠	3◇	pass	pass
3♠	all pass		

If East passes RHO's 1♡ response, North-South are likely to play the contract in some number of diamonds. But even though East doesn't have a fourth club, with 14 HCP in aces and kings, his hand seems to be worth a bid.

Note how the takeout double brings West into the picture so that he is now willing to compete all the way to the three-level with his 5-4 in the black suits. East-West do quite nicely in their spade contract, losing a trump, two hearts and a diamond. North-South are likely to make nine tricks in diamonds but will go down if they take the push to the four-level.

2. N-S vulnerable

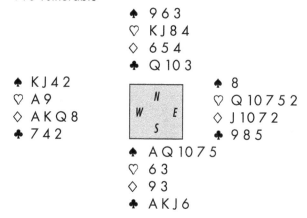

		♠ 9 6 3	
		♡ K J 8 4	
		◇ 6 5 4	
		♣ Q 10 3	

♠ K J 4 2
♡ A 9
◇ A K Q 8
♣ 7 4 2

♠ 8
♡ Q 10 7 5 2
◇ J 10 7 2
♣ 9 8 5

♠ A Q 10 7 5
♡ 6 3
◇ 9 3
♣ A K J 6

West	North	East	South
1NT	pass	2◇*	2♠
dbl	pass	3♡	all pass

This was the table result, where South did bid his five-card suit. South's hand is pretty good although you don't know how strong the transfer bidder is. Passing for now and balancing later is also a viable option.

Unlike the responder, when the 1NT bidder doubles it's for takeout only when an overcall is passed around to him. An immediate double in direct seat, as here, is penalty-oriented.

If East decides to pull the double with his extremely poor hand, he should bid 3◇ rather than 3♡ — partner already knows he has five hearts. Had he done that, his side would have landed in an eight-card fit and got out for down one.

West was livid with his partner for removing the double, but 2♠ is cold, even on the best defense of three top diamonds. South ruffs and leads a heart. Once the king is set up as a trick, he then cashes one high trump and plays four rounds of clubs. Try as they may, the defenders cannot get a sixth trick. Opener's lack of any good intermediates in the trump suit come back to haunt him, as the hand is an open book for South after the double reveals the bad trump break.

3.   Neither vulnerable

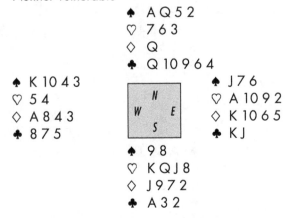

♠ A Q 5 2
♡ 7 6 3
◇ Q
♣ Q 10 9 6 4

♠ K 10 4 3
♡ 5 4
◇ A 8 4 3
♣ 8 7 5

♠ J 7 6
♡ A 10 9 2
◇ K 10 6 5
♣ K J

♠ 9 8
♡ K Q J 8
◇ J 9 7 2
♣ A 3 2

West	North	East	South
pass	pass	1◇	1♡
dbl	2♡	all pass	

It's a case of now or never for South over 1◇, as his decision won't get any easier if he passes. LHO will respond 1♠ and opener will rebid 1NT. Now South has little choice but to pass and defend. So, with a suit headed by the KQJ, he tosses in the four-card overcall.

West barely has enough for a negative double and North raises partner's major. West might compete to 3◇ at his next turn, but advancer is going to persist in the heart suit regardless.

A heart contract will often make eight or nine tricks in practice. If East-West lead trumps to stop declarer from ruffing diamonds in dummy, they will lose a trump trick and South can establish dummy's club suit for discards. Otherwise, he can finesse in spades and cross-ruff in the pointed suits.

4.   N-S vulnerable

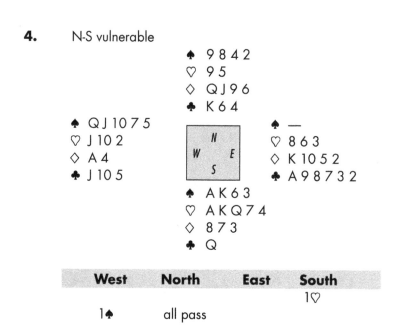

♠ 9 8 4 2
♡ 9 5
◇ Q J 9 6
♣ K 6 4

♠ Q J 10 7 5
♡ J 10 2
◇ A 4
♣ J 10 5

♠ —
♡ 8 6 3
◇ K 10 5 2
♣ A 9 8 7 3 2

♠ A K 6 3
♡ A K Q 7 4
◇ 8 7 3
♣ Q

West	North	East	South
			1♡
1♠	all pass		

This was an amusing deal from a club game, and I was the guilty party in the West chair. It seemed so automatic to overcall 1♠ with a suit headed by the QJ10 that I forgot the warning signs. To start with, the opening bid was in a major suit, and that meant I was probably going to be on lead if they had a heart fit. Secondly, I had the death holding of three cards in their suit. Most important, however, was that when you tally up the loser count, I had nine of them: three each in clubs and hearts, two in spades and another in diamonds. If you overcall and partner has any semblance of a fit, your side will likely get overboard in a competitive auction.

A great many pairs treat a new suit by the partner of the overcaller as a one-round force, so East was reluctant to bid his clubs on what might be a total misfit.

The supreme irony of this hand is that had I passed, LHO would have responded 1♠ and opener would have then jumped to 3♠ or 4♠. Then I'd be smugly defending a high-level contract with a good five-card holding in their suit.

This was a classic instance of poetic justice, where I made a dubious overcall and wound up with egg on my face.

5. Both vulnerable

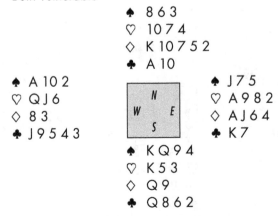

	♠ 8 6 3	
	♡ 10 7 4	
	◇ K 10 7 5 2	
	♣ A 10	
♠ A 10 2		**♠ J 7 5**
♡ Q J 6		**♡ A 9 8 2**
◇ 8 3		**◇ A J 6 4**
♣ J 9 5 4 3		**♣ K 7**
	♠ K Q 9 4	
	♡ K 5 3	
	◇ Q 9	
	♣ Q 8 6 2	

West	North	East	South
pass	pass	1◇	pass
1NT	pass	pass	dbl
pass	2♡	all pass	

South passed the 1◇ opening rather than double with his soft 12-count and only three-card support for hearts. He then fell from grace, however, by balancing when LHO's 1NT response came back to him. At this point, North had a choice of evils. He could pass the double of 1NT, a contract that was likely to make. Or he could remove to the stronger of his three-card majors (which is what he did), landing in an inglorious 3-3 heart fit and going down four vulnerable.

The danger here was that East-West had not found a trump suit, so it was quite possible that North-South did not have a playable fit either. The real problem with South's action, though, was that he was aceless and had three queens as part of his 12-count. To balance with a flat hand like this, you need your values to be aces and kings.

6.   E-W vulnerable

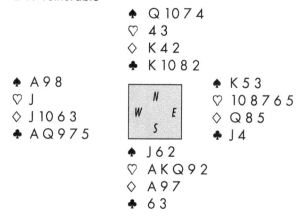

♠ Q 10 7 4
♡ 4 3
◇ K 4 2
♣ K 10 8 2

♠ A 9 8
♡ J
◇ J 10 6 3
♣ A Q 9 7 5

♠ K 5 3
♡ 10 8 7 6 5
◇ Q 8 5
♣ J 4

♠ J 6 2
♡ A K Q 9 2
◇ A 9 7
♣ 6 3

West	North	East	South
	pass	pass	1♡
dbl	pass	1♠	pass
pass	dbl	1NT	pass
pass	dbl	pass	pass
2♣	dbl	all pass	

West's choice here was between a 2♣ overcall and a takeout double. Although the clubs are not bad and he has only three spades, the double would meet with an approving eye from most experts.

East is right to bid 1♠ over the double, as he'd need a better hand (around 8-10) to suggest notrump as a contract. It's his best suit, even if there are only three of them.

Note what North did over the double. He just waited. With 8 HCP and good holdings in two of the enemy suits, he knew the opponents might not have a fit and was not inclined to take them off the hook by bidding. His subsequent doubles were penalty-oriented, since he had already denied a heart fit and limited his hand by the failure to redouble. The opponents then vainly tried to find greener pastures and came to rest in 2♣. If West had gone with the 2♣ overcall instead, that would have gone two passes to a reopening double by South, left in by North.

More than half of the East-West pairs avoided -200 or -500, though. After the takeout double, North often bid 1♠ or 1NT, which the opponents were only too glad to pass out.

In talking with several expert players about this deal, I discovered that they also bid over the double rather than pass. That's not my way of thinking on the North cards, as I'd be smelling blood, but I seem to be in the minority.

5

The Preemptive Melee

As I mentioned earlier in the book, the bridge world at large is a good deal friskier with its preemptive style in the here and now. There are still pairs who like to be sound in their actions, but a greater number will tend to be moderately light or extremely light when they preempt.

The purpose of this chapter is not to recommend one style of preempting over another: that is up to you and your partner. We will, however, touch upon several issues that relate to preempts and sacrifices.

Third-seat Preempts

With partner having passed originally, you can take a certain amount of liberty when preempting in third seat. For example, it would not be unusual to see a non-vulnerable 3◇ opening in third chair on this rather miniscule hand:

♠5 ♡J43 ◇K987542 ♣J10

On the flip side, though, the bidder might choose for tactical reasons to pre-empt on a hand he would have opened at the one-level in first or second seat. We have a couple of examples, beginning with:

♠2 ♡AJ ◇KQ108432 ♣J73

In first seat, the hand would be too strong point-wise for a 3◇ preempt, and you would likely open 1◇ instead. After two passes, however, the thought processes for the person holding these cards might be along these lines:

- With no length in either major suit and partner having passed, it's unlikely that our side can make game.
- If I open 1◇, then the opponents will be able to get in cheaply with a major suit. Moreover, if I keep bidding diamonds, partner will expect a better hand and more in the way of defense, so...
- I'm going to open 3◇ and deprive them of two levels of bidding space. It's what I'd have to do eventually if I want to buy the contract any-way, so why not get it over with in one fell swoop?

The decision to open with a 'heavy' preempt in third seat bore fruit on this occasion, as the four hands were:

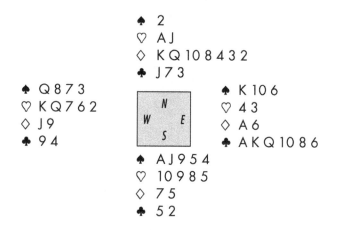

<pre>
                         ♠ 2
                         ♡ A J
                         ◇ K Q 10 8 4 3 2
                         ♣ J 7 3
        ♠ Q 8 7 3   ♠ K 10 6
        ♡ K Q 7 6 2   N   ♡ 4 3
        ◇ J 9   W   E   ◇ A 6
        ♣ 9 4   S   ♣ A K Q 10 8 6
                         ♠ A J 9 5 4
                         ♡ 10 9 8 5
                         ◇ 7 5
                         ♣ 5 2
</pre>

If North were to open 1◇, East would conveniently be able to overall 2♣ or even, if the mood took him, 1NT. East-West would be able to exchange information and, in the end, either sell out to 3◇ or bid on to 4♣.

A 3◇ opening, by contrast, presents East with a real headache. Does he overcall clubs at the four-level or venture 3NT? The latter contract could be an easy make if partner has as little as the ♠A and some heart length.

Now let's move over to the West hand and the decision he faces if partner overcalls 3NT. Should he leave it there or bid 4♣ (Stayman in many partnerships), intending to settle in a major suit? Either could be right — it's just a guess.

For our next example, you are not vulnerable against vulnerable opponents, with this appealing distribution:

♠A J 10 8 6 4 3 2 ♡A J 7 ◇— ♣9 6

Again, if you were in first or second seat, a 4♠ opening could turn out to be a mistake as your partner, who might easily have enough for a slam to make, would likely pass. In third seat, you have no such fears – you need three or four useful cards for slam and he can't possibly have them. Again, since your final destination will be 4♠, you might as well go right there immediately.

This time, once the curtain is raised on all four hands, we're looking at:

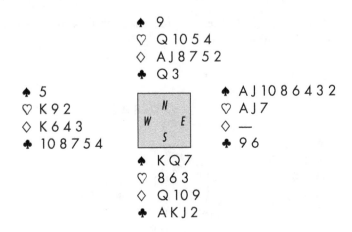

♠ 9
♥ Q 10 5 4
♦ A J 8 7 5 2
♣ Q 3

♠ 5
♥ K 9 2
♦ K 6 4 3
♣ 10 8 7 5 4

♠ A J 10 8 6 4 3 2
♥ A J 7
♦ —
♣ 9 6

♠ K Q 7
♥ 8 6 3
♦ Q 10 9
♣ A K J 2

Over a 1♠ opening, it's easy for North-South as South would overcall 1NT and his side would reach the notrump game after a Stayman inquiry. For East to bid 4♠ at that point would be a complete roll of the dice as he could easily be defeating the enemy contract. With the ◇K onside and the ♣Q available as an entry, South cannot be prevented from making nine tricks in notrump, and will take ten or eleven if the opponents don't find a heart switch.

Over an opening 4♠, though, South may or may not double. The standard for most partnerships is that doubles of preempts up to 4♡ are takeout-oriented, while a double of 4♠ shows enough cards to beat the contract but doesn't have to be a trump stack. If South were to double, North would probably leave it in, but also might be wondering if his side could make five of a red suit.

More on Responding to a Weak Two-bid

In the second chapter, I noted that the 2NT 'feature ask' over a weak two-bid is no longer universal as the suit quality is not exactly written in stone nowadays. As a result, a fair number of partnerships use some form of Ogust for the 2NT inquiry.

Aside from 2NT, the partner of the weak two-bidder can also introduce a suit of his own, which leads us to a sad story for these two hands:

♠ K 9
♥ 10 3
♦ K Q J 10 8 7
♣ 10 7 3

♠ A J 6
♥ K J 9 7 6
♦ A 6 2
♣ K 5

West opened 2◇ and East bid 2♡, which he intended as forcing. His plan was to see if there was a heart fit and then bid 3NT if partner was unable to support. However, West passed and there was much gnashing of teeth by responder. The problem was, of course, that the 2◇ opener thought that 2♡ was merely contract improvement and that he was not obligated to bid again.

If you are playing with someone for the first time, you should assume that a new-suit response to a weak two-bid is a one-round force, just as if you'd opened at the one-level. I do know of some partnerships who agree that a 2♡ or 2♠ response to 2◇ can be passed, but at the same time, the hand will have at least invitational strength. If the 2◇ bidder has a fit or is on the top of his range, he is expected to keep the bidding alive.

So what should West do over the 2♡ response? He has two options:

- He could repeat his excellent diamond suit, but even better...
- He could bid 2♠. This does not show length, as you don't open a weak two-bid with a side four-card major. This action shows a better-than-minimum hand, with a high-card value in the suit bid.

Regardless of how the weak two-bidder proceeds, East will follow up with 3NT with this particular hand.

On the assumption that a new suit over a weak two-bid is forcing (or at least invitational), what is opener to rebid? There are three routes to choose from:

- With three-card support, he can raise. As a matter of fact, even with a doubleton headed by the queen or better, he can support, as partner will have at least six of his suit or a very good five-card holding.
- With a maximum or near-maximum hand and an outside value, he bids that suit (e.g. the 2♠ bid in the last example). This will help the partnership to reach a suit game or 3NT.
- With shortness in partner's suit and no high card on the side, he just rebids his own suit. Responder will then set the contract.

We'll now look at three pairs of hands to show how it all shakes out in practice.

♠ K 7		♠ Q J 9 6 4 2
♡ 6 4	N	♡ A K 9
◇ K Q 9 7 6 2	W E	◇ A 4
♣ 9 4 2	S	♣ Q 8

West	North	East	South
2◇	pass	2♠	pass
3♣	pass	4♠	all pass

Since opener has a top honor in partner's long suit and his own suit is no better than advertised, the two-card raise is the most reasonable course to take and the partnership thus gets to an excellent 4♠ contract.

♠ 9 7		♠ A K 8 5 4 2
♡ A J 9 7 3 2	N	♡ K
◇ K J 2	W E	◇ A 9 8 4
♣ 9 7	S	♣ A 10

West	North	East	South
2♡	pass	2♠	pass
3◇	pass	3♠	pass
4♠	all pass		

Here, with two small in partner's suit, the 2♡ opener should not raise immediately. Since he is on the top of his range, what he can do is bid 3◇ to show where his outside strength is. Partner repeats his spades and opener can now raise to game, knowing there's an eight-card fit.

♠ A Q 10 9 7 5   ♡ 6 4   ◇ 10 5 4   ♣ 8 7

You open 2♠ on this hand, and partner responds 3◇. Unlike the first two examples, this is a dead minimum. It's also unlikely that you have an eight-card fit in spades as partner hasn't gone directly to 4♠ or made an Ogust inquiry with 2NT. With three-card diamond support, however, you can scrounge up a raise to 4◇, which only promises a fit and not a maximum hand, else you'd either have gone all the way to game or bid a new suit to show a high-card value.

If you play a new suit over a weak two-bid as forcing, then you may have the opportunity to make a useful lead-directing bid, as witness our next deal:

E-W vulnerable

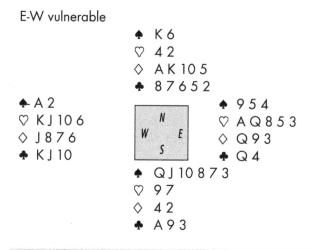

```
                    ♠ K 6
                    ♡ 4 2
                    ◇ A K 10 5
                    ♣ 8 7 6 5 2
  ♠ A 2                              ♠ 9 5 4
  ♡ K J 10 6          N              ♡ A Q 8 5 3
  ◇ J 8 7 6       W       E          ◇ Q 9 3
  ♣ K J 10            S              ♣ Q 4
                    ♠ Q J 10 8 7 3
                    ♡ 9 7
                    ◇ 4 2
                    ♣ A 9 3
```

West	North	East	South
			2♠
dbl	3◇	4♡	all pass

With the ◇AK in his hand, North would like to attract that lead from partner as there might be a possible ruff. He therefore bids 3◇, which is forcing (new suit!) to at least 3♠. East, with 10 HCP and a five-card suit opposite a takeout double, jumps to 4♡.

South obediently leads a diamond and now the defense collects two tricks plus a ruff in that suit along with the ♣A for down one.

If North passes or raises spades, the 4♡ contract makes as South will almost certainly lead the ♠Q. Declarer will win, draw trumps and then force out the ♣A, setting up a winner in that suit for a diamond pitch.

This treatment of a new-suit bid as lead-directing over a takeout double is called McCabe.

How Vigorously to Raise?

In contrast to earlier times, virtually all partnerships now use a jump raise below game after a takeout double or overcall of a one-bid as being preemptive in nature. This has been a positive development for bidding accuracy in competitive auctions. However, players tend to get carried away in these leaps, and the final result can be less than satisfactory.

The thing to keep in mind is that unlike in a weak two-bid or preempt auction, when partner opens the bidding at the one-level he will have at least

12 points and conceivably more. Because of that, you shouldn't blithely assume that the contract belongs to the opponents if you have a great fit but little or no defense. Suppose you have:

♠ 7   ♡ J 8   ♢ Q 10 8 5 3 2   ♣ A 9 7 3

Partner opens 1♢ and RHO passes. You play 2♢ as an inverted raise, showing 10+ points, you can bid 3♢ (preemptive), 4♢ (more preemptive) or the full 5♢ on these cards. Which is it going to be?

One of the opponents has a lot of points and/or major-suit cards, and it's likely to be LHO as the player on your right hasn't bid. Bidding 3♢ may not suffice to keep them out of the auction. Jumping to 5♢ will be fine if they can make game in a major, but you do have one defensive trick of your own and partner has opened, so they're not a cinch to have game their way. The preemptive action that makes the most sense here is 4♢. It suggests a very distributional hand and not that many high-card values, as you've carried your side beyond 3NT. Now, if the opponents bid a major, you can safely leave it to partner to decide whether or not to defend or bid on.

The full deal this time is:

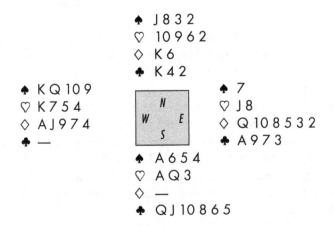

```
              ♠ J 8 3 2
              ♡ 10 9 6 2
              ♢ K 6
              ♣ K 4 2
♠ K Q 10 9                    ♠ 7
♡ K 7 5 4        N            ♡ J 8
♢ A J 9 7 4   W     E         ♢ Q 10 8 5 3 2
♣ —              S            ♣ A 9 7 3
              ♠ A 6 5 4
              ♡ A Q 3
              ♢ —
              ♣ Q J 10 8 6 5
```

If you bid 5♢, South will either pass or make an ambitious takeout double. Either way, North will choose to defend and your contract will fail by a trick.

After a 4♢ raise, however, South will surely make a takeout double. His side has a 4-4 fit in spades but North may bid hearts, the cheaper of his four-card majors. Even if they get to spades, West holds length in both majors and will elect to defend. He won't double hearts but might take a piece of 4♠. If West doesn't go on to 5♢ himself, East should respect that decision as he's pretty much told his story.

Another hand to consider with South the dealer and everyone vulnerable:

♠Q 4 2   ♡K 10 2   ◇Q 10 9 7 5 4   ♣Q

The auction has gone:

West	North	East	South
			pass
pass	1♣	1◇	pass
?			

Again some kind of diamond raise seems to be in order, but how many? There is, since you have 9 HCP and a good fit, a possibility that your side has the majority of the points and could easily be on for game. Not raising diamonds directly but cuebidding 2♣ to show a limit raise or better would be an alternative here. But most players would be fixated on bidding some number of diamonds.

Unlike the last deal, where you expected the opponents to have a major-suit fit, that may not be the case here since you have three cards in each of those suits. No bid is quite ideal. The 2♣ cuebid might be an overbid in the eyes of some, while 3◇ would be an underbid. Jumping to 5◇ is an outright gamble that the opponents have a major-suit fit, and it could easily be that neither side can make game. Meanwhile, 4◇ would suggest massive support but not be overly committal. It keeps partner involved and at the same time, gives the opponents just enough rope to hang themselves.

The whole story this time is:

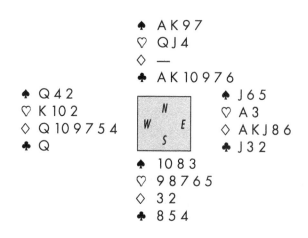

```
                    ♠ A K 9 7
                    ♡ Q J 4
                    ◇ —
                    ♣ A K 10 9 7 6
  ♠ Q 4 2                          ♠ J 6 5
  ♡ K 10 2           N            ♡ A 3
  ◇ Q 10 9 7 5 4   W   E          ◇ A K J 8 6
  ♣ Q                 S            ♣ J 3 2
                    ♠ 10 8 3
                    ♡ 9 8 7 6 5
                    ◇ 3 2
                    ♣ 8 5 4
```

Over a preemptive 4◇ raise, North will find it difficult to keep quiet with his fine hand, and will likely make a takeout double. The good news for his side is that they have a fit in two suits, but South is totally devoid of high cards. All game contracts will go down at least two tricks. If West bids 5◇, opener will still double but South will leave it in and hope for the best, which in this case is a plus score.

In our final example, you are not vulnerable against vulnerable opponents:

♠3 ♡K 10 8 6 4 ◇10 4 ♣Q 10 6 5 4

The auction has commenced with:

West	North	East	South (you)
1◇	2♣	dbl	?

The opponents rate to have an eight- or nine-card fit on this one, but partner may also have four of them. Still, a direct leap to 5♣ certainly seems reasonable on this holding.

Was it the right thing to do? Well, let's see the actual deal:

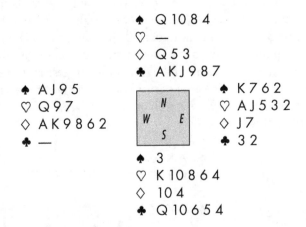

```
                    ♠ Q 10 8 4
                    ♡ —
                    ◇ Q 5 3
                    ♣ A K J 9 8 7
♠ A J 9 5                           ♠ K 7 6 2
♡ Q 9 7          N                  ♡ A J 5 3 2
◇ A K 9 8 6 2   W   E               ◇ J 7
♣ —                S                ♣ 3 2
                    ♠ 3
                    ♡ K 10 8 6 4
                    ◇ 10 4
                    ♣ Q 10 6 5 4
```

It's close, but 4♠ their way likely goes down a trick, as does your 5♣. However, when you have extreme shape, someone else at the table might have wild distribution as well. Your action has left opener with a real problem. Some experts will say that he should double rather than bid, but there are a lot of hands that East can have that would give 5♣ an excellent play. At the table, West is likely to bid five of a pointed suit, thinking slam might even be a possibility.

Getting What You're Entitled To when the Opponents Preempt

It can be difficult coping with a preemptive opening bid. The next deal is one that resulted in much consternation for the North-South pair.

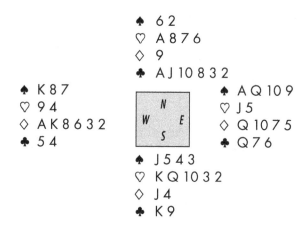

```
                    ♠ 6 2
                    ♡ A 8 7 6
                    ◇ 9
                    ♣ A J 10 8 3 2
    ♠ K 8 7                        ♠ A Q 10 9
    ♡ 9 4            N             ♡ J 5
    ◇ A K 8 6 3 2   W     E       ◇ Q 10 7 5
    ♣ 5 4               S          ♣ Q 7 6
                    ♠ J 5 4 3
                    ♡ K Q 10 3 2
                    ◇ J 4
                    ♣ K 9
```

With neither side vulnerable, the auction went:

West	North	East	South
2◇	pass	3◇	pass
pass	4♣	all pass	

North guessed the ♣Q to make his contract, but the result was an average-minus as slightly more than half the field played in hearts, two in partscore and four in game. It's likely that the West hand opened 1◇ rather than 2◇ at some tables, enabling North-South to enter the bidding more conveniently.

Since North-South can make 4♡ easily, there was some intense discussion afterward as to which member of the partnership should have found a bid. When I emailed the deal to a dozen of my friends, five of them thought North should either bid 3♣ directly or balance with a double instead of bidding 4♣ at his second turn. Four thought that South ought to make a takeout double after the raise to 3◇. The other three found no particular fault and chalked up the result to the East-West pair's weak two-bid and raise.

If you turned North's ♣J into the queen, I'd wager that just about everyone would overcall 3♣. The reason he should bid immediately is that he knows his hand is the one that has the more attractive distribution, and he has another suit as well as clubs. South has him beat by one in high-card points, but North has a better hand in playing strength.

This brings me to some advice from a friend of mine. He says, 'the only effective defense to a preempt is an overbid.' This requires some clarification. It does not mean that you should be stepping in with balanced 11- or 12-point hands. However, if you're in the ballpark for the needed shape but don't have the moon and the stars point-wise, you shouldn't let that deter you.

We'll go through some more examples to illustrate the point. For the next one, East is the dealer and East-West are vulnerable:

♠ 9		♠ 10 8 4 2
♡ K 7 2	N	♡ A J 10
◇ K Q 10 8 3	W E	◇ J 9 6 5
♣ A 9 8 2	S	♣ K Q

South opens 2♠. Of the two hands, West's has the more appropriate shape for competing, and he should bid 3◇. Yes, he'd rather have a sixth diamond or 15 HCP as opposed to 13, but his suit is good and the outside values are aces and kings. After a direct 3◇ overcall, East-West might reach game, as East will try for notrump with a 3♠ cuebid and, when his partner doesn't cooperate, may well bid 5◇.

Another one, with neither side vulnerable:

♠ 9 7		♠ A K
♡ Q 9 7 6	N	♡ 8 5 2
◇ K J 8	W E	◇ Q 10 4 3
♣ A K 5 4	S	♣ Q 9 7 3

South opens 3♠. There is certainly some risk in doubling on the West cards as it may push the auction to the four-level and North may be laying in wait with a good hand. Be that as it may, West has reasonable shape for a takeout double even though he's not brimming over with a lot of points. Note that if he passes, East will be leery about balancing since he has even fewer points and only three cards in the unbid major. East-West might then suffer the indignity of defending 3♠, while having an excellent play for 3NT their way.

We're not done yet. For this one, South deals and East-West are vulnerable:

♠ A J 7 5 3		♠ Q 10
♡ A 9 7 3	N	♡ K J 8 6
◇ K 5	W E	◇ A 9 8 6 4
♣ J 6	S	♣ 8 2

South opens 3♠. This time, West has two decisions to make. The first is whether to compete at all. If he does, then which of 3♠ or a takeout double does he go with? Of course, 4♡ by East-West isn't laydown, but if either major-suit finesse succeeds, it will probably come home.

If West passes, East will be hard-pressed to take action at his turn. Even if he does bid 3◊, the heart fit may be lost entirely.

A salient point on each of these examples is that if the direct hand passes and the next player furthers the preempt, the competing side has an even tougher row to hoe.

Speaking of which, we'll now look at two more auctions that feature a weak two-bid and a raise. RHO could be just making a nuisance bid with nothing much to speak of, but other times he'll have a good enough hand to go plus at the three-level with some expectation of defeating your contract if you take a bid. Still, as the expression goes, you pay your money and take your chances if you are in possession of a decent hand. So here we go, West being the dealer and North-South vulnerable:

♠A 10 ♡Q 10 7 5 ◊A Q 10 4 ♣Q 8 5

West	North	East	South (you)
2♠	pass	3♠	?

You have 14 HCP with North having passed the weak two-bid. On top of that, your side is vulnerable. Should you pass or live on the edge with a take-out double? It's very close, as there is no real clue from the auction whether you should be bold or prudent. At the table, South chose not to get shut out and made a takeout double. The layout of all four hands was:

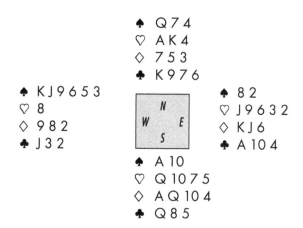

North could bid the clubs over the takeout double, but the 4-3-3-3 shape is not the greatest and languishing at the four-level in a minor suit is seldom going to yield a good result at matchpoints. Instead, he will likely either bid

3NT or leave in the double. The notrump game turns out to be a roaring success due to the friendly lie of the diamonds, allowing North-South to take eight red-suit tricks plus at least two more in the blacks, making ten or eleven winners in all. If North leaves the double in, that will also be quite profitable, as declarer can only muster five or six tricks, down three or perhaps even four if the defense is accurate.

To close out this section, here is one more hand to ponder. West is the dealer and both sides are vulnerable. You're in the South chair:

♠ 10 ♡ A Q 7 6 2 ◇ K Q 9 2 ♣ K 10 6

West opens 2♠, partner passes and RHO boosts opener to 3♠. Same points as in the previous hand, and you have a fifth heart. In this case, you can either double or venture a 4♡ bid. Which is it going to be?

Sad to say, it doesn't matter; the result won't be so glorious for your side on this occasion as North doesn't have the same tickets as he did on the previous deal:

♠ 9 5 3 ♡ K 10 9 ◇ 8 3 ♣ Q 8 7 4 2

Even so, four of either rounded suit is not an awful contract. The real killer for your side is that the weak two-bidder has a singleton club and with that suit dividing 4-1, you're bound to go down two in either 4♣ or 4♡.

All these examples were taken from actual play. Generally, you'll be rewarded for bidding aggressively but with a certain degree of good sense over the opponents' preempts. You will occasionally encounter a setback, but that's part of being active rather than passive. Don't get discouraged when adversity strikes, because the highs will outnumber the lows when all is said and done.

Sacrificing

A 'paying' sacrifice, when the amount your contract goes down is not as much as the opponents would have got for making their game, gives most players a rush of adrenalin. At IMPs, it often doesn't matter much either way — the difference between -500 and -620 isn't usually a big deal. At matchpoints, though, that can be a difference of half a board or more. Often when you look at the results, however, they aren't as good as you thought they might be. Sometimes you go down one too many. Sometimes it turns out their contract was beatable, or maybe they had a higher-paying contract than the suit they were in.

Many top bridge players use an expression, 'Jesus saves', which is their way of saying that taking sacrifices is vastly overrated and not all that productive.

This is not to say that you should totally refrain from sacrificing. Sometimes the cost of being wrong will be negligible and you are quite certain the opponents will make their game. But you should not be cutting it too close. For example, if the vulnerability is favorable, I will not sacrifice if I expect the best-case scenario to be down three. If that turns into down four, it's going to be a cold zero even if their game is making. So my objective in that situation would be to have at least some chance of holding our contract to down two, giving me some margin for error. At all other vulnerabilities, my target would be coming up one trick short of my bid. Other experts may have different criteria, but the theme is the same in that they don't get caught up in the sacrificing mania.

Here is your first challenge on whether to sacrifice. You are South, not vulnerable against vulnerable opponents, holding these cards:

♠ K J 10 6   ♡ 8 3   ◊ 10 9 6   ♣ 10 9 5 4

The auction so far has gone:

West	North	East	South
1◊	1♠	dbl	3♠*
pass	pass	4◊	pass
4♡	pass	pass	?

Your jump to 3♠ was preemptive. Should you bid 4♠ now that the opponents have reached game?

The answer is an emphatic 'no'. There are three reasons for letting them play in 4♡ instead of taking the sacrifice:

- Your hand is so balanced. There is no way of telling how many your side will go down in 4♠.

- Opener has four hearts but has also shown a minimum hand by passing your 3♠. It was only after his partner competed to 4◊ that he now went back to hearts.

- Finally, you've told your story with your preemptive 3♠ raise. Partner had all the information he needed to take the sacrifice himself. Since he has chosen not to, he has some hope of beating their contract.

What happens if you pass? Or bid 4♠ on your own? Here's the full picture:

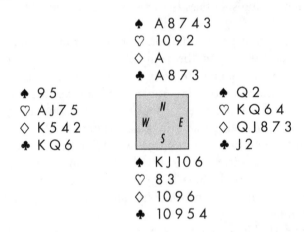

```
              ♠ A 8 7 4 3
              ♡ 10 9 2
              ◇ A
              ♣ A 8 7 3
♠ 9 5                          ♠ Q 2
♡ A J 7 5        N             ♡ K Q 6 4
◇ K 5 4 2    W       E         ◇ Q J 8 7 3
♣ K Q 6          S             ♣ J 2
              ♠ K J 10 6
              ♡ 8 3
              ◇ 10 9 6
              ♣ 10 9 5 4
```

Against 4♡, partner will start out with the ◇A and then underlead his ♠A at Trick 2. You win with the ten and then play your highest diamond back to give him a ruff. Back comes another spade and another diamond ruff, whereupon North cashes the ♣A for down three.

If you decide to bid on, somehow, partner isn't all that impressed when 4♠ goes down one. Your explanation that you thought 4♡ would make gets a two-word reply from him: 'Jesus saves'.

In our next example, it's the good hand that is faced with the decision of whether to sacrifice. Sitting East with neither side vulnerable, you have:

♠A J 7 5 ♡A 2 ◇9 8 ♣A K 6 5 2

The opponents arrive in 4♡ with the bidding having gone:

West	North	East (you)	South
pass	pass	1♣	dbl
3♣*	pass	pass	3♡
pass	4♡	?	

Partner's 3♣ raise over the double was preemptive. So here they are in 4♡. It doesn't look as if you have more than one club trick on defense, if that, and your two outside aces. Should you take the sacrifice?

First, consider how many tricks you might lose in 5♣. None in clubs, probably a couple of diamonds, and one heart. That's down one already. In spades, there is likely one trick to lose, possibly two. The best you can hope for, then, is down two, with down three a possibility.

Meanwhile, are you sure they are going to make 4♡? You're assuming a trick each in clubs, hearts and spades. Your ♠J might become another trick, or partner might have a spade or diamond card for his 3♣ bid since he can't have much in clubs. All things considered, sacrificing is too big a parlay and you should leave them in their contract.

At the table, the East player did push on to 5♣, and the complete layout was:

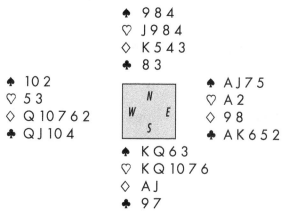

Much to his chagrin, partner had only four clubs, not five as he'd expected. East-West would have defeated 4♡, and 5♣ went down two. Yes, it was un-lucky West didn't have the fifth club and so they had a couple of tricks in that suit in defense, but if there had been a spade honor in dummy, South would have had two tricks to lose in that suit.

Before you get cold feet on sacrificing, though, next up are a couple of hands where saving will have a lot more going for it. Here you are South and are dealer with neither side vulnerable:

♠7 ♡Q87 ◇Q742 ♣QJ974

The auction so far:

West	North	East	South
			pass
2♠	3◇	4♠	?

It's true partner might be able to defeat 4♠ all on his own, but you have noth-ing resembling a defensive trick. Unlike the first two examples, your distribu-tion is such that a 5◇ contract should not be too expensive, and might come close to making on some days.

On the actual layout, the result will be down one in 5◊. They will get two top hearts and a ruff, but nothing else. Defending 4♠, partner can never get to your hand for a club through declarer's king, and declarer can ruff out the hearts to establish winners for minor-suit discards.

And to wrap up, we have this East hand for you, with South dealer and neither side vulnerable.

♠9 5 3 2   ♡J 9   ◊A J 10 8   ♣Q 10 8

After a pass on your left, partner opens 3♣ and RHO overcalls 3♠. You suspect that the opponents can make four of a major but pass for now, just in case they don't have an eight-card fit. The bidding continues:

West	North	East (you)	South
			pass
3♣	3♠	pass	4♣
pass	4♠	?	

Now the picture is more complete. LHO with his cuebid has advertised a spade fit, so partner will have one or none. Clubs should not be a problem, so assume one spade, two hearts, and either one or no diamonds to lose depending on what partner has in the suit. This is a hand on which you *do* want to take a sacrifice, as you have little or no chance of defeating 4♠. It turns out that 5♣ is down two, and while the opponents can make eleven tricks in hearts, they're not likely to take the push. Your -300 is a good score, as several East-West pairs sell out to a 4♠ contract.

1. Both vulnerable, you are West with this hand:

♠ Q J 9 8 7 6 3   ♡ A   ◇ A Q 2   ♣ K 10

The auction has begun with:

West (you)	North	East	South
		2♡	dbl
?			

What action do you take?

2. Neither vulnerable, you are North:

♠ A Q 4   ♡ Q 10 9 8 6 3   ◇ 10   ♣ Q 9 3

The bidding has gone:

West	North (you)	East	South
	pass	2♠	3♣
3♠	?		

Pretty nice hand with support for partner and a suit of your own; what now?

3. You hold these cards as East with North-South vulnerable:

♠ Q 9   ♡ K 7 5   ◇ K Q J 10 8 7 2   ♣ 5

The auction so far has been:

West	North	East (you)	South
			pass
pass	1♣	?	

Nice suit with 11 HCP; what action do you take?

4. You're North for this one, with East-West vulnerable:

♠ K Q J 8 7 5 4   ♡ —   ◇ A J 2   ♣ 10 6 3

Your decision here comes after an opening bid and a response:

West	North (you)	East	South
		1♣	pass
1♡	?		

5. You are North yet again, with North-South vulnerable:

♠ J 9 4 3   ♡ —   ◇ A K 10 7   ♣ Q 10 9 3 2

RHO has opened 2♡. With this meager 10-count, is it best to pass, overcall or make a takeout double?

6. Voids seem to be the order of the day if you are North, as this time you have:

♠ A 8 4   ♡ Q 5   ◇ —   ♣ A Q 10 8 7 4 3 2

The auction has commenced with:

West	North (you)	East	South
			pass
1◇	?		

The vulnerability is favorable, you have a lot of clubs and partner is a passed hand. Do you go to 5♣ immediately or take it slower with a 2♣ overcall?

1. Both vulnerable

```
                      ♠ K 5
                      ♡ 9 8 4 3 2
                      ◇ 8 7 5
                      ♣ J 7 4
 ♠ Q J 9 8 7 6 3                      ♠ —
 ♡ A                                  ♡ K Q J 10 6 5
 ◇ A Q 2                              ◇ 10 6 4
 ♣ K 10                              ♣ Q 9 5 2
                      ♠ A 10 4 2
                      ♡ 7
                      ◇ K J 9 3
                      ♣ A 8 6 3
```

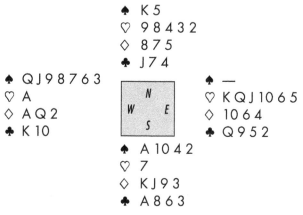

West	North	East	South
		2♡	dbl
redbl	pass	pass	2♠
dbl	all pass		

If South had passed, West likely would have looked for game by introducing his seven-card spade suit. After the takeout double, however, the chances of a fit in that suit have been greatly reduced. He can redouble to show a very good hand and hold a spade bid in reserve for later. North-South are in a heap of trouble now. North will likely pass whereupon the doubler will bid spades, being unwilling to go to the three-level. West lands on that with both feet, and North will have to decide whether to play a likely 4-2 fit or try escaping to a minor suit via 3♣ or 2NT. There is indeed a better fit in clubs or diamonds, but after partner's redouble, East can double 3♣ and West will put the axe to anything else.

If West does not appreciate the opportunity that beckons and woodenly bids 2♠ over the double, North-South will gladly leave well enough alone and defend whatever contract the opponents end up in.

2.   Neither vulnerable

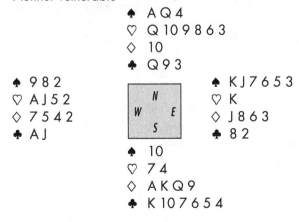

♠ A Q 4
♡ Q 10 9 8 6 3
♢ 10
♣ Q 9 3

♠ 9 8 2
♡ A J 5 2
♢ 7 5 4 2
♣ A J

♠ K J 7 6 5 3
♡ K
♢ J 8 6 3
♣ 8 2

♠ 10
♡ 7 4
♢ A K Q 9
♣ K 10 7 6 5 4

West	North	East	South
	pass	2♠	3♣
3♠	4♡	all pass	

After East opens a weak two-bid, South doesn't have a wealth of high cards but with 4-6 in the minor suits, the hand contains too much playing strength to pass, so he bids 3♣.

West's 3♠ suffers from the drawback that he doesn't have a spade honor, but he expects the opponents' contract to make and his side's contract to produce seven or eight tricks, so he offers up the raise.

The fate of the board now rests with North. Although he has club support, bidding game in the minor isn't a good option since both 4♡ and 3NT may score better. Each of those bids has something going in its favor. Bidding 4♡ should promise club tolerance and leaves open a retreat to 5♣ if overcaller is short in hearts. However, because South hasn't made a takeout double, there might not be a heart fit. Meanwhile, 3NT will turn out well if the opponents lead their suit, and after partner's raise, East might well do that. The worry is if they lead diamonds instead, but South's high cards have to be somewhere besides clubs, and he could have the other minor adequately stopped.

On this deal at least, Bob Hamman is right in saying that if 3NT is one of the possible contracts, then that should be your choice. While a diamond lead severs the communication between the two hands, the clubs are friendly and North would take nine or ten tricks. With the 4-1 break in hearts, 4♡ is doomed to failure, as is 5♣.

Results:

North-South	+460	1 pair
	+140	3 pairs
	–50	5 pairs
	–100	2 pairs
	–470	1 pair

The results for this deal are not totally surprising. The 140s for North-South could have been the result of North opening 2♡ and playing it there. Otherwise, his side played game in either hearts or clubs, going down one and sometimes two. One brave North ventured 3NT and hit the jackpot, making eleven tricks.

3.   N-S vulnerable

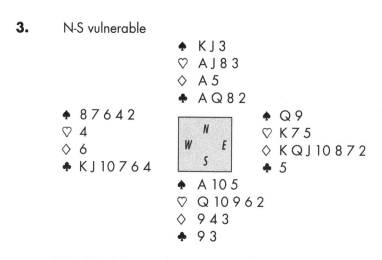

```
              ♠ K J 3
              ♡ A J 8 3
              ◇ A 5
              ♣ A Q 8 2
♠ 8 7 6 4 2                    ♠ Q 9
♡ 4            N              ♡ K 7 5
◇ 6         W     E           ◇ K Q J 10 8 7 2
♣ K J 10 7 6 4    S           ♣ 5
              ♠ A 10 5
              ♡ Q 10 9 6 2
              ◇ 9 4 3
              ♣ 9 3
```

West	North	East	South
			pass
pass	1♣	3◇	pass
pass	dbl	pass	3♡
all pass			

At the table, our East opted for the 'heavy' 3◇ preempt instead of 1◇, influenced no doubt by the fact that West had passed originally and there likely wasn't a game for his side. This came back around to North, who made a takeout double. While some type of reopening is expected at the one- or two-level, opener wouldn't do that at a higher level unless he had extra values.

While South knows partner should have a very good hand, it doesn't have to be the full 19 HCP. He's faced with the choice of jumping to game in hearts (as he might do at teams) or conserving a plus by bidding 3♡.

The outcome of the deal is that declarer has ten easy tricks in hearts, even with the trump king offside. If East overcalls 1◇, then South has enough to respond 1♡, and North will then drive to game.

4. E-W vulnerable

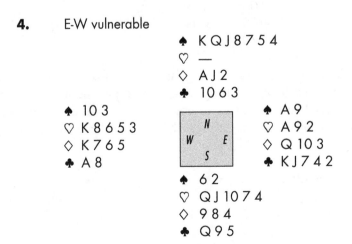

♠ K Q J 8 7 5 4
♡ —
◇ A J 2
♣ 10 6 3

♠ 10 3
♡ K 8 6 5 3
◇ K 7 6 5
♣ A 8

♠ A 9
♡ A 9 2
◇ Q 10 3
♣ K J 7 4 2

♠ 6 2
♡ Q J 10 7 4
◇ 9 8 4
♣ Q 9 5

West	North	East	South
		1♣	pass
1♡	3♠	pass	pass
dbl	pass	4♡	all pass

Some Norths may go for maximum preemption by leaping all the way to 4♠. However, that leaves the opponents little choice but to double and take whatever plus they have coming to them.

Another friend once made the comment that '3♠ is the most preemptive bid in bridge', in that it leaves the opponents having to chance the four-level. It also has the advantage of involving partner, should the other side keep bidding. He can then take the non-vulnerable sacrifice himself or elect to defend.

Aside from the general principle, there are a couple of reasons not to bid 4♠ on North's cards. The first is his terrible holding of three small in opener's suit. The second is that his void in hearts suggests that the opponents might be catching a foul break in the trump suit if they have a fit in responder's major.

As you can see, 4♡ by East-West has no play, losing a spade, diamond and two or three heart tricks. If North jumps to 4♠ instead, that will come around to West; West still doubles and the carnage will be fearful. If a club is led, the defenders get two top clubs and a ruff. After that, they still have two diamonds, a heart and the ♠A to come.

5.   N-S vulnerable

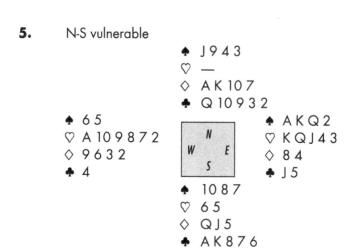

```
                    ♠ J 9 4 3
                    ♡ —
                    ◇ A K 10 7
                    ♣ Q 10 9 3 2
♠ 6 5                                  ♠ A K Q 2
♡ A 10 9 8 7 2          N              ♡ K Q J 4 3
◇ 9 6 3 2         W          E         ◇ 8 4
♣ 4                     S              ♣ J 5
                    ♠ 10 8 7
                    ♡ 6 5
                    ◇ Q J 5
                    ♣ A K 8 7 6
```

West	North	East	South
			pass
2♡	dbl	4♡	5♣
all pass			

Over RHO's weak two-bid, North heeds the adage, 'the only effective defense to a preempt is an overbid', and makes a takeout double. While his hand is not bursting with high-card values, he has the ideal shape and two defensive tricks.

East leaps to 4♡ and now South can either bid 5♣ or double, showing points but no clear action. Although he has no singletons, with a nice five-card suit and 10 HCP, I think he should expect the minor-suit game to have a decent play. If South doubles, North might pull to 4NT to play in a minor suit, but he could also leave it in.

On this layout, 5♣ will make a fair amount of the time. If West leads a top heart or one of the minor suits, declarer can draw trumps and then toss a spade on dummy's fourth diamond.

With his jump to 4♡, East missed a chance to direct the defense. Over North's double, he could have bid 2♠, which is forcing because it's a new suit. North-South may still bid 5♣, since 4♡ is cold, but now West will lead his doubleton spade and his side will manage to take the first three tricks and at least go plus on the board.

6.   E-W vulnerable

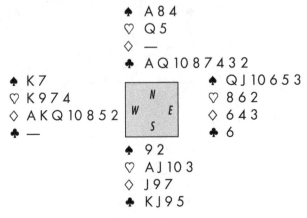

```
                    ♠ A 8 4
                    ♡ Q 5
                    ◇ —
                    ♣ A Q 10 8 7 4 3 2
  ♠ K 7                              ♠ Q J 10 6 5 3
  ♡ K 9 7 4          N               ♡ 8 6 2
  ◇ A K Q 10 8 5 2  W   E            ◇ 6 4 3
  ♣ —                 S              ♣ 6
                    ♠ 9 2
                    ♡ A J 10 3
                    ◇ J 9 7
                    ♣ K J 9 5
```

West	North	East	South
			pass
1◇	5♣	pass	pass
5◇	all pass		

After LHO's jump to 5♣, West decided to persist with his diamonds. Since partner could still have as many as 9 points and not be able to bid at the five-level, opener was hoping that East had enough in the major suits that 5◇ would be a possible make.

The bad news was that partner didn't have the required stuff and that by ducking one round of spades, North-South were able to defeat the contract by two tricks. However, the silver lining in the cloud was that the opponents had a cold game and, if they had gone on to the six-level, would have made twelve tricks on anything but a spade lead.

On the bidding shown above, it is hard for either member of the North-South partnership to double the final contract. South has too many clubs, and North has just one sure trick outside of his long suit.

Even though South passed originally, North should not be in such a hurry to bid an immediate 5♣. For one thing, since his void is in diamonds, the opponents may not have a major-suit fit. If he simply makes a two-level over-call, the auction is unlikely to die there. As it turns out, partner will cuebid 2◇, showing a limit raise, which will have a twofold effect. First, North may indeed think more seriously about a possible slam. Meanwhile, West can now assume that partner will be virtually broke and that he won't be able to make 5◇.

6
Exploring for Game

The interesting thing about pairs is that doing well doesn't involve being uniformly aggressive or conservative in your bidding style. There are three components to the mantra of the seasoned matchpoints player:

1) Don't sell out cheaply. Never let the opponents play a suit contract at the one-level. If they've shown a fit and stop at two of their suit, you are likely to have one as well and should try to compete. That said, you need to recognize the auctions where they have a true fit and those where they may not. Here are two sequences in a 2/1 auction:

West	North	East	South
1♠	pass	2♠	

West	North	East	South
1♠	pass	1NT	pass
2♣	pass	2♠	

In the first auction, East-West are known to have an eight-card fit. You should not make the same assumption with the second example. In fact, East's 2♠ is more apt to be a two-card preference; the opponents might not have an actual fit and it is therefore more dangerous to compete.

2) If possible, try and get the other side out of their 1NT contract. Granted, they have not established a fit and you may not have one either, so it's a risky proposition. However, since notrump is the highest-scoring contract and the final outcome could be very much lead-dependent, there is a growing tendency to bid in this type of scenario. This next deal profoundly illustrates the difference between teams and pairs, with both sides vulnerable:

```
                    ♠ K Q J 9
                    ♡ J 10 7 6 4
                    ◇ 10 9
                    ♣ Q 10
   ♠ A 10 3 2              ┌──────┐        ♠ 8 5 4
   ♡ 9 8                   │   N  │        ♡ K Q
   ◇ K 7 2              W  │      │  E     ◇ J 8 5 4 3
   ♣ J 9 8 5               │   S  │        ♣ A K 4
                          └──────┘
                    ♠ 7 6
                    ♡ A 5 3 2
                    ◇ A Q 6
                    ♣ 7 6 3 2
```

West	North	East	South
		1◇	pass
1♠	pass	1NT	pass
pass	?		

At teams, there is no way the North hand would get involved with such a humble five-card suit, especially with his side vulnerable. Playing matchpoints, however, the holder of these cards reasoned that defending 1NT was only likely to be right if a spade were led, which might be too much to expect from partner. South was likely to have between 8 to 12 HCP, with the opponents having stopped in a partscore. North therefore balanced with 2♡, which turned out to be a make, as would the opponents' 1NT contract have been. You could argue that he was lucky to catch four-card support from partner, and that East might well have had some length to go with his KQ. Yes, that's true, but then 1NT would have made eight tricks instead of seven, with 2♡ only going down one.

A word of advice, however. The point when you should be contemplating your decision in passout seat is when LHO rebids 1NT, *not* when RHO passes. When the auction comes back to you, it's essential that if you bid, you do so in tempo, because otherwise the opponents will sense your doubt.

3) Where you shouldn't get too optimistic is in chasing marginal games and slams, particularly when you either don't have a fit or have just a minimal one of eight cards. If you don't consider game to be a solid favorite to make, the best course is to settle for the partscore and try to make an extra trick in the play of the hand. This third point will be the focus of this chapter.

When the partnership has found a major-suit fit, that's a pretty good thing. It will pay quite well score-wise, and now your only decision is whether to content yourself with a partscore or try for game.

In 2/1, which most readers will be playing, a 1NT response followed by two of partner's major could either be a weak three-card raise or a two-card preference with 6-9 HCP. In these auctions, opener will generally call it quits unless he has in the neighborhood of 17-18 points for his two-level rebid.

The single raise is 'constructive', which for most people means about 8-9 HCP. As I've mentioned in a previous book, *Two over One: A First Course*, that is not the best way of evaluating the quality of responder's hand. I use the approach of 'cover cards', first introduced by Bobby Goldman in his book *Aces Scientific*.

Cover cards are defined as follows:

Any ace or king	=	one cover card
queen of trumps	=	one cover card
outside singleton	=	one cover card
outside queen	=	half a cover card
outside doubleton	=	half a cover card

Keep in mind this is an approximation. For example, an outside queen may be either useless or a full trick depending on what partner has in the suit. Similarly, a doubleton is of no value if opener has the same or fewer cards than you do, but a definite asset if he has length in that suit. I've found, however, that this tool has served me well in the twenty-some years since I've begun using it.

Once you have added up the number of cover cards, you can support opener's major according to this table:

Number of Cover Cards	Type of Raise
1.5 or fewer	'Destructive' i.e. 1NT then 2 of partner's suit
2 to 2.5	'Constructive', immediate raise
3 to 3.5, with three-card support	1NT and then 3 of partner's suit
3, with four-card support	Jump in partner's major suit
4 or more	Force the auction to game

I've left out one holding, where responder has four-card support and 3.5 cover cards. You could go either way on this one, but it will likely be sufficient to produce game in most cases.

Here are a few quick examples to show how cover card evaluation out-shines the mere counting of points. Partner has opened 1♠:

♠ K J 3   ♡ J 9 4   ◇ Q 10 8 6   ♣ J 6 2

Yes, you have 8 HCP, but the cover card tally here is 1.5, 1 for the king and 1/2 for the queen. You should bid 1NT and then 2♠.

♠ Q 9 7   ♡ J 9 5 4   ◇ A 8 6 3   ♣ 6 2

Although you have one point fewer, you have 2.5 cover cards here, as the queen of trumps and the ◇A count as one each, and the doubleton club for another half. You can therefore raise to 2♠ directly.

Now partner has opened 1♡ and you've been dealt this:

♠ K 7 5   ♡ K J 4   ◇ J 7 6 2   ♣ Q 4 2

In the strict point-counter's world, the single raise tops out at 9 HCP and this hand would respond 1NT followed by 3♡. However, it's a truly terrible 10 points, flat and full of unsupported queens and jacks. It has 2.5 cover cards, one for each king and a half for the outside queen. Going by the above table, then, it's only worth a two-level raise.

♠ A 7 5   ♡ Q 10 4   ◇ K J 3 2   ♣ 4 3 2

Here we've got the same 10 points, but 3 cover cards in the form of the ♠A, ◇K and queen of trumps. This collection qualifies for 1NT forcing and then 3♡.

The beauty of using cover cards to determine your first action is that it leaves opener in a good position to know whether he should bid game or at least invite. A typical opening hand will have seven losers (using Losing Trick Count). For each cover card responder shows, you can mentally subtract one loser — partner has it 'covered'. If your total loser count is getting near to three, then you are in the game zone. For example, the auction has commenced with:

West	East
1♡	2♡
?	

and West's hand consists of:

♠ K Q J ♡ A K 7 5 3 ♢ Q 7 5 3 ♣ 9

With a loser each in spades, hearts and clubs plus another two in diamonds, his LTC total is five. Partner has shown at least two cover cards with his direct raise, so game is definitely a possibility. Yet the diamond holding is somewhat tenuous and responder could have wasted values in the club suit. You therefore need some way to find out whether partner's values are in the right place.

Trying for Game

Whether it's opener's or responder's major that has been supported, there is one more or less standard way of trying for game and a popular alternative.

Carrying on from the last section, West's hand after 1♡ – 2♡ was:

♠ K Q J ♡ A K 7 5 3 ♢ Q 7 5 3 ♣ 9

In order to find out if his side has decent chances for game, he would bid 3♢ here, which is a **help-suit game try**. He is asking his partner to focus on his holdings in the red suits, diamonds and hearts, and bid accordingly. We can now examine four hands East might have to see how he reacts to partner's game try:

♠ 6 4 ♡ Q 4 2 ♢ 10 4 2 ♣ K Q 8 7 4

Yes, the clubs are nice, but 10xx of diamonds is going to be of little or no help in the suit opener is asking about. North should decline with 3♡.

♠ 6 4 2 ♡ 8 6 4 ♢ A K 10 6 ♣ J 8 2

The answer here to, 'Do you have help in diamonds?' is an emphatic 'Yes'. Responder will happily accept the game try with a jump to 4♡.

♠ 6 4 2 ♡ Q 9 8 6 ♢ 8 ♣ K J 10 5 2

South has nothing in the way of high-card assistance for partner here, but his singleton along with four trumps means declarer will be able to ruff losers in dummy. With this hand he should also go on to 4♡.

♠ 8 6   ♡ Q 6 4   ◇ 8 6 4 2   ♣ A Q 8 7

Responder has 2.5 cover cards here, but his diamond holding couldn't be worse. He has too many of them and no honor strength. He puts the brakes on with 3♡ and the partnership stops in their last makeable contract.

In the example we've just gone through, the suit opener was asking for help in was four cards in length. However, he can bid the same way even if he has fewer cards in the suit. Here is a new pair of hands:

♠ K Q 10 9 5		♠ J 8 6
♡ 8	N	♡ A 5 4 3
◇ A K J 9	W E	◇ 7 5
♣ Q 10 8	S	♣ K 9 6 3

West	East
1♠	2♠
?	

After his spades are raised, opener wants to try for game. However, his side four-card suit doesn't really need help because it is so strong. Clubs are the suit where he needs some high cards from partner, and he makes his try with 3♣. Responder's hand now looks very good, and he duly bids the game.

If opener had bid 3◇ rather than 3♣, responder would have a coin-toss on whether to accept. The ♡A is useful and the doubleton diamond is an okay holding, but he has only three trumps and the ♣K could easily be facing shortness in partner's hand.

I once made the comment to my friends that any time opener's six-card major is raised, he should bid game regardless of point-count. That could be a slight exaggeration, but it really isn't that far off the mark. Having a sixth card in your suit reduces the possibility of having trump losers. Also, it's not a huge concern if you need to ruff when the opponents try to cash their winners as you have enough length to withstand continued leads of their suit. I've since revised my advice to say that you should at least try for game when partner supports your six-card major.

I understand that you might take some convincing, so here are some examples. You have this hand as West:

♠ —   ♡ A K 10 8 6 2   ◇ A 10 8 7   ♣ A 6 5

The auction has gone:

West	East
1♡	2♡
?	

This is a hand on which you'd certainly want to try for game. Why not just bid it and let the chips fall where they may? The opponents may not have a picnic on their opening lead, and responder could easily have enough values in the minor suits for 4♡ to have excellent chances. The complete layout is:

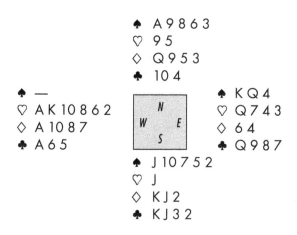

```
              ♠ A 9 8 6 3
              ♡ 9 5
              ◇ Q 9 5 3
              ♣ 10 4
♠ —                           ♠ K Q 4
♡ A K 10 8 6 2      N         ♡ Q 7 4 3
◇ A 10 8 7       W     E      ◇ 6 4
♣ A 6 5             S         ♣ Q 9 8 7
              ♠ J 10 7 5 2
              ♡ J
              ◇ K J 2
              ♣ K J 3 2
```

Partner has 5 wasted points in the spade suit, the king-jack of clubs are sitting over dummy's queen, and yet game is cold as you can ruff two diamonds in dummy. If North were to lead the ♠A or his doubleton club, the contract would make with an overtrick.

Even if you don't have that many points or such nice distribution, you should still be inclined to try for game, as witness our next example:

♠K 10 9 6 4 2   ♡9   ◇K J 8 3   ♣A Q

You've opened 1♠ and partner has given you a boost to 2♠. On total points alone, your side only gets up to 22. Also by the cover card formula you fall short, as it's a six-loser hand with partner showing 2 to 2.5 cover cards. However, there is a finesse available in the club suit and with at least a nine-card fit, you should be okay in the trump suit. A help-suit game try of 3◇ would be a reasonable choice here. Partner would accept with either of these hands:

♠A 8 5 3   ♡Q 7 6   ◇Q 9 5 4   ♣6 3

♠ A 8 5 ♡ Q 7 6 2 ◇ Q 5 ♣ 9 6 3 2

In both instances, you'd want to be in game. It's virtually ironclad opposite the first hand and has lots of play on the second, as you can ruff a diamond and test both black suits, making if trumps are 2-2 or the ♣K is onside.

Here's another one to illustrate the principle of trying for game:

Opener		Responder
♠ —		♠ 9 8 7 5 2
♡ A 10 8 6 4 2	N	♡ K 9 3
◇ K 9 7 5 4	W　E	◇ A 10 8
♣ A 3	S	♣ 10 9

First off, responder's hand is worth an immediate 2♡ bid as it has two cover cards with the king of trumps and the outside ace. Opener has a mere 11 HCP, but after partner's raise the 6-5 distribution justifies a game try of 3◇. Responder should not get cold feet now just because he is minimum for his original bid. He's been asked a specific question about the red suits, where all his values are located. He ought to show complete faith in the process by going on to 4♡. With 'just' 18 HCP between them, this is a super contract to be in, and it would take horrible splits in both red suits for it to go down.

While help-suit game tries are reasonably effective in looking for game, both players must guess about wasted values (points opposite shortness). Opener has also described his hand to a certain extent with the suit he needs assistance in, and this gives the opponents information to work with as they defend.

The most widely used alternative was popularized by Eric Kokish. The gist of Kokish game tries is that after a raise, the cheapest bid by opener is artificial and asks partner where his high-card values are. In that way, the asker doesn't have to reveal his distribution and can make his ultimate decision based on what partner shows. The other actions besides the cheapest suit by opener are also game tries, but showing a singleton or void in the bid suit.

Here are the two major-suit raise auctions and we can see how Kokish works in each of them:

Opener	Responder	
1♠	2♠	
2NT		Asks where partner will accept a HSGT
3♣/3◇/3♡		Short-suit GT, singleton/void in bid suit
3♠		Partnership agreement

Opener	Responder
1♡	2♡
2♠	Asks where partner will accept a HSGT. If responder has spade values, he will now bid 2NT, otherwise he'll now bid the minor he has stuff in.
2NT	Game try with short spades
3♣/3◇	Short-suit game try, singleton/void in bid suit
3♡	Partnership agreement

Now we can move on to specific examples of Kokish game tries in action.

```
    ♠ A Q 9 8 7 2           ♠ J 5 4 3
    ♡ 8 3          N         ♡ 6 2
    ◇ A J      W       E     ◇ Q 10 8 5
    ♣ K J 4        S         ♣ A Q 5
```

The auction would go:

West	East
1♠	2♠
2NT*	3♣
3◇	4♠

As you can see, opener needs help in more than one suit, so he begins with the artificial 2NT, whereupon partner shows a high card in the club suit. That improves West's holding considerably and he now bids 3◇, which is a further game try asking if partner has something useful in diamonds. Responder has length and two honors, so he goes on to game.

If East had nothing much in diamonds but held the ♡A or ♡K, he would bid 3♡, and that would have been enough for opener to bid game.

On these hands, 4♠ is a good place to be and will make if either pointed-suit finesse works.

Next one:

```
    ♠ A Q 5                         ♠ 8 7 4
    ♡ K Q 10 7 6      N            ♡ A 8 4
    ◇ 5           W       E        ◇ K J 7 3
    ♣ K J 4 2         S            ♣ 7 6 5
```

West	East
1♡	2♡
3◇	3♡
pass	

This time opener has shortness, which he shows with 3◇. That is a complete turnoff for East, who quickly retreats to 3♡. They are glad to stop short, as nine tricks will probably be the limit of the hand.

One sequence that you should discuss with your partner is when opener bids three of the agreed major, i.e. 1♡ – 2♡; 3♡. Some pairs use the '1-2-3 stop' convention, which means that this action is not invitational but obstructive, trying to prevent the other side from coming into the auction with a fit of their own. Other partnerships use the re-raise of the major as asking responder how good his trumps are.

Hamman Game Tries

To grasp the underlying principle, we'll quote from the man himself, who was interviewed in the April 2007 issue of *The Bridge World*.

'I do enjoy being a critical examiner of Prevailing Wisdom. One of the bones that I have to pick with P.W. is that scientific exploration of the choice between game and part-score is of much utility when the final strain is highly probable. I am especially reluctant to explore delicately, then stop at the three-level after perhaps giving the opponents the information needed to beat the contract; in some of these cases, using the bulldozer approach yields a made game. I take the position that my consistent usage of this tactic gives me license to call it the Hamman Game Try: Bid game and try to make it.'

On some hands, you might indeed want to inquire about partner's holding in a certain suit if you figure to be safe at the three-level if partner rejects the game try. However, there are a great many others that it's best to sail into game with the expectation that it will have a play or might benefit from a friendly lead. Here is one shining example that Mr. Hamman would be proud of. You are in the West chair and everyone is vulnerable. You've been dealt:

♠K Q 10 8 6   ♡Q   ◊A J 10 7   ♣A 10 4

The auction begins with 1♠ by you and a raise to 2♠ by partner. Although the loser count is six, there are spot cards aplenty in the long suits, making the hand worth a game try. Rather than advertise your shape via a help-suit game try, it seems best just to vault into game and give LHO a blind lead. That pays off handsomely for you, as the four hands are:

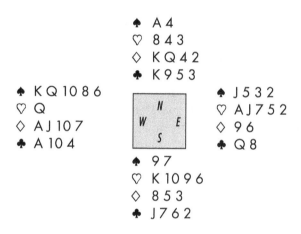

With no other suits mentioned, North will likely start out with the ◊K, which is an absolute disaster for his side, as declarer will only have one loser in the suit. Had West rebid 3◊ instead of going straight to game, North would have led either the ace and another trump or a heart instead.

Continuing along with another example, you pick up these cards as South:

♠K Q 6 5 2   ♡A 9   ◊8   ♣A J 10 3 2

You've opened 1♠ and partner has replied with 2♠. There are two reasons to dispense with science and just blast to game. Your loser count is five, and partner's constructive raise shows 2 to 2.5 cover cards. Moreover, your club suit doesn't really need any help. Whether partner has an honor, a singleton, two small or even three small, prospects will always be good for establishing tricks in your second suit.

Does the bullish approach yield dividends for you on this deal? Well, let's take a look:

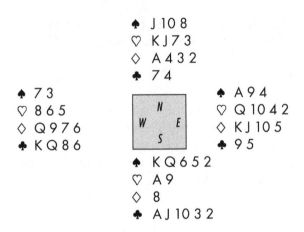

```
              ♠ J 10 8
              ♡ K J 7 3
              ◇ A 4 3 2
              ♣ 7 4
♠ 7 3                        ♠ A 9 4
♡ 8 6 5         N           ♡ Q 10 4 2
◇ Q 9 7 6    W     E        ◇ K J 10 5
♣ K Q 8 6       S           ♣ 9 5
              ♠ K Q 6 5 2
              ♡ A 9
              ◇ 8
              ♣ A J 10 3 2
```

On a straight jump to 4♠, West naturally leads the ♣K, which once again brings a smile to declarer's face, as his second suit can now be established with one ruff and then he'll draw trumps. I don't know about you, but after the last two deals, I'm going to have some harsh words for any bridge authors who tell us the king is a good lead from an unsupported king-queen against a suit contract.

If South had mentioned clubs at any point in the auction, the lead would have probably been a diamond or, even more likely, a trump. The defense would have fared much better on either of those leads.

Three Forms of Drury

Because even in the 1950s third-seat opening bids could be light and intended for lead-directional purposes, Doug Drury suggested an artificial response that allows a passed partner to show a good supporting hand for opener's major without having to venture to the three-level. A 2♣ bid showed this hand and then opener's rebid indicated whether he was interested in game, with a 2◇ rebid saying 'no'. Along the way, several innovative minds expanded on the idea and there are now three commonly-used variations of Drury:

- Reverse Drury. Here, 2♣ shows a fit for partner's major and invitational values, but opener now declines the game try by retreating to two of the agreed suit. Anything else promises solid values and game interest.

- Two-way Drury, where either minor suit is a raise of opener's major with 10-11 points. The difference is that 2♣ shows three-card support and 2◇ promises at least four of opener's major suit.

- Fit Drury, which means any two-level response in a new suit guarantees support for the major and is a concentration of values in the bid suit. If North were to open 1♡ in third seat, responder could bid 2◊ on either of these hands:

♠ 5 2 ♡ K 10 6 ◊ A J 9 5 2 ♣ Q 7 3
♠ 5 2 ♡ K 10 6 4 ◊ A Q J ♣ J 7 3 2

On the first hand, South has support and length in the suit he is bidding. In the second example, he doesn't have as much length but just about all his outside high cards are in diamonds, so that is the suit he mentions as opposed to the nondescript clubs.

Before we move on to our final topic, we'll look at a few examples of auctions where the convention is used. The partnership is assumed to be using Reverse Drury.

♠ A 10 9 8 6 4		♠ K 5 3
♡ A K 6	N	♡ 10 4
◊ J 10 9	W E	◊ A 8 2
♣ Q	S	♣ K 10 7 3 2

The auction might go:

West	East
	pass
1♠	2♣
2◊	4♠

Opener has 15 HCP and a six-card suit, and when partner bids 2♣ to show a fit and a maximum passed hand, he wants at least to try for game. You can always use a help-suit game try in these auctions and West continues with 2◊, as any of the top three honors in responder's hand will produce at least a trick out of the suit. East needs to show some enthusiasm rather than just bidding 2♠, and can either jump to game as shown or leave the final decision to opener with a jump to 3♠.

Here, 4♠ is where the partnership belongs, as declarer can ruff a heart and force out the ♣A to establish a winner in that suit for a diamond pitch.

For our next one, I'll just give you North's hand:

♠QJ972 ♡AJ542 ◇6 ♣A2

The auction has proceeded as follows:

North	South
	pass
1♠	2♣*
?	

With 5-5 in the majors, North isn't going to sign off. He could settle for a game probe with 2♡, or disdain any attempt at science and leap to 4♠ — the Hamman game try.

What is the outcome of charging into game? Well, this time the four hands are:

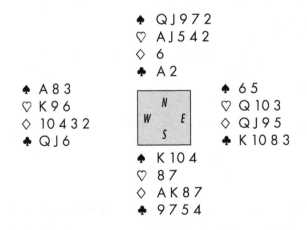

```
                    ♠ QJ972
                    ♡ AJ542
                    ◇ 6
                    ♣ A2
    ♠ A83                        ♠ 65
    ♡ K96            N           ♡ Q103
    ◇ 10432      W     E         ◇ QJ95
    ♣ QJ6            S           ♣ K1083
                    ♠ K104
                    ♡ 87
                    ◇ AK87
                    ♣ 9754
```

With hearts breaking 3-3, game will always make for North-South but there is an overtrick at stake. If North sails into 4♠ without further ado, East will probably lead the ◇Q. Declarer wins and can either take a club discard or, a bit more accurately, lead a heart to the ace and a second round of the suit. The defense shifts to a trump, but it's too late as North ruffs his third heart high, notes the 3-3 break, sheds his club on the high diamond and then plays on trumps. All he will lose is a heart and a spade.

If North rebids 2♡, partner might not think too highly of his hand and may well sign off. Even if North-South subsequently reach game, East might now lead a trump to prevent declarer from ruffing out the suit. If the opponents defend accurately, they can get out all the trumps before declarer can negotiate a ruff and hold him to ten tricks.

Responder's Game Tries when His Major Is Supported

Our example auction in this discussion is:

West	East
	1◇
1♠	2♠

Does opener guarantee four-card support for his raise? This is a matter that the partnership ought to have a firm agreement on. For example, would you mind if opener were to support your major on either of these hands?

♠A93   ♡A932   ◇KQJ94   ♣6
♠KJ4   ♡92   ◇A10875   ♣KQ6

If the answer is 'Yes, I play that opener must have four-card support', East can try for game with a natural 2NT or a help-suit game try in a new suit.

The partnerships who have agreed that opener might sometimes be raising with three-card support would typically use the cheapest bid here to ask for more precise information. In this case, 2NT would be artificial and partner would describe his hand further like this:

3♣	Three-card support, minimum values (second hand)
3◇	Three-card support, maximum hand (first hand)
3♡	Four-card support and a minimum
3♠	Four-card support and a maximum

This structure is only necessary if you allow opener to raise a major suit with three of them. Otherwise, you needn't bother and can just play it simple with help-suit game tries.

1. With North-South vulnerable, you are sitting East with this as your hand:

♠K 10 7 6   ♡7 5 2   ◇J 8   ♣A Q 10 4

Partner opens 1♡. How would you go about raising his suit — an immediate 2♡ or a three-card limit raise via 1NT forcing and then 3♡?

2. Both vulnerable, you're now South and your hand is:

♠K J 5 3   ♡A K 8 4 3   ◇Q 5   ♣K 7

You've opened your longer major and partner has raised to 2♡. Do you try for game on these cards?

3. You're South again for this one, with East-West vulnerable.

♠A K 10 7 6 4   ♡9 5   ◇4 2   ♣A K 10

Partner gives you a single raise when you open 1♠. Your partnership has agreed to use Kokish game tries. Does this hand qualify?

4. This time, with neither side vulnerable, you've been dealt as South:

♠8 6   ♡K Q 10 6 4   ◇A 9   ♣A Q J 8

You have the same decision facing you when you open 1♡ and partner raises to 2♡. What's your pleasure?

Regardless of what your answer was, you end up as declarer in a heart contract. West has led the ♣6. Here is the dummy that greets you:

♠ A K J 3
♡ 9 8 7
◇ 4 3
♣ 10 4 3 2

	N	
W		E
	S	

♠ 8 6
♡ K Q 10 6 4
◇ A 9
♣ A Q J 8

East thinks for awhile and puts up the ♣K at Trick 1. How do you play the hand?

1.   N-S vulnerable

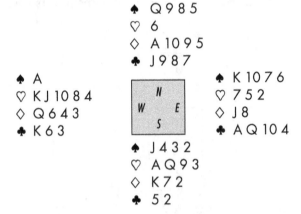

```
            ♠ Q 9 8 5
            ♡ 6
            ◇ A 10 9 5
            ♣ J 9 8 7
♠ A                              ♠ K 10 7 6
♡ K J 10 8 4      N             ♡ 7 5 2
◇ Q 6 4 3     W       E         ◇ J 8
♣ K 6 3           S             ♣ A Q 10 4
            ♠ J 4 3 2
            ♡ A Q 9 3
            ◇ K 7 2
            ♣ 5 2
```

West	North	East	South
			pass
1♡	pass	2♡	all pass

In terms of both high-card points (10) and cover cards (3), East could respond a forcing 1NT and then jump to 3♡ to show a three-card limit raise. If he does, opener may well bid game, but will at best only come to nine tricks

There are a couple of reasons for him to value the hand more conservatively. One is the ◇J, which is located in a short suit and unlikely to be a working card. The other is the meager quality of the three-card support.

If responder settles for 2♡ as his first action, opener won't go any further as he has six losers and not much extra in the way of high cards.

2.   Both vulnerable

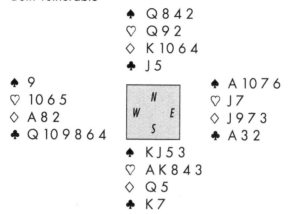

	♠ Q 8 4 2	
	♡ Q 9 2	
	◇ K 10 6 4	
	♣ J 5	

West	North	East	South
		pass	1♡
pass	2♡	pass	2♠
pass	3♠	pass	4♠
all pass			

This was the actual bidding. North-South deserve some credit for having located their 4-4 spade fit. The heart game essentially needs both major suits to divide evenly and the ♣A to be onside as well. Meanwhile, 4♠ has slightly more chances, although both contracts will go down because of the 4-1 spade break.

However, South was a bit pushy in trying for game. Yes, he has 16 HCP, but his loser count is six, and responder is suggesting 2 to 2.5 cover cards for his constructive raise. In fact, the ♠Q, which he counted as half a cover card initially, turns out to be worth a full trick to opener. Even with all that, it's not a game you'd really want to be in.

As I have emphasized several times before, experienced players like to go plus at matchpoints, and will not be overly aggressive in trying for game. In this case, the loser count and a third of the points being in the short suits are reasons for opener to dampen his enthusiasm.

3.   E-W vulnerable

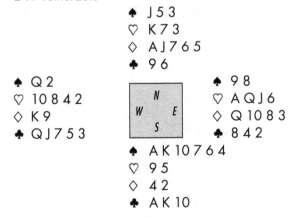

       ♠ J 5 3
       ♡ K 7 3
       ◇ A J 7 6 5
       ♣ 9 6

♠ Q 2   ♠ 9 8
♡ 10 8 4 2   ♡ A Q J 6
◇ K 9   ◇ Q 10 8 3
♣ Q J 7 5 3   ♣ 8 4 2

       ♠ A K 10 7 6 4
       ♡ 9 5
       ◇ 4 2
       ♣ A K 10

West	North	East	South
			1♠
pass	2♠	pass	2NT*
pass	3◇	pass	3♡
pass	4♠	all pass	

This is a shining example of at least trying for game when your six-card major is raised. Although the South hand initially counted a loser in his long suit, for a total of six, that possibility is greatly reduced once he knows partner has support.

A hand like this where opener's long suits are of good quality is tailor-made for Kokish game tries. South bids the artificial 2NT and partner shows a top honor in diamonds, usually the ace or king. That is enough for opener to try again with 3♡, whereupon responder accepts by going to 4♠.

This deal, like the one before it, shows how giving value to certain features is an approximation. For instance, the ♡K turns out to be useless because the ace is offside. The good news is that the doubleton club, which North assumed was half a cover card, was worth a full trick because opener had three cards in the suit. The 6-3 fit improved the chances of the contract making, and the ♠J in responder's hand made it an even better proposition.

4.　Neither vulnerable

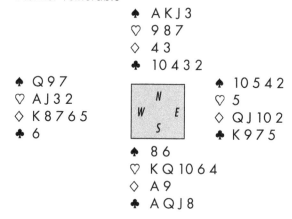

```
              ♠ A K J 3
              ♡ 9 8 7
              ◇ 4 3
              ♣ 10 4 3 2
♠ Q 9 7                        ♠ 10 5 4 2
♡ A J 3 2          N           ♡ 5
◇ K 8 7 6 5    W       E       ◇ Q J 10 2
♣ 6                S           ♣ K 9 7 5
              ♠ 8 6
              ♡ K Q 10 6 4
              ◇ A 9
              ♣ A Q J 8
```

West	North	East	South
pass	pass	pass	1♡
pass	2♡	pass	4♡
all pass			

With 16 HCP and two suits of excellent quality, South uses the Hamman game try and bashes into 4♡. Regardless of the form of game, you are entitled to use whatever table feel you have, and East's hesitation in putting up his ♣K at Trick 1 suggests that the lead might have been from shortness.

Since dummy entries are limited, it's best to preserve them and lead the king of trumps from hand. West takes the ace and then shifts to a diamond, which goes to the ten on your right as you take the ace. Only now do you go to table with a spade to play a second round of trumps as East shows out. You are in peril of going down since West has two trump winners and will be able to get to partner's hand in diamonds for a club ruff. You will have to take the spade finesse and hold your breath. When you open your eyes, the jack has held and you are able to get rid of a diamond.

While leading from an unsupported king is something that players don't often fancy, there is a case to be made for a diamond lead here. If West catches partner with either the queen or ace, then he's in good shape to continue the suit and force declarer to ruff. As it turns out, this defense would have likely defeated the 4♡ contract.

7

Bidding on the Borderline

When you and your partner have a free run during the auction, you have to make several choices, both about the strain and the level of the final contract. In a pairs game, there is always the temptation of forsaking the lowly minor suit and going for the higher-paying contract of notrump or a major suit. Similarly, there is the credo 'pluses are always good at matchpoints' and you will have to decide how aggressive you should be in trying for games and slams.

Part of making the right decision is using good hand evaluation, but it's also important to recognize certain situations and know which approach is likely to work out best. There are also tools and guidelines that can assist you in the process.

We'll begin with a deal where you have a decent hand for your initial bid. Both sides are vulnerable and you hold as East:

♠A 3 ♡Q 4 3 2 ◊J 7 4 ♣K 6 5 4

The auction has gone:

West	East
1♠	1NT*
2◊	?

Partner's two-level rebid can be anywhere from 11 or 12 points all the way up to a bad 18-count. The options here for responder are a cautious preference to 2♠ or an invitational 2NT. Point-wise, East has the approximate values required for 2NT in this sequence. Should that be his bid?

Neither action would be wrong, but the disconcerting factor about this hand is the lack of spot cards in the rounded suits. If you added some texture, such as the ♡10 and the ♣9, you'd be better equipped to handle whichever suit the opponents led. I held these cards and took the conservative route by bidding 2♠. This would not have ended the auction if opener held an unbalanced hand of a good 16 or 17 points, as he'd take a further call and our side would still reach game. On the flip side, West is going to subside if he has 15 points or an uninspiring 16-count.

Was I a hero or a bum when the smoke cleared? It turned out well for me this time as the complete layout was:

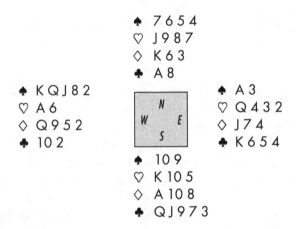

```
                    ♠ 7 6 5 4
                    ♡ J 9 8 7
                    ◇ K 6 3
                    ♣ A 8
    ♠ K Q J 8 2          N          ♠ A 3
    ♡ A 6                           ♡ Q 4 3 2
    ◇ Q 9 5 2      W         E      ◇ J 7 4
    ♣ 10 2              S           ♣ K 6 5 4
                    ♠ 10 9
                    ♡ K 10 5
                    ◇ A 10 8
                    ♣ Q J 9 7 3
```

A 2NT bid from East would end the auction, and South would lead the ♣Q. East has seven winners but if North-South discard correctly they can defeat the contract. On the run of the spades, South will have to throw one of his clubs and keep two cards each in diamonds and hearts. If he bares down to the ◇A, he can be endplayed into leading away from his ♡K.

What you might argue concerning this deal as an example is that poor West has dead-minimum values for his opening bid. All right, then, let's switch the ♣10 and ♣Q, so that he now has 14 HCP. South will lead the jack from his J109 sequence and the result is exactly the same. Even if we bolster opener's club holding to Q10 doubleton, while chances are better for eight tricks, nine winners are still far, far away.

The deal we've just talked about does not mean that we should always take the low road in the bidding. Our next example occurs in a 1NT auction. With East-West vulnerable, you are South and have been dealt:

♠J 8 7 6 ♡A 5 ◇A K 8 6 ♣A 6 4

The bidding has commenced with:

North	South
	1NT
2♡	?

For those of you unfamiliar with 'super-accepts' after a Jacoby transfer response, opener might sometimes jump to three of partner's major instead simply bidding 2♠ if he has a maximum hand and at least four of the suit. South's point-count here is 16 rather than 17, but it's easily worth the super-accept because all of his points are sure tricks, with the outside king supported by the ace of that suit.

The bolder choice pays off handsomely in this case, as the four hands are:

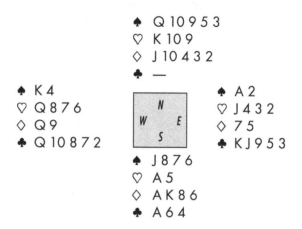

Here, 4♠ makes with an overtrick and would have ten winners even if the ◇Q does not fall.

If South simply bids 2♠ over the transfer, responder might like his shape but still will pass as opener might have only two spades. The problem for North-South here is that a new suit by an unpassed hand over the transfer is natural and game-forcing, so North isn't good enough to bid 3◇ over 2♠.

The Issue of Three-card Raises by Opener

Before we move on to other topics in this chapter, I will touch briefly again upon one that partnerships ought to have a dialogue and agreement on: that is whether it's fine for opener to support partner's major with a three-card holding if the hand looks right for it.

Some players are adamant that you should not, while others do it regularly. I fall somewhere in the middle of the two extremes. Here are three examples to illustrate the heart of the matter. You are West, and this has been the start of the auction:

West	East
1◇	1♠
?	

♠ K J 6   ♡ 4   ◇ A Q 8 5 4   ♣ K 9 6 2

I wouldn't object to a 2♠ raise on these cards. Your other choice would be to rebid 2♣ – if responder passes, you'll be in a makeable contract, but the same might be true for spades, which will score much better. Let's say partner takes a 2◊ preference. You might still be wondering if you're in the right spot. But if you now take a third bid with 2♠, responder is going to expect a much stronger hand. An immediate 2♠ raise is very descriptive of your range and the fact that you have a ruffing value compensates somewhat for the lack of a fourth trump.

♠ Q J 6   ♡ 4 2   ◊ A K 8 5   ♣ A 9 6 2

The reason some openers would consider 2♠ rather than 1NT here is that they have misgivings about the small doubleton in the unbid major. The notrump rebid is not likely to miss a 5-3 spade fit as responder will head in that direction most times. Yes, 1NT could be a slightly worse contract if partner has four spades and two or three hearts, but all in all, there will be a fair number of 1NT bidders here. Of course, 2♠ will have its advocates too, but not as many as on the previous hand.

♠ Q J 6   ♡ J 4 2   ◊ K Q 8 5   ♣ A 9 6

The pendulum swings dramatically the other way on this hand. With 4-3-3-3 shape, it is far more advisable to rebid 1NT than 2♠. Sure, you don't have a full stopper in the heart suit, but this is a hand that is not in the least suit-oriented.

Notrump Versus a Minor Suit

Typically, if a partnership's only eight-card or better fit is in a minor suit and they have the combined values for game, they will try mightily to play in notrump. They will only give up on that notion if one partner lacks a high card in the other's short suit. Where the choice between notrump and the minor occurs is when it's a partscore hand or when one of the two players is inviting game. Then you have to weigh the safety of the known fit against the inclination to strive for the higher-paying contract.

Your first decision comes as responder, sitting West and your side vulnerable. You have these cards as partner opens 1♣:

♠ J 6 4   ♡ J 5 4   ◊ Q 9   ♣ A Q 7 4 3

There are two feasible options here: one is to respond 1NT, the other is to support clubs with some degree of enthusiasm. If you're playing inverted minor-suit raises, you could bid 2♣. For partnerships that use game-forcing single raises and a jump in the other minor as 'criss-cross', showing 10-11 HCP, 2◊ would be the route to take.

As 10-point hands go, this one is not all that sparkling. You have balanced distribution, with the queens and jacks all being unsupported honors. Moreover, the forward-going action commits your side to 2NT or the three-level. A fair number of experienced players would downgrade this collection to a 9-count and bid 1NT. True, you don't have a full stopper in either major, but a notrump response is a limited action and makes no such promises.

What is the outcome when the deal is completed? Well, here's the whole story:

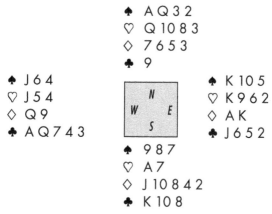

```
                    ♠ A Q 3 2
                    ♡ Q 10 8 3
                    ◊ 7 6 5 3
                    ♣ 9
   ♠ J 6 4                          ♠ K 10 5
   ♡ J 5 4          N               ♡ K 9 6 2
   ◊ Q 9         W     E            ◊ A K
   ♣ A Q 7 4 3      S               ♣ J 6 5 2
                    ♠ 9 8 7
                    ♡ A 7
                    ◊ J 10 8 4 2
                    ♣ K 10 8
```

Since North is probably going to lead one of the major suits against 1NT, declarer is in good shape and will eventually take four clubs, two diamonds and two tricks in whichever major is led.

If West responds 2♣, the partnership might also arrive in notrump, but at least one and maybe two levels higher, and with South on lead. Since he has five diamonds, that will be his opening salvo and now the defense will collect six tricks.

Now we'll move you over to the South chair, with North the dealer and East-West vulnerable:

♠9 7 3　♡K 5 2　◊A 9 4　♣Q 8 4 2

The auction to this point has been:

West	North	East	South
	1♣	1♡	1NT
2♡	pass	pass	?

Rather than support what might be a three-card suit, you bid 1NT at your first turn with a stopper in their suit and totally flat 4-3-3-3 shape. West then raises his partner's overcall and it comes back around to you. Because of the raise, it's now likely partner has actual club length. So do you pass, double, support clubs now, or persist in notrump? We can eliminate pass as your side has more than half the deck, and the heart quality is not good enough to venture a double, which partner will probably take as penalty. What is opener's distribution likely to be? It's not written in stone, but he hasn't competed to the three-level as he might have with shortness in the enemy suit. Your expectation would be that he has balanced or semi-balanced distribution. Nothing has changed about your hand in that it hasn't suddenly transformed into one where you'd rather play a suit contract, so you might as well bid 2NT. There is actually a slight inference that you're bidding with a fit for partner's suit rather than multiple stoppers in East's suit. If your hand were:

♠ 9 7 3 ♡ K Q 9 2 ◇ A 9 4 ♣ 8 4 2

you certainly would have doubled since the opponents are vulnerable.

When all is said and done, the complete deal is:

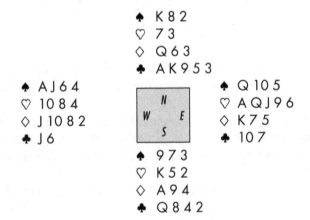

```
              ♠ K 8 2
              ♡ 7 3
              ◇ Q 6 3
              ♣ A K 9 5 3
♠ A J 6 4                   ♠ Q 10 5
♡ 10 8 4          N         ♡ A Q J 9 6
◇ J 10 8 2    W     E       ◇ K 7 5
♣ J 6             S         ♣ 10 7
              ♠ 9 7 3
              ♡ K 5 2
              ◇ A 9 4
              ♣ Q 8 4 2
```

On a heart lead and continuation, you don't have much choice in the line of play: you can lead a spade to the king right off the bat, or take your five club winners and exit a heart. Your 2NT contract will make or at worst, be down one. Meanwhile, 3♣ will go down unless the opponents do you a favor in the diamond suit. Their 2♡ contract will also make, so in bidding on, you've improved on that result.

Before you get the impression that abandoning the minor-suit fit is always the best policy, here are a couple of more examples that show it isn't necessarily so. In the first one, you are sitting West and hold:

♠ Q J 10 8   ♡ Q 8   ♢ J 10 3   ♣ A J 6 5

The start of the auction has been:

West	East
	1♢
1♠	2♢
?	

Does your hand justify inviting game? The answer is yes, since partner can have up to 15 points for his rebid. While some people I've consulted like 2NT as West's follow-up, I can't agree. Opener is going to have an unbalanced hand, and it's a guess as to where his shortness might be. The action I would take is 3♢. If East passes, we'll have a good play for nine tricks, while a notrump game will probably fail if the opponents lead their best suit. If he has extras, any continuation such as 3♡, 3♠ or 3NT by him would be very much to your liking. Here are a couple of hands partner might have:

♠ K 6   ♡ 10 4   ♢ A K Q 9 8 7   ♣ Q 7 2
♠ 6   ♡ K 10 4   ♢ A K Q 9 8 7   ♣ Q 7 2

On the first hand, he will carry on to 3NT over 2NT and the opponents will run the heart suit and get the ♠A to boot. Over 3♢ he will probably show his spade stopper, and you may be able to stop in 4♢.

The second hand is a different story. In either case, if opener doesn't bid 3NT himself, he'll show his outside high card with 3♡, whereupon your concern about that suit is alleviated and you can settle in the notrump game.

In our last example, you are East, partner is the dealer and neither side is vulnerable:

♠ A J 10 7 5   ♡ Q   ♢ K 9 2   ♣ 7 5 4 2

The auction has kicked off with:

West	East
1♡	1♠
2♣	?

There are two higher-paying contracts than clubs that you can suggest on your rebid, namely 2♠ or 2NT. Passing is also a thought, but opener would jump shift only if he had a nice 18 points, so he could still have quite a good hand. Bidding 3♣ is just as invitational as 2NT, and keeps our side in an eight-card or better fit if opener has a minimum hand. What he has is:

♠K 4 ♡A K 9 8 6 ◇6 ♣A J 10 9 6

With the lack of a notrump bid from you, the games he will look for are clubs or possibly spades, either of which should make. If you had rebid 2NT, he would have bid 3NT with a source of tricks in both rounded suits. Opposite your hand, 3NT is not hopeless, but needs spades to be friendly.

Notrump Versus a Major Suit

When a partnership has an eight-card fit in a major suit and has no game ambitions, they will almost never consider notrump, as the suit contract will often play a trick better. When the pair is about to bid game or slam, however, they may succumb to the lure of playing in notrump in the hope of gaining the extra 10 points when there is no difference in the tricks to be made. There are two scenarios where the decision may arise, and we'll look at each of them in turn.

1) A strong notrump hand with 4-3-3-3 distribution sees partner transfer to a major and then bid 3NT. He must now decide whether to leave it there or go back to the 5-3 fit in responder's major.

If opener has no ruffing value, it seems reasonable to pass 3NT instead of going back to the major suit. After all, both contracts might have the same number of tricks. How does it play out in real life? I sifted through 25-30 deals and the results were consistent. Here are four of them.

<table>
<tr><td>
♠ K 9 3
♡ A Q 2
◇ 10 8 3
♣ A Q 7 3
</td><td>
N
W   E
S
</td><td>
♠ J 10 4
♡ K J 10 9 3
◇ Q 9
♣ K 10 8
</td></tr>
</table>

West opens 1NT, after which responder transfers to hearts and then offers a choice of games with 3NT. If opener passes, the defense leads diamonds and collects the first five tricks plus the ♠A for down two.

Ah, you might say, but opener had an unstopped suit so he should have gone back to hearts. On to the next one:

```
    ♠ A 10 5                      ♠ Q J 9 8 3
    ♡ A 8 4          N            ♡ 3 2
    ◇ A 9 8      W       E        ◇ K 10 7 3
    ♣ K 9 8 6        S            ♣ A 2
```

Over partner's strong notrump, East transfers to spades and then bids 3NT. Opener has a high card in every side suit along with his 4-3-3-3 shape, so it feels right to pass. Unfortunately, North has a natural heart lead and the ♠K behind the ace. So the 3NT contract goes down one, while 4♠ has only three losers.

Well, is it just a bad run of luck? After all, notrump would have had the same tricks if the spade finesse had worked. The next hand up is:

```
    ♠ Q 9 3                       ♠ A K 7 6 2
    ♡ K Q 9 3        N            ♡ J 10 7
    ◇ A Q 7      W       E        ◇ K 9 5
    ♣ K 10 2         S            ♣ 9 5
```

The landscape is familiar: strong notrump by West and partner transfers to spades and then continues with 3NT. Once more, opener has 4-3-3-3 distribution with a high card in every side suit. What happens this time if he passes? The four hands are:

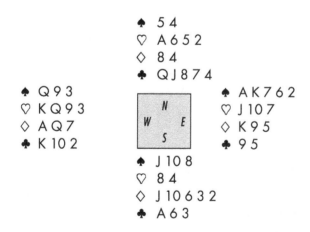

```
                        ♠ 5 4
                        ♡ A 6 5 2
                        ◇ 8 4
                        ♣ Q J 8 7 4
    ♠ Q 9 3                            ♠ A K 7 6 2
    ♡ K Q 9 3          N               ♡ J 10 7
    ◇ A Q 7       W        E           ◇ K 9 5
    ♣ K 10 2          S               ♣ 9 5
                        ♠ J 10 8
                        ♡ 8 4
                        ◇ J 10 6 3 2
                        ♣ A 6 3
```

Although hearts are the unbid major, North is probably going to lead a club, whereupon South wins the ace and plays one back. Declarer holds up and wins the third round of the suit. He has nine top tricks but cannot develop extra winners in hearts without surrendering the lead to North, who has the long clubs. Meanwhile, with the ♣A onside, 4♠ will make five.

Of course, playing in notrump instead of the major suit *can* sometimes be a rewarding endeavor, as we'll see on the last of our exhibits:

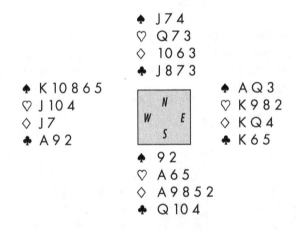

♠ K 10 8 6 5   ♠ A Q 3
♡ J 10 4   ♡ K 9 8 2
◇ J 7   ◇ K Q 4
♣ A 9 2   ♣ K 6 5

This is the same approximate hand for the 1NT opener as the previous two, and we'll assume he passes 3NT again rather than go back to the 5-3 spade fit. South leads a diamond and there look to be nine tricks for sure, with five spades and two in each of the minor suits. The source of possible overtricks is in the heart suit, in which declarer is missing the ace but will be able to develop three winners if the queen is in the right place.

Do the notrump bidders come out ahead on this deal? The answer is yes, as this is the whole story:

```
                    ♠  J 7 4
                    ♡  Q 7 3
                    ◇  10 6 3
                    ♣  J 8 7 3
  ♠ K 10 8 6 5                   ♠ A Q 3
  ♡ J 10 4            N          ♡ K 9 8 2
  ◇ J 7           W     E        ◇ K Q 4
  ♣ A 9 2            S           ♣ K 6 5
                    ♠  9 2
                    ♡  A 6 5
                    ◇  A 9 8 5 2
                    ♣  Q 10 4
```

With the ♡Q lying nicely, all you'll lose is the two red aces and will have your moment of triumph for playing in notrump rather than spades.

The bottom line, then, is that leaving the contract in 3NT with 4-3-3-3 shape after a transfer auction is by no means a sure thing. LHO will be starting out with his longest suit, and you'll need to have multiple stoppers as in the last of our four deals. If you don't, you'll only beat out the pairs that are in the major-suit fit if the cards are lying well for you.

2) Partner has shown 18-19 balanced with a jump to 2NT on his second bid and you also have a balanced hand with a five-card major. The question here for responder is whether to just raise to 3NT or check back to see if opener has three-card support for you.

The answer hinges on what the combined point-count between the two hands is known to be. As Woolsey points out in his book, if the total is in the 28-30 point range, then notrump will often come to the same number of tricks as the major suit. If you have slightly less, with 25-27 points, the 5-3 fit could well be the superior alternative.

As people were fond of saying way back when, 'the proof is in the pudding', so we can examine some deals to find out if that assumption holds true. Our first pair of hands is:

♠ A 10 2
♥ Q J 10 6
♦ A K Q
♣ Q 7 6

	N	
W		E
	S	

♠ K J 9 6 4
♥ K 9
♦ 10 6 4
♣ K J 10

The auction has gone:

West	East
1♣	1♠
2NT	?

With his 11 HCP, responder knows the two hands total at least 29 or 30 points. Even if there is a 5-3 spade fit, notrump may well yield the same number of tricks. Will that indeed be the case? Here is the full deal:

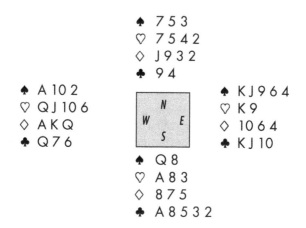

           ♠ 7 5 3
           ♥ 7 5 4 2
           ♦ J 9 3 2
           ♣ 9 4

♠ A 10 2
♥ Q J 10 6
♦ A K Q
♣ Q 7 6

♠ K J 9 6 4
♥ K 9
♦ 10 6 4
♣ K J 10

           ♠ Q 8
           ♥ A 8 3
           ♦ 8 7 5
           ♣ A 8 5 3 2

North will probably flip a coin on his lead against 3NT, but it won't matter. Both 3NT and 4♠ will take the same number of tricks, depending on whether declarer can guess where the ♠Q is.

Moving on:

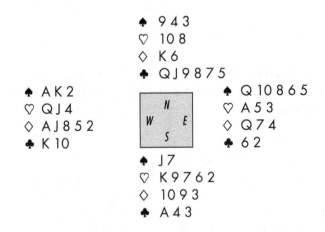

```
♠ A K 2                    ♠ Q 10 8 6 5
♡ Q J 4          N         ♡ A 5 3
◇ A J 8 5 2   W     E      ◇ Q 7 4
♣ K 10           S         ♣ 6 2
```

The bidding so far is:

West	East
1◇	1♠
2NT	?

Tallying up the points, East knows there are 26 or 27 HCP between the two hands, leaving the partnership just short of the threshold where he'd simply raise to 3NT and not consider the major-suit contract. He should therefore check back for three-card support.

The full deal is:

```
              ♠ 9 4 3
              ♡ 10 8
              ◇ K 6
              ♣ Q J 9 8 7 5
♠ A K 2                         ♠ Q 10 8 6 5
♡ Q J 4           N             ♡ A 5 3
◇ A J 8 5 2   W       E         ◇ Q 7 4
♣ K 10            S             ♣ 6 2
              ♠ J 7
              ♡ K 9 7 6 2
              ◇ 10 9 3
              ♣ A 4 3
```

After two rounds of clubs, notrump isn't very good at all, needing a miracle lie in the diamond suit to make the same number of tricks. Spades, by contrast, will lose only a club and a diamond, scoring up eleven tricks with ease.

3) Partner has opened 2NT and you have sufficient values for game and a balanced hand with at least one four-card major.

Here again the borderline for the notrump versus major choice is 28 points. As responder, you should look for the major fit if you know for a certainty that your side has less than that. To illustrate, here's a 2NT opening:

♠K 8 3 2 ♡A K 6 4 ◇A K 3 ♣A 5

and two slightly different responding hands:

♠ 1 0 9 5 ♡J 8 5 3 ◇Q J 8 ♣K Q 4
♠ 1 0 9 5 ♡J 8 5 3 ◇Q J 8 ♣K 6 4

On the first hand, responder with his 9 HCP can tell there is little chance of slam, but elects to bypass a Stayman inquiry. With 4-3-3-3 shape and a 29-30 combined point, 3NT may (and does) take the same number of tricks as hearts.

It's a different story when you take the ♣Q away, leaving the partnership with 27 points total, only slightly more than they need for game. If the opponents lead clubs, the two stoppers will be dislodged before you can establish the extra winners in the major suits. Playing in the 4-4 heart fit, declarer has the time to work on spades.

Before we move on to the next topic, we'll consider one more hand for responder. As South, you hold these cards:

♠1 0 8 4 ♡A Q 1 0 6 ◇1 0 9 8 6 ♣K 7

Partner has opened 2NT, and this time you have a doubleton instead of 4-3-3-3 distribution. Should you now go searching for a 4-4 heart fit?

The slight change doesn't matter, as you have the king in your doubleton suit and know once again that your side has at least 29 points. That is above the borderline and you can raise to 3NT with a fair amount of confidence that it will produce the same tricks as hearts.

The complete deal on this occasion is:

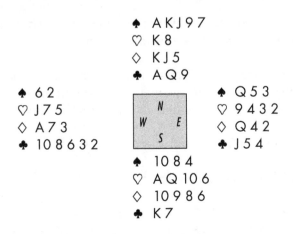

North-South do have an eight-card fit in a major, but it's in spades, not hearts. However, unless East somehow finds a diamond lead from his ◊Q42, notrump will make the same or more tricks than spades. Probably he will either lead a straightforward heart or, if he tries to find partner in his short major, a spade. Wouldn't that be a pleasure?

The 4-Point Principle

Thus far, our focus has mostly been on where to play the contract, in a suit or notrump. Just as crucial for the partnership, though, is the decision about how high to go in the bidding. Do we content ourselves with a partscore or try for game? Are there times when we should be looking for or bidding slam?

The same friend that gave me the advice on dealing with preempts also told me about something he called the '4-point principle'. The gist of it is that for every 4 points partner has shown in the bidding, give him the dream card of your choice, and imagine that hand opposite yours. For example, suppose he has opened 1NT. That will be 15-17 HCP, and translates to four 'dream cards'. If he opens a suit and then rebids cheaply in notrump, his range is 12-14 and the maximum number of useful cards he will have is three.

The 4-point principle is most accurate when partner is known to have a balanced hand. There are some auctions in which he might have both high card and distributional features. For example, North-South have the following auction:

North	South
1◊	1♠
2♣	

What we know is that opener is minimum in terms of high-card points, and will normally have three useful honor cards. Other than having support for your major, though, we have no inkling of whether he is balanced or unbalanced, as he could be either.

With our guideline in place, we can use it to determine how far to venture on each of the following hands. To begin with, you are in the South chair and no one is vulnerable:

♠743 ♡K98532 ◇QJ8 ♣10

The auction has kicked off with:

North	South
1NT	2◇*
2♡	?

You have 6 HCP with a six-card suit. Could there be a game for your side? The 4-point principle says no. Even if you give partner the something like the ♠AK, ♡A and ◇A, it's not enough for game to struggle home unless he also has four-card heart support. That is unlikely because North has not super-accepted with a jump to three of your major. You should therefore pass as game will be a long shot at best.

In the next hand, you are West and both sides are vulnerable:

♠KJ93 ♡AKQ642 ◇107 ♣4

The auction you've had to this point is:

West	East
1♡	2◇
2♠	2NT
3♡	4♡
?	

You've shown your 6-4 distribution and partner has not cooperated. Since he hasn't raised your hearts earlier, responder should have a doubleton heart. You can expect a hand in the vicinity of 12-14 points. Should you be trying for slam?

The odds are against it. Give partner the ◇AK and the ♠A: there is still going to be a club to lose and a missing honor in the spade suit. That means slam is never going to be a claimer and you should refrain from going any further. Partner's actual hand is:

♠A65 ♡75 ◇AK542 ♣Q107

Here, 6♡ would not be hopeless but it needs some good things to happen, like diamonds to be 3-3 or spades dividing evenly with the queen onside. Alas, even eleven tricks are beyond your reach this time as the trumps are 4-1.

On this next example, you can also use the 4-point principle to good effect. You are North and both sides are vulnerable:

♠AK ♡KQJ95 ◇KJ4 ♣972

The partnership uncovers a fit immediately:

North	South
	1♣
1♡	2♡
?	

And here you are, with a nice 17-count and a good five-card suit. Is the partnership in slam territory?

Close, but you'll likely be a trick short. With opener having shown a minimum, you are entitled to three useful cards according to the 4-point principle. Make them the ♣AK and a red ace. That still won't be enough, as you'll have a club and the missing ace to lose, and possibly a diamond as well.

Partner's hand was:

♠754 ♡A1083 ◇A98 ♣A104

So you have two losers in the club suit for sure, and perhaps another one in diamonds.

Although the 4-point principle has you stopping short in the examples so far, we can gaze upon the world more optimistically on this next one. You are North and neither side is vulnerable:

♠8 ♡K753 ◇AK7542 ♣85

Partner got the ball rolling with a 2NT opening bid. From there it went:

North	South
	2NT
3♣	3♠
?	

Do you shut it down in 3NT or try for a slam in your long suit with 4◇?

Since partner has shown 20-21 points, that translates to five useful cards. Make them the ♡AQ, the ◇Q and the ♣AK, and that gives you a play for 6◇. If you bid 4◇, partner will cooperate and you'll wind up in slam, as this is his hand:

♠A Q J 5   ♡A 10 2   ◇9 6 3   ♣A K Q

The diamond slam is a reasonable contract, even with partner having wasted values in spades. If trumps are 2-2, you are home free. If they split 3-1, then you will need to get rid of two small hearts out of your hand. One will go on the extra club winner, and in spades you can take either the simple finesse or the ruffing finesse to dispose of another heart from hand.

One more for the road, with you sitting West and both sides vulnerable:

♠K Q 10 7 6 4   ♡K J 6 3   ◇9   ♣A K

The auction gets high rather quickly:

West (you)	North	East	South
	pass	1♣	3◇
3♠	pass	4♠	pass
?			

Partner could have a minimum hand, but three 'dream cards' consisting of the ♠A and ♡AQ opposite what you have will produce a slam. You should therefore show your outside ace with 5♣ and see how partner reacts.

Opener has some wastage in the minor suits, but good holdings in the majors as his hand is:

♠A J 5 2   ♡A 8   ◇Q 10 4   ♣Q J 7 6

He will cooperate with 5♡, and you can proceed on to 6♠, which is a very good contract.

More Slam Decisions — Is It Worth the Effort?

Before moving on to the quiz section, I have a quartet of examples where one player has to decide whether to try for slam. In some of them, you may have to bypass a notrump game or major-suit contract to look for bigger things. Here we go!

With both sides vulnerable, you hold as South:

♠ K Q 10 4 ♡ J 7 ◇ 5 4 2 ♣ A Q J 8

You're in the hot seat after the auction has begun:

North	South
1◇	1♠
2♡	?

Partner has shown 17 or more points with his reverse into 2♡, and you're in a possession of a hand that would have opened. Is this a potential slam hand?

Yes, it might be. However, to make the try you'd have to go past 3NT, the highest-paying game contract. This hand may look gaudy, but you have nothing to write home about in partner's long suits and too many queens and jacks where his shortness is going to be.

You can take the middle road on this hand and bid 3◇ if your partnership is using the Ingberman convention over reverses. With this agreement, a direct raise of one of partner's suits is game-forcing while 2NT is a relay to 3♣ and is used for all the weaker hand types. By raising first and then bidding 3NT, you are indicating mild slam interest. Partner's hand is:

♠ 3 ♡ A K 10 4 ◇ A K Q J 7 3 ♣ 6 4

A diamond slam is not a bad one to be in. If the opponents don't lead clubs it will have an excellent play and even if they do, it will make if the finesse succeeds.

Our next example features a choice between game in a major suit or looking for slam in a minor suit.

```
        ♠ A 8                    ♠ K 7 6 5 3
        ♡ 9            N         ♡ A Q J 10 5 2
        ◇ A Q J 4   W     E      ◇ —
        ♣ Q J 10 4 3 2    S      ♣ K 5
```

East is as the crossroads after:

West	East
1♣	1♡
2♣	2♠
3◇	3♠
3NT	?

Notrump is the furthest thing from responder's thoughts, so he isn't going to leave it there. From his point of view, there might be a slam in clubs if partner has the ♠A. However, if East bids 4♣ and all opener can do is bid game, he is going to regret missing out on playing 4♡. In a team game, you wouldn't lose any sleep over playing in the minor suit. At pairs, though, it matters a whole lot. The more practical choice here is to insist on your long and strong major and bid 4♡. It is what most of the field is liable to do anyway.

Your next challenge is as East:

♠K ♡QJ52 ◇Q93 ♣AJ642

This is how the auction has progressed:

West	East
1♣	1♡
1♠	2◇*
3◇	?

Your 2◇ was fourth-suit forcing, and partner's raise was natural, implying 4=0=4=5 distribution. Again you're faced with the decision of bidding 3NT or agreeing clubs as trumps and looking for slam. Since opener has not limited his hand and can have anywhere from 12 to 17 points, you lack the information needed to apply the 4-point principle. He could have four useful values, and that would be enough for your side to make 6♣. The chances of slam are much higher on this hand and you can leave it up to partner with 4♣. In fact his hand is:

♠AQ96 ♡— ◇KJ87 ♣K9853

At this point, opener will likely shrug his shoulders and bid 6♣. Since you haven't bid 3NT, he can expect you to have enough fillers in his suits for it to have a play.

In conclusion, we have this pair of hands:

♠ A 7		♠ K Q 10 9 6 5
♡ A Q 7	N	♡ 8 5 3
◇ A 10 4 2	W E	◇ 6
♣ K Q 6 5	S	♣ A J 7

The auction goes:

West	East
1◇	1♠
2NT	3♠
3NT	4♣
?	

As an aside, whenever partner jumps to 2NT after a one-level opening, *any* major-suit bid shows extra length. With only five spades, responder would use a checkback inquiry. Both 3♠ and 4♠ promise a six-card suit, with East's continuation here indicating slam interest in accordance with the Principle of Fast Arrival.

Opener decides to protect his heart holding with 3NT. East is going to place the contract in spades, but along the way, he can show his ♣A. That improves partner's club holding so he can now ask with 4NT. When the reply shows two keycards with the ♠Q he can inquire about kings, settling in 6NT if partner shows the ◇K and no ♡K.

1. Neither side vulnerable, you're East and are looking at:

♠A93 ♡A932 ◇KQJ94 ♣6

The bidding so far has been:

West	East
	1◇
1♠	?

What is your second call?

2. For this one, East-West are vulnerable and you are sitting West:

♠J72 ♡A6532 ◇QJ95 ♣3

Here's the auction to this point:

West	East
	1NT
2◇*	2♡
?	

What now?

3. Back over to the East seat for our next one. North-South are vulnerable:

♠KJ9874 ♡Q98 ◇K7 ♣A9

Partner seems enthused by your opening bid:

West	East
	1♠
4♡	?

Responder's 4♡ was a splinter raise, generally 11-14 HCP with at least four spades and shortness in the bid suit. Will you sign off in game or try for slam?

4. You are North with neither side vulnerable, and your hand is:

♠ J 6 5 3 ♡ A J 7 3 ◇ K Q J ♣ J 4

Your partner should obviously be playing for money, as the auction has gone:

North	South
	2♣
2◇	2NT
?	

What is your bidding plan from here on in?

5. Remaining in the North seat with East-West vulnerable, your hand now is:

♠ Q 6 ♡ K J 6 2 ◇ A 5 2 ♣ K 8 7 5

North	South
	1♣
1♡	2NT
?	

Partner has shown a strong balanced hand and you also have opening values. Is it time to go all the way to slam?

6. You are West for this one, with both sides vulnerable:

♠ J 9 7 5 4 3 ♡ 3 ◇ A 9 5 ♣ K 10 2

Partner opens 1NT. After transferring to spades, do you commit to game or just invite?

7. Both sides are vulnerable and North is the dealer. You are South, and your hand consists of:

♠ A ♡ 7 5 4 ◇ A 10 9 5 3 ♣ A J 10 6

West	North	East	South
	pass	pass	1◇
2♡	2♠	3♡	pass
pass	4◇	pass	?

Do you go any further?

1. Neither vulnerable

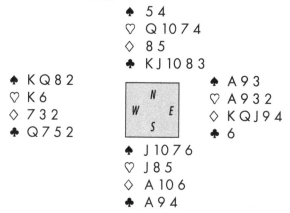

```
                    ♠ 5 4
                    ♡ Q 10 7 4
                    ◇ 8 5
                    ♣ K J 10 8 3
  ♠ K Q 8 2                      ♠ A 9 3
  ♡ K 6           N              ♡ A 9 3 2
  ◇ 7 3 2     W       E          ◇ K Q J 9 4
  ♣ Q 7 5 2       S              ♣ 6
                    ♠ J 10 7 6
                    ♡ J 8 5
                    ◇ A 10 6
                    ♣ A 9 4
```

West	North	East	South
		1◇	pass
1♠	pass	2♠	all pass

Since the East hand lacks the values to reverse into 2♡, the only feasible choices are 2◇ and the three-card raise to 2♠.

It's a matter of picking your poison, as neither call is totally descriptive of what responder has. Some experts, including one of my consultants, balk at raising a major as opener with only three-card support under any circumstances. Others would consider repeating the original suit to be just as big a lie, as partner will assume you have at least six diamonds rather than just five.

Regardless of what opener does, the partnership will subside in a partscore. If he rebids 2♠, responder won't try for game. It's close, but the 4-point principle means he can assume three useful cards and that won't be enough to get him up to ten tricks. If opener continues with 2◇, West shouldn't invite with 2NT as he has only one stopper in each of the unbid suits and no helpful card in diamonds. Responder could make an encouraging noise with 3◇, but East will either pass or bid 3♠, definitely avoiding notrump.

Playing 2♠, declarer will wind up with nine or ten tricks. A diamond contract also fares well, with eleven tricks being the likely result. That will be fine if the spade bidders can only muster nine tricks, but comes out second-best if they tally up +170. As for the pairs that end up in notrump, they will lose five clubs plus the ◇A, being held to seven tricks.

2.   E-W vulnerable

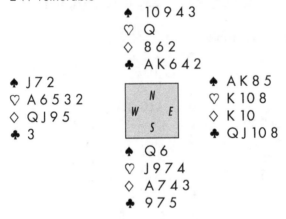

♠ 10 9 4 3
♡ Q
♢ 8 6 2
♣ A K 6 4 2

♠ J 7 2
♡ A 6 5 3 2
♢ Q J 9 5
♣ 3

♠ A K 8 5
♡ K 10 8
♢ K 10
♣ Q J 10 8

♠ Q 6
♡ J 9 7 4
♢ A 7 4 3
♣ 9 7 5

West	North	East	South
pass	pass	1NT	pass
2◊*	pass	2♡	pass
2NT	pass	4♡	all pass

This is another of those 8-point hands opposite a strong notrump opening. After the transfer, responder has four options to choose from:

- Pass, which yields a plus for his side, but could miss a game if opener is at the top of his range with a fit. The 4-point principle suggests that game will be touch-and-go even if East has a maximum with three hearts.

- 3♡, which is invitational but promises a six-card suit. Opener will assume an eight-card fit even if he has only two hearts and will bid according to the strength of his hand.

- 2NT, which is correct on heart length and values, but there will be some nervousness on responder's part about the singleton in clubs.

- 3◊, which is the best description of West's shape. However, in most partnerships this is game-forcing. Responder is a bit shy of the values for that action.

If West tries for game, opener will accept and choose hearts over notrump. There is one piece of good luck with the ♠Q falling doubleton. The downer, though, is the bad split in the trump suit: he will lose two tricks there plus the minor-suit aces for down one.

You'll notice that 3NT is the only makeable contract on this hand. However, it's not that realistic a destination and normally takes one trick fewer than the major suit without the 4-1 trump break. Such is bridge on the borderline.

3.   N-S vulnerable

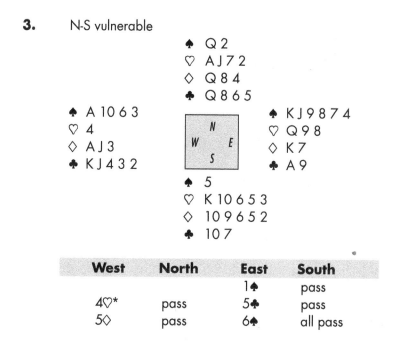

	♠ Q 2	
	♡ A J 7 2	
	◇ Q 8 4	
	♣ Q 8 6 5	

West	North	East	South
		1♠	pass
4♡*	pass	5♣	pass
5◇	pass	6♠	all pass

East can use a combination of the 4-point principle and partner's splinter raise to decide whether to go slamming in this case. He has a six-loser hand. With partner known to be short in hearts, two of them can be ruffed. Since West has shown 11-14 HCP, three 'dream cards' will be enough to bring him up to twelve tricks.

Opener at the table elected to cuebid 5♣. Partner reciprocated with 5◇, making a sure trick out of East's king, and he then duly bid the slam. Another option for East would be just to check on keycards with a 4NT inquiry, as it was just possible that responder had the ♠Q rather than the ace, and then the contract would have been off two fast tricks.

4.   Neither vulnerable

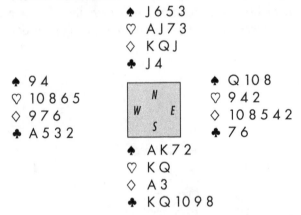

	♠ J 6 5 3	
	♡ A J 7 3	
	◇ K Q J	
	♣ J 4	

♠ 9 4		♠ Q 10 8
♡ 10 8 6 5	N	♡ 9 4 2
◇ 9 7 6	W E	◇ 10 8 5 4 2
♣ A 5 3 2	S	♣ 7 6

	♠ A K 7 2	
	♡ K Q	
	◇ A 3	
	♣ K Q 10 9 8	

West	North	East	South
			2♣
pass	2◇	pass	2NT
pass	6NT	all pass	

South could have opened any of 1♣, 2NT, or 2♣ at his first turn. Very few players nowadays would open 1♣, so it's a choice of treating the hand as a 21-count or upgrading it to a 2♣ opening as South did here.

The two four-card majors in responder's hand are a red herring. North has 13 HCP and is assuming partner will have 22-24 with a balanced hand. That puts his side well above what is required for a small slam but not quite enough for the grand. His thoughts should be that notrump will produce the same number of tricks as a 4-4 fit and he can go directly to 6NT.

There are exactly 6 HCP missing on this deal, an ace and the ♠Q. Since the latter honor is guarded, 6♠ is doomed to failure. In 6NT, declarer simply forces out the ♣A and scores up twelve tricks easily.

Even if you switch the black queens, 6♠ and 6NT will probably make the same number of tricks, as both will need the clubs to be friendly.

5.   E-W vulnerable

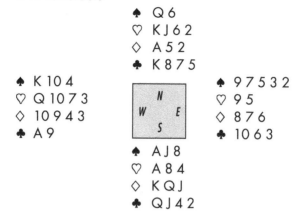

```
                        ♠ Q 6
                        ♡ K J 6 2
                        ◇ A 5 2
                        ♣ K 8 7 5
  ♠ K 10 4                              ♠ 9 7 5 3 2
  ♡ Q 10 7 3         N                  ♡ 9 5
  ◇ 10 9 4 3      W      E              ◇ 8 7 6
  ♣ A 9              S                  ♣ 10 6 3
                        ♠ A J 8
                        ♡ A 8 4
                        ◇ K Q J
                        ♣ Q J 4 2
```

West	North	East	South
			1♣
pass	1♡	pass	2NT
pass	3NT/4NT	all pass	

Responder has 13 HCP opposite partner's 18-19 balanced. Using the 4-point principle, he can place five useful cards in opener's hand but it won't be enough for slam to be laydown. As it turns out, 6NT needs two successful finesses and a 3-3 heart break. If you took away South's third heart and gave him a fifth club, 6♣ would then come down to a 50% shot, only needing the ♠K to be onside. Meanwhile, 6NT would still not be a good contract.

North-South should not have a problem in avoiding slam on this hand as responder can invite with a quantitative 4NT, and opener will quickly decline.

The 4NT raise fails to convey the message of a decent club fit, though. If responder can show club support and mild slam interest, then that would be the best way forward. For example, if they use the unbid minor, 3◇, as checkback for major-suit holdings, then 3♣ is freed up for that purpose. However, if the agreement is that 3♣ is always the checkback inquiry, then North only has 3NT or an optimistic 4NT available to him.

6.   Both vulnerable

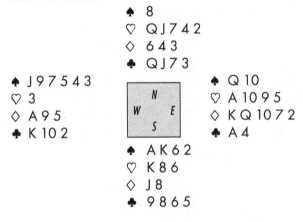

```
                  ♠ 8
                  ♡ Q J 7 4 2
                  ◇ 6 4 3
                  ♣ Q J 7 3
♠ J 9 7 5 4 3                      ♠ Q 10
♡ 3                               ♡ A 10 9 5
◇ A 9 5                           ◇ K Q 10 7 2
♣ K 10 2                          ♣ A 4
                  ♠ A K 6 2
                  ♡ K 8 6
                  ◇ J 8
                  ♣ 9 8 6 5
```

West	North	East	South
	pass	1NT	pass
2♡*	pass	2♠	pass
4♠	all pass		

If East-West had been playing both Jacoby and Texas transfers, responder would have got there faster via 1NT – 4♡; 4♠.

East didn't have much choice other than to open 1NT with his 2=4=5=2 shape and 15 HCP. The hand isn't quite strong enough for a 1◇ opening followed by a reverse into hearts, especially with not knowing how useful his ♠Q10 will be.

Responder's decision is whether to transfer and invite or just to bid game. If you choose to use the 4-point principle, the two black aces, the ◇K and a minor-suit queen will offer game a reasonable play.

If West takes the low road and follows up with 3♠ after the transfer, opener should not be fixated on his point-count but should look a bit deeper. Since partner will have six or more of his major, the ♠Q10 is a pretty good holding. He also has two aces and a source of tricks with the good five-card diamond suit. All in all, this is a pretty respectable hand, somewhat better than the 15 HCP would suggest, and East would be justified in carrying on to game.

7.   Both vulnerable

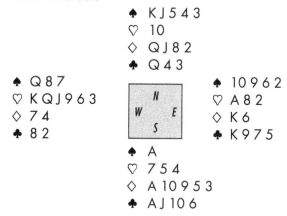

♠ K J 5 4 3
♡ 10
◇ Q J 8 2
♣ Q 4 3

♠ Q 8 7
♡ K Q J 9 6 3
◇ 7 4
♣ 8 2

♠ 10 9 6 2
♡ A 8 2
◇ K 6
♣ K 9 7 5

♠ A
♡ 7 5 4
◇ A 10 9 5 3
♣ A J 10 6

West	North	East	South
	pass	pass	1◇
2♡	2♠	3♡	pass
pass	4◇	pass	5◇
all pass			

For South, the question is whether to bid 5◇ once partner has supported his long suit. With responder being a passed hand, there can't be more than 23 or 24 high-card points between the two hands, so it will be a thin game. Most of the North-South pairs will likely be in a partscore or defending a heart contract by the opponents. Do you expect game will be a favorite to make?

Just looking at the bidding, this is what we can reasonably expect from the North hand:

- He will have 9-11 points.
- He rates to have five spades (six is unlikely because he didn't open a weak two-bid) and at least four diamonds.
- Because North has gone on to the four-level after East supported hearts, he will almost certainly have no more than one card in their suit, if that.

As for South, while his hand is minimum point-wise, it also has three attractive features:

- He has a fifth diamond, guaranteeing his side will have a nine- or ten-card fit.
- There are no wasted values in the heart suit, with three small opposite partner's known shortness.

- Most importantly, he has a second suit that is quite respectable, with three of the top five honors.

Finally, since West has preempted, he won't have many high-card values outside his long suit, so if a finesse is required, it is likely to succeed. Taking it all into consideration, opener should feel there will be a good shot at eleven tricks in diamonds. Although 5◊ is going to be an anti-field bid to a certain extent, you shouldn't let the form of the game deter you if you are confident in your hand evaluation.

As you can see by looking at all four hands, the contract has excellent chances, needing only one of the minor-suit kings to be onside. Not surprisingly, both are favorably placed and declarer makes twelve tricks, losing only a heart.

North has pretty much the hand that you would expect from the bidding, and even if you moved the ♣Q over to the spade suit, 5◊ would be a good place to be.

8
Does the Three-level Belong to the Opponents?

Aside from being able to defend accurately, your success at matchpoints will depend largely on managing to win your share of the partscore battles. Most players learn at a certain point that they aren't going to score well by meekly allowing the opponents to play their two-level contracts. Consequently, they grit their teeth and enter the fray if they have the values and shape to do so. That's the first hurdle. The next one comes when both sides have a fit and one of them has bid to three of their suit. Does the other pair go any further?

There is an expression you may have heard of sometime in the course of your bridge experience, that being, 'The five-level belongs to the opponents'. Obviously, that refers to high-level auctions. An analogous question, which will be the focus of our discussion here, is, 'Does the three-level belong to the opponents?'

To serve as our backdrop, we'll use the following auction:

West	North	East	South
1♠	2♡	2♠	3♡

It's quite possible that either opener or overcaller might bid game now that his suit has been raised, but for the time being we'll assume that it's a partscore hand.

If West has a sixth spade or East has four-card support, that player will continue on to 3♠ at his turn. However, suppose neither member of the partnership has extra length in spades. That gives East-West eight total trumps; the trump count for North-South is up in the air but it will be at least eight. Applying the Law of Total Tricks, the most likely outcomes are that both three-level contracts will go down or one will make and the other will not. (By the way, a good agreement to have in this frequently-occurring auction is to play maximal doubles. With this agreement, with both sides having bid and raised, a double by opener shows game interest while 3♠ is strictly competitive.)

If West lacks a sixth trump, when should he bid 3♠? If he has a good minimum hand of 14-15 points, then he should make the effort. The more unbalanced his hand is, the more appealing it would be to compete further. Even 5-4-2-2 distribution would give his side additional chances for that pivotal extra trick. Here are two hands with which opener might consider bidding on:

♠QJ983 ♡85 ◇AK97 ♣A4
♠AK1054 ♡7 ◇J865 ♣KQ9

Vulnerability might also factor into your calculations. When the opponents are vulnerable and you are not, then even if you go down it will be a good result if the opponents are going to make their contract. For example, if you were to have something like:

♠KQ1097 ♡96 ◇KQ10 ♣QJ9

Then 3♠ by your side might well go down, but with your nice trump holding it is unlikely to be doubled. Meanwhile, you don't have particularly high expectations for the number of tricks you will take on defense. On a good day, you might take three, but on a bad day you might only have one, so let's average it out at two. The opponents will be a favorite to bring home nine tricks in 3♡. Should you be worried that they might bid game if you compete in your spade fit? It could happen, but if that is LHO's inclination, what you do isn't going to make a whole lot of difference.

Moving over to responder's side of the table, he may have the final say if the auction continues:

West	North	East	South
1♠	2♡	2♠	3♡
pass	pass	?	

East has already seen opener cast his vote by passing instead of bidding on to 3♠ himself. With four trumps, East will naturally compete further, but what if he only has three? Then about the only hand where he might overrule partner in his choice to defend is something like:

♠K83 ♡6 ◇KJ943 ♣10762

Any heart losers are covered via ruffs. If the opponents lead trumps, then partner has the reasonable five-card diamond suit to work on for extra tricks.

Other than the above hand, though, responder is best off passing with 6-7 points. If he has 8-9 for the raise and a relatively balanced hand, he can indeed dip his toes back in the water, but the way to show his values is with a double rather than a 3♠ bid. This double is not strictly for penalties, as both sides have a fit. It shows a maximum hand for the previous raise and, on aver-

age, at least two defensive tricks. Opener can then elect to defend or retreat to
3♠. Either of these hands would qualify for a double of 3♡:

♠863 ♡QJ6 ◇A987 ♣Q106
♠754 ♡K73 ◇96 ♣AJ842

The thing you see in both cases is that the trump holding is nothing to write
home about, so declarer in 3♠ might not be able to cope with foul splits.
The defensive trick expectation on both hands is two for sure, with decent
chances at a third. Assuming the double is left in, East will lead the ♠8 on
the first hand, denying anything higher in that suit so that partner will have
a good idea of what to do from there. With the second hand, he can start out
with the ◇9, hoping to collect an eventual diamond ruff in addition to the ♡K
and ♣A.

Having concluded the lead-in to our topic for this chapter, we can now
move on to some examples from actual play. The first one is not a happy
story for the East-West pair:

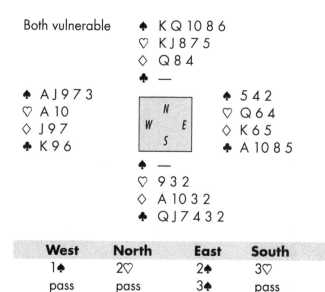

	Both vulnerable	♠ K Q 10 8 6
		♡ K J 8 7 5
		◇ Q 8 4
		♣ —

♠ A J 9 7 3   ♠ 5 4 2
♡ A 10   ♡ Q 6 4
◇ J 9 7   ◇ K 6 5
♣ K 9 6   ♣ A 10 8 5

♠ —
♡ 9 3 2
◇ A 10 3 2
♣ Q J 7 4 3 2

West	North	East	South
1♠	2♡	2♠	3♡
pass	pass	3♠	pass
pass	dbl	all pass	

North's 2♡ overall may not be to everyone's taste, but it's not totally outlandish and certainly led to a good result on this hand. The raises by East and
South are normal, as is West's pass of 3♡. With an eight-loser hand, there will
be very little play for 3♠ from his perspective.

East felt obliged to compete further since he had 9 HCP for his single raise. However, although his hand is maximum point-wise, it's totally

balanced and the trumps are downright pitiful. Finally, the ♡Q may take a trick on defense but is not going to be worth much on offense. As you can see, 3♠ by West does not turn out well. In the final analysis, bidding on is not the way to go on the East cards. The only sensible options are to pass or double.

A 3♡ contract by North-South can be beaten, although it comes close to making on a spade lead as declarer can ruff back and forth in the black suits. The killing lead from East, one that will net his side +800, is a trump. Should he find it? My two consultants feel that it's too tough, but I think there is a case to be made for it. Yes, it may give up a trick you might otherwise have scored, but since the most the opponents have is 19 high-card points between them, it's hard to imagine them getting to nine tricks without ruffing losers in dummy.

Those of you who have read either or both of Larry Cohen's books on the Law of Total Tricks know that the Law generally holds true, and if there is an exception there is a logical reason for it. We'll begin our tour with a couple of deals in which each side has an adequate fit but not an excess of trumps. As South with neither side vulnerable, you have:

♠ 6 4   ♡ A J 9 6   ◇ K Q 5 4   ♣ A 8 6

The auction has gone:

West	North	East	South
	2♠	pass	pass
3♡	pass	pass	?

Your hand will have some tricks for partner in a spade contract and some of you might be tempted to go on to 3♠. However, the total trumps for the two sides will be 16 or 17, and that is why you should defend. Both three-level contracts may go down, and even if the opponents have a nine-card fit, your four-card trump holding may cause declarer some headaches in a heart contract. Partner's hand is:

♠ Q 10 8 7 3 2   ♡ —   ◇ J 7 3   ♣ K 5 3 2

Partner is going to use his 'Well, our side wasn't vulnerable' excuse to justify his sketchy weak two-bid. If you bid 3♠, that contract loses three spades, a club and a diamond. As it turns out, they have a nine-card heart fit but are unable to cope with the 4-0 split and will also go down.

Sometimes it's tough to resist the urge to bid on. For the next hand, you're South, not vulnerable against vulnerable opponents:

♠ K J 4 2   ♡ A K J 8 5   ◇ 9 7 4   ♣ 2

The bidding to this point has been:

West	North	East	South
	pass	1◇	1♡
dbl	2♡	3♣	?

Your suit has been raised and you have opening values plus an unbalanced hand. Won't 3♡ have a decent play here?

Well, maybe, but you should be leaving it up to partner. If he passes, then you're on an eight-card fit. Your three small in East's suit is a cause for concern, while West has made a negative double, indicating he's sitting over your spades. The opponents seem to have a club fit, but may also have just eight between them.

If you hold your tongue, the auction is not yet over. West may convert to 3◇, in which case you're still in the ball game if you so choose. If he passes 3♣, then partner may have the values and/or distribution to carry on to 3♡. As it turns out, he'll go quietly, his hand being:

♠ A 8 7   ♡ Q 10 7   ◇ 8 6 5   ♣ Q 10 4 3

There are no surprises here, as you have four minor-suit tricks to lose in 3♡, plus one or two more in spades. You don't even have the satisfaction of their contract making, as you'll cash your major-suit winners and declarer can't handle the bad trump split.

Let's now look at a complete deal where there is a similar decision to make:

Both vunerable

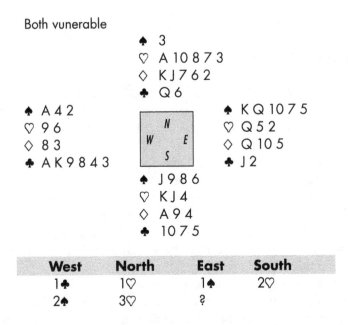

```
                  ♠ 3
                  ♡ A 10 8 7 3
                  ◇ K J 7 6 2
                  ♣ Q 6
♠ A 4 2                          ♠ K Q 10 7 5
♡ 9 6          N                 ♡ Q 5 2
◇ 8 3       W     E              ◇ Q 10 5
♣ A K 9 8 4 3     S              ♣ J 2
                  ♠ J 9 8 6
                  ♡ K J 4
                  ◇ A 9 4
                  ♣ 10 7 5
```

West	North	East	South
1♣	1♡	1♠	2♡
2♠	3♡	?	

North goes on to 3♡ after partner's raise based on his 5-5 distribution.

First let's consider the East hand. It has 10 HCP, but nothing other than queens and jacks outside the spade suit, with the ♡Q looking to be particularly nebulous in value. It's hard to say whether the hand is offensive or defensive in nature. East is best off passing, leaving it to opener to have his say.

If the bidding comes around to West, he can be reasonably certain that his side's fit is precisely eight cards. His source of tricks in clubs argues in favor of bidding, yet at the same time, his hand also contains three likely defensive tricks.

In fact, after two rounds of clubs, the ♠A and a third club, North-South are no cinch to make 3♡. Moreover, if East-West do press on to 3♠, South might double. He would be expecting to go +140 in his side's contract, with partner marked for shortness in spades. Since a one-trick set against 3♠ will not be adequate compensation, he'll raise the stakes in attempt to get the precious +200. This is a common theme in partscore tussles at matchpoints, where players will make doubles that they would never even contemplate at teams.

On this example, both sides anticipated being successful in their contract. Sometimes a player will bid in the expectation of going down if the colors are favorable, willing to trade -50 or -100 against the other side making their contract. Well, that's fine if they do, but if that's not the case you might have gone plus by defending. Also, the price sometimes could be too high, as witness this deal:

E-W vulnerable

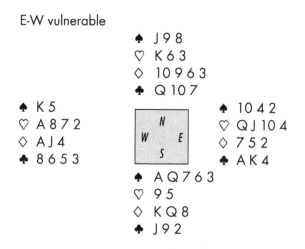

	♠ J 9 8	
	♡ K 6 3	
	◇ 10 9 6 3	
	♣ Q 10 7	
♠ K 5		♠ 10 4 2
♡ A 8 7 2		♡ Q J 10 4
◇ A J 4		◇ 7 5 2
♣ 8 6 5 3		♣ A K 4
	♠ A Q 7 6 3	
	♡ 9 5	
	◇ K Q 8	
	♣ J 9 2	

West	North	East	South
	pass	pass	1♠
dbl	2♠	3♡	3♠
pass	pass	dbl	all pass

South has a seven-loser hand, and partner's single raise is likely only going to cover two of them, so he is not bidding 3♠ to make. He's doing it to try to escape cheaply for -50 against the -140 he expects the opponents will tally up in their 3♡ contract.

East's double isn't penalty, just an announcement that he was bidding 3♡ on a maximum passed hand rather than just to compete. With 10 HCP and two defensive tricks, he certainly has the values to do so. West has three tricks of his own and leaves in the double. It turns out his ◇J will also take a trick and North-South go down two for -300, a shared top for East-West as the results are:

East-West	+300	2 pairs	East-West	+140	3 pairs
	+140	3 pairs		+100	2 pairs
	+100	3 pairs		+50	3 pairs
	+50	2 pairs		−140	2 pairs

I have two sets of results here. The ones on the left reflect what happened in real life, with 3♠ going down two. Two East-West pairs lost one of their tricks on defense. The scores on the right are those that would have occurred if the ◇J had been in the East hand instead of belonging to the West player. Then 3♠

goes down one and, if the defense slips up, could make. Again, the double is necessary to turn a very poor score for East-West into something better than average.

On the preceding two deals, one pair had reason to double the opponents' three-level contract. Sometimes, it's harder for them to do, as we'll see in this example:

N-S vulnerable

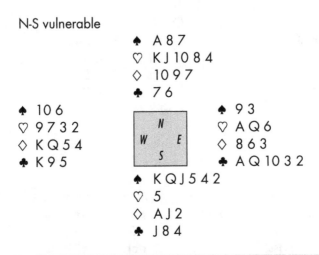

```
                    ♠ A 8 7
                    ♡ K J 10 8 4
                    ◇ 10 9 7
                    ♣ 7 6
  ♠ 10 6                              ♠ 9 3
  ♡ 9 7 3 2              N            ♡ A Q 6
  ◇ K Q 5 4          W       E        ◇ 8 6 3
  ♣ K 9 5                S            ♣ A Q 10 3 2
                    ♠ K Q J 5 4 2
                    ♡ 5
                    ◇ A J 2
                    ♣ J 8 4
```

West	North	East	South
pass	pass	1♣	1♠
dbl	2♠	pass	pass
3♣	pass	pass	3♠
all pass			

On his third turn, instead of bidding 3♣, West could have doubled again, showing the values to compete but with no clear direction. That would have led to opener bidding his clubs again.

South here is bidding 3♠ expecting it to have a play, as he has 12 HCP with a six-card suit. If West leads the ◇K, 3♠ is an easy make. However, if he begins with a low club, spot-on defense can beat the contract. East needs to be able to lead diamonds through twice before hearts are set up, but it may not be obvious how to maneuver that.

There isn't much of a case to be made for either player doubling 3♠. East has a minimum hand and West has already taken two calls on a mere 8 HCP. Besides, in successfully pushing the opponents to the three-level, they will achieve a good result if they can beat it, as several East-West pairs might sell out to 2♠.

You'll note, by the way, that this deal is an exact match for the Law of Total Tricks, as there are 17 total trumps (9 for North-South, 8 for East-West), and also 17 tricks (8 for North-South and 9 for East-West on best defense).

As Larry Cohen himself points out, the Law is not an absolute rule, and there are factors that will lead to the total tricks exceeding or falling short of what you would expect from the combined trump holdings for each side. Our next example will be a good illustration of when this might happen:

Neither vulnerable

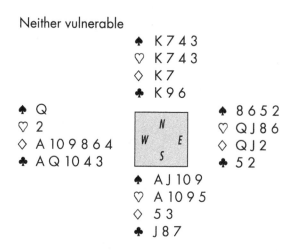

	♠ K 7 4 3	
	♡ K 7 4 3	
	◇ K 7	
	♣ K 9 6	
♠ Q		♠ 8 6 5 2
♡ 2		♡ Q J 8 6
◇ A 10 9 8 6 4		◇ Q J 2
♣ A Q 10 4 3		♣ 5 2
	♠ A J 10 9	
	♡ A 10 9 5	
	◇ 5 3	
	♣ J 8 7	

West	North	East	South
			pass
1◇	dbl	1♡	1♠
2♣	pass	2◇	pass
pass	2♠	pass	pass
3◇	pass	pass	3♠
all pass			

West has the most attractive distribution with 6-5 in the minor suits. North has a more balanced hand but support for both majors, hence his takeout double over 1◇. East musters up a 1♡ response and later takes a preference to partner's diamonds. South bids spades, eventually gets raised and competes to the three-level.

If you add up each side's best fit, the total is seventeen, yet the number of tricks available is eighteen, nine in either major and nine in diamonds. There are two factors at work here, one being opener's shape and the other being North-South having a double fit.

Speaking of double fits, there is the occasional deal where both sides have one, and finding that out will be crucial in determining who will buy the contract:

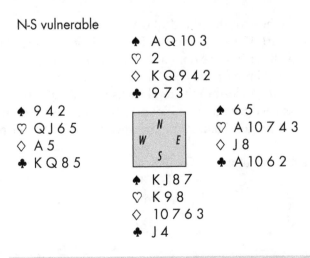

N-S vulnerable

```
                    ♠ A Q 10 3
                    ♡ 2
                    ◇ K Q 9 4 2
                    ♣ 9 7 3
♠ 9 4 2                              ♠ 6 5
♡ Q J 6 5          N                 ♡ A 10 7 4 3
◇ A 5          W       E             ◇ J 8
♣ K Q 8 5          S                 ♣ A 10 6 2
                    ♠ K J 8 7
                    ♡ K 9 8
                    ◇ 10 7 6 3
                    ♣ J 4
```

West	North	East	South
1♣	1◇	1♡	2◇
2♡	2♠	3♡	3♠
all pass			

In the bidding, you invariably need to be thinking ahead. Since hearts out-rank diamonds and East is almost certain to compete at the three-level in the agreed major, North should realize the necessity of discovering whether his side has a spade fit. If he lazily bids 3◇ over 2♡, then he will be left on a straight guess once the opponents persist with their heart suit. However, if he takes the time to introduce his other suit, partner will be happy to compete to 3♠.

Before we move on to the quiz, let us consider one more scenario, with you as South in this auction:

West	North	East	South
	1♣	1♠	2♣
2♠	3♣	3♠	?

To compete further, you'll need to go on to the four-level, and there are lots of bad things that could happen if you do, namely:

- Their contract might have been going down.
- Your contract could be defeated by multiple tricks.
- There is a much greater chance of your being doubled at the four-level.
- Worst of all, if the opponents have misjudged and can actually make ten tricks in spades, you're now giving them a chance to rectify their mistake.

For either of you to bid 4♣ here, a nine-card or better fit is highly recommended. Without that in your favor, the outcome is usually going to be tragic for your side. Also, you should have enough on defense to beat four of their major and be prepared to double, because if they make it, you're getting a zero or close to it anyway.

With that pep-talk over and done with, we're ready to move on to a pair of case studies. To begin with, you're sitting North and your side is vulnerable. You've been dealt these cards:

♠ 8   ♡ J 8 7   ◇ A Q 10 8 7   ♣ A K J 2

The auction has been:

West	North	East	South
	1◇	2NT*	3◇
3♠	?		

Let's analyze the bidding. The opponents don't necessarily have a fit, since West has not competed in either of partner's rounded suits. What he is certain to have, though, is a long and strong suit of his own. Partner has raised your diamonds, so he will have four or perhaps even five of them. Point-wise, he should have somewhere in the 8-10 range. He could have some spade length, although whether he actually does is up in the air at this point.

If you do manage to defeat their 3♠ contract, down one might be the best you can hope for. Will 4◇ make your way? It may not be ironclad, but you'll have a fighting chance at bringing it home. The vulnerability is such that passing will seldom result in a good score. Bidding on is a decent two-way shot. Even if you go down, who's to say they weren't going to make their contract? It's quite possible that they can. With partner's support combined with your trump quality and fast tricks, you're unlikely to get doubled.

The full deal is:

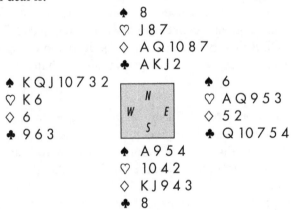

♠ 8
♡ J 8 7
♢ A Q 10 8 7
♣ A K J 2

♠ K Q J 10 7 3 2
♡ K 6
♢ 6
♣ 9 6 3

♠ 6
♡ A Q 9 5 3
♢ 5 2
♣ Q 10 7 5 4

♠ A 9 5 4
♡ 10 4 2
♢ K J 9 4 3
♣ 8

True, the opponents would go down in 3♠, losing two pointed aces, two high clubs and a club ruff. They wouldn't be too distressed at -50 or -100, though, since the deal belongs to your side in diamonds. Indeed, 4♢ will likely make five in practice, as East will lead his singleton in partner's suit which allows declarer to play the ace and king of clubs and discard a heart. He can then give up two hearts and make the rest of the tricks on an eventual cross-ruff.

Your final assignment will be in the South chair with both sides vulnerable. Your hand consists of:

♠9 8   ♡K 3   ♢A Q 9 8 6 4   ♣J 10 3

The bidding has been:

West	North	East	South
pass	1♣	2♣*	2♢
2♡	3♢	3♡	?

What can each side make in their known fit? In a diamond contract, you are assuming three major-suit losers. The trump suit shouldn't be a problem as North has raised, and the same applies to clubs. If there is a missing card and a finesse needs to be taken, it will likely succeed as East has ten or more cards in the majors.

On defense, you should be able to score three tricks in the minor suits and there is a fair chance of your getting the ♡K, since the Michaels bidder will have the ace of that suit most of the time. Your plan, then, should be to go one level higher in your minor-suit fit and then double 4♡ if they bid it.

The complete deal is:

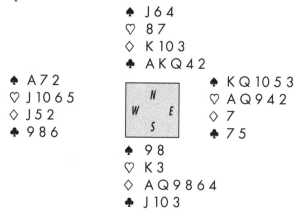

```
                  ♠ J 6 4
                  ♡ 8 7
                  ◇ K 10 3
                  ♣ A K Q 4 2
  ♠ A 7 2                        ♠ K Q 10 5 3
  ♡ J 10 6 5         N          ♡ A Q 9 4 2
  ◇ J 5 2        W       E      ◇ 7
  ♣ 9 8 6            S          ♣ 7 5
                  ♠ 9 8
                  ♡ K 3
                  ◇ A Q 9 8 6 4
                  ♣ J 10 3
```

The assessment of each side's trick-taking potential as described above is correct here, as North-South do indeed have ten tricks their way and East-West will only get nine in hearts or spades. This is another case of the number of tricks exceeding the total trumps, and that is mainly because each side has a fit in two suits.

QUIZ

1. As South with your side vulnerable, you hold:

♠ J 9 8 4 3 2 ♡ Q 5 4 ◇ Q 10 ♣ A Q

The auction has been:

West	North	East	South
	pass	1◇	1♠
pass	2♠	dbl	pass
3♣	pass	pass	?

Do you leave the opponents be or push on to 3♠?

2. You're in the West seat, and your side is vulnerable again. You've picked up this hand:

♠ J 10 9 4 2 ♡ 10 ◇ A 9 8 2 ♣ Q J 5

The bidding has slowly gained momentum up to the three-level:

West	North	East	South
		1♣	pass
1♠	dbl	redbl*	2♡
2♠	pass	pass	3♡
?			

Opener's second call was a support redouble, promising exactly three spades. At that point his strength is unknown, and he could have either a minimum hand or extra values, but once he passes your 2♠, he'll be in the 12-15 range. At any rate, South has now competed to 3♡. Is that all she wrote, or do you bid 3♠?

3. You're North and holding this rather modest hand with the opponents vulnerable:

♠ A 10 5 ♡ 10 7 3 ◇ 9 3 ♣ J 9 8 5 3

Both sides are duking it out again:

West	North	East	South
			1♢
1♠	pass	1NT	2♣
2♡	3♣	3♡	pass
pass	?		

Your side has nine clubs at least, perhaps ten of them. The opponents have no spade fit but have found their calling in the heart suit, where they might have eight or nine between them. Should you bid up to the four-level?

4. For this one, you are South with neither side vulnerable. Your reward in high cards is miniscule to say the least:

♠ J 8 7 4 2   ♡ 6 2   ♢ 9 5   ♣ Q J 8 4

You've only bid at gunpoint so far:

West	North	East	South
		pass	pass
1♡	dbl	2♡	pass
pass	dbl	pass	2♠
3♡	pass	pass	?

When partner showed a very good hand with his second takeout double, you had to bid your spades. Now the opponents are in 3♡ and you're out of it if that's your choice. They will have eight or nine hearts between them and you should have a nine-card spade fit. What is your pleasure?

5. You're North and have a somewhat better hand this time, with East-West vulnerable:

♠ 8 7 4   ♡ A K 5   ♢ Q 8 7 5   ♣ J 6 4

Naturally, since this chapter is all about the three-level, you can guess that the auction is going to be like this:

West	North	East	South
			1♣
1♡	1NT	2♡	3♣
3♡	?		

What are your options here? And which one do you like best?

6. For some thirty years, *The Bridge World* magazine had a feature about three times a year called 'You Be the Judge'. In it, a deal that ended in a disastrous result was given and the panel was asked to apportion the blame between each partner and name the worst bid of the auction. So we're going to do that here, with neither side vulnerable and these being the East-West hands:

```
    ♠ K 9 3 2              ♠ 6 4
    ♡ J 9 4 3 2      N     ♡ Q 8 6 5
    ◇ 10          W     E  ◇ K Q J 8 3
    ♣ K Q 5          S     ♣ 9 2
```

The auction went:

West	North	East	South
	1♣	1◇	pass
1♡	1NT	2♡	3♣
3♡	dbl	all pass	

By opening 1♣ and then rebidding 1NT with partner showing no signs of life, North is showing a strong balanced hand, likely too good for 1NT. The defense against 3♡ doubled goes the ♣J to the ace and a spade back. Declarer loses two tricks each in the major suits plus the two minor suit aces for -300.

What percentage of the blame do you assign to East and West?

In your opinion, what is the worst bid of the auction?

1.   N-S vulnerable

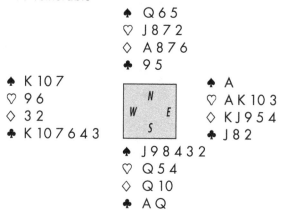

	♠ Q 6 5		
	♡ J 8 7 2		
	◇ A 8 7 6		
	♣ 9 5		

♠ K 10 7   ♠ A
♡ 9 6   ♡ A K 10 3
◇ 3 2   ◇ K J 9 5 4
♣ K 10 7 6 4 3   ♣ J 8 2

♠ J 9 8 4 3 2
♡ Q 5 4
◇ Q 10
♣ A Q

West	North	East	South
	pass	1◇	1♠
pass	2♠	dbl	pass
3♣	all pass		

There are two things of note concerning this auction. East with his 16-count is worth a further bid, even with partner not having acted over South's 1♠. However, rather than compete over 2♠ in a red suit he should double, which is for takeout and keeps all avenues open. His side's best fit is actually in clubs and they will never get there if he rebids 3◇ or 3♡.

South needs to realize that despite having a nine-card fit, bidding 3♠ would not be the greatest of ideas because his hand gets a negative adjustment according to the Law of Total Tricks with its feeble long suit and three queens. If you aren't a LOTT *aficionado*, overcaller's hand can be evaluated in terms of losers, of which there are eight. For his single raise, partner will typically have two useful cards. On a real good day, he might have a third one, but your contract will be down two vulnerable most of the time, occasionally down one. Even undoubled, North-South will get a bad score, and if one of the opponents happens to find a double, it won't be pleasant.

The Souths who abide by the credo 'discretion is the better part of valor' will allow East-West to play the hand in clubs, making ten or eleven tricks handily. Those who venture 3♠ find out that West is indeed going to double with his ♠K107 and then lead one of the red suits to try for a ruff. When the smoke clears, overcaller goes down two or three and (one hopes) learns that not all nine-card fits are created equal.

2. E-W vulnerable

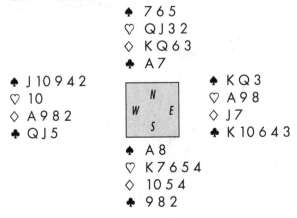

```
                  ♠ 7 6 5
                  ♡ Q J 3 2
                  ◇ K Q 6 3
                  ♣ A 7
♠ J 10 9 4 2                      ♠ K Q 3
♡ 10              N               ♡ A 9 8
◇ A 9 8 2      W     E            ◇ J 7
♣ Q J 5          S               ♣ K 10 6 4 3
                  ♠ A 8
                  ♡ K 7 6 5 4
                  ◇ 10 5 4
                  ♣ 9 8 2
```

West	North	East	South
		1♣	pass
1♠	dbl	redbl*	2♡
2♠	pass	pass	3♡
3♠	all pass		

At West's third turn, he knows his side's major-suit fit is eight cards because of opener's support redouble. As for North-South, it's quite possible they have a combined holding of nine hearts because South was willing to compete to the three-level.

Even though there are just 17 total trumps, it's possible there will be nine tricks available in both three-level contracts. The key here is that responder has a good holding of two honor cards in the suit partner opened. Unlike the previous deal, all his cards seem to be working here so it's quite reasonable for him to bid on.

In 3♡, North-South would have lost a trick in each suit to make their contract. The play is a bit trickier for East-West in 3♠, but that can also be made. On a heart lead, declarer will have to drive out the ♣A before playing on trumps, even though it may allow North to score a club ruff. If he does that, West should prevail, losing just two trumps, a club and a diamond.

3.   E-W vulnerable

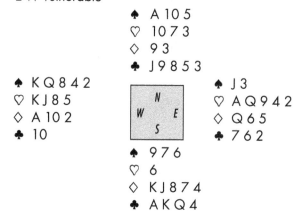

```
              ♠ A 10 5
              ♡ 10 7 3
              ◇ 9 3
              ♣ J 9 8 5 3
♠ K Q 8 4 2                    ♠ J 3
♡ K J 8 5          N          ♡ A Q 9 4 2
◇ A 10 2      W        E      ◇ Q 6 5
♣ 10               S          ♣ 7 6 2
              ♠ 9 7 6
              ♡ 6
              ◇ K J 8 7 4
              ♣ A K Q 4
```

West	North	East	South
			1◇
1♠	pass	1NT	2♣
2♡	3♣	3♡	all pass

With five-card support for opener's second suit and an outside ace, North might feel inclined to compete to the four-level, especially with the vulnerability in his favor. However, as I mentioned previously in the chapter, these situations leave no margin for error.

Responder ought to surmise that the opponents have a nine-card heart fit, as partner has shown nine or ten minor-suit cards. Also, the spades will be dividing evenly. It would not be a surprise if East-West were able to make 4♡ their way. Consider what their thought processes will be if you bid 4♣: 'Gee, we expected to score +140 or better, and what we'll get from defending their contract won't match it, so all we can do now is bid 4♡ and hope for the best.'

It turns out here that 4♡ can't be defeated, as West ruffs the second club and then proceeds to knock out the ♠A. With spades splitting evenly, he won't have any difficulty in making the contract.

You might be taken aback by the 1NT bid, suppressing the five-card heart suit. The reason for it is that an advance in a new suit at the two-level following an overcall would require 10 or more points, just as it would after an opening bid. East had enough values to keep the bidding alive, but 1NT was his only feasible action.

The results on the board are quite interesting:

North-South	+130	1 pair		−200	1 pair
	+110	2 pairs		−500	1 pair
	+90	2 pairs		−620	1 pair
	−140	2 pairs		−790	1 pair
	−170	1 pair			

Some East-West pairs did not compete all that much beyond an initial over-call and at their tables North-South got to play clubs at the two-level. A second group are the East-West pairs who got to their heart fit but did not attempt to play game. Finally, we have the North-South pairs who refused to go quietly in the partscore battle. They wound up having their opponents bid game – that explains the three big numbers for East-West.

4.   E-W vulnerable

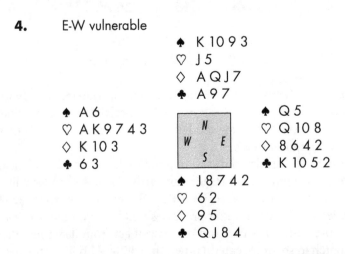

West	North	East	South
		pass	pass
1♡	dbl	2♡	pass
pass	dbl	pass	2♠
3♡	pass	pass	?

It's a very close decision for South, even with his threadbare hand. Partner for his two doubles will have at least 15 HCP along with four spades. That gives North-South a nine-card fit, and since partner will have at most two hearts, the opponents have the exact same number of their agreed suit. It's possible, then, that both three-level contracts make. Even if 3♠ goes down, it could still be the winning action if 3♡ by East-West comes home.

How do the contracts fare? If North leads either a trump or ace and another club, 3♡ will go down. If he leads a spade, calamity will strike as declarer flies with the queen and loses only three diamonds and the ♣A. How about 3♠? Well, declarer has a chance if he gets the trump suit right and leads to the king on the first round. Double-dummy, East-West can beat it with a club lead or one high heart and a club shift. Now West can climb on the first round of spades and get over to his partner's hand in hearts to obtain his club ruff.

5.   E-W vulnerable

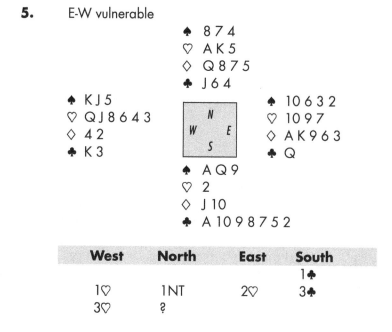

	♠ 8 7 4	
	♡ A K 5	
	◇ Q 8 7 5	
	♣ J 6 4	

♠ K J 5   ♠ 10 6 3 2
♡ Q J 8 6 4 3   ♡ 10 9 7
◇ 4 2   ◇ A K 9 6 3
♣ K 3   ♣ Q

♠ A Q 9
♡ 2
◇ J 10
♣ A 10 9 8 7 5 2

West	North	East	South
			1♣
1♡	1NT	2♡	3♣
3♡	?		

Opener doesn't have a wealth of high cards for his 3♣ rebid, but a seven-card suit needs to be mentioned a second time.

The most discernible options for North are to double, trying for the +200 that would get North-South a near-top, or to go one level higher in partner's suit. Bidding 4♣ would turn out better, as 3♡ makes due to the extremely fortunate lie of the spade suit. A North-South 4♣ contract has chances, but may go down one for the same reason.

There is another thought for North, and that is to bid 3NT, figuring his double stopper in hearts will keep the opponents at bay while he sets up his tricks. That contract is still beatable, but I'll let you have fun exploring the play of the hand on your own.

6.   Neither vulnerable

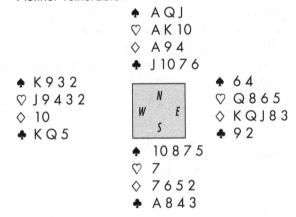

```
                        ♠ A Q J
                        ♡ A K 10
                        ◇ A 9 4
                        ♣ J 10 7 6
  ♠ K 9 3 2                              ♠ 6 4
  ♡ J 9 4 3 2          N                 ♡ Q 8 6 5
  ◇ 10             W        E            ◇ K Q J 8 3
  ♣ K Q 5              S                 ♣ 9 2
                        ♠ 10 8 7 5
                        ♡ 7
                        ◇ 7 6 5 2
                        ♣ A 8 4 3
```

West	North	East	South
	1♣	1◇	pass
1♡	1NT	2♡	3♣
3♡	dbl	all pass	

The panel consensus was that East's overcall was light but reasonable. Some might quibble with his 2♡ raise, but that's not a particularly strong action – with significant extra values he could have doubled 1NT. The culprit on this deal, I'm afraid, is West. With partner having overcalled in his singleton, he has no pressing reason to be declaring the hand, as 3♣ might easily be going down. I would give him 77% of the blame and say that 3♡ was the worst bid.

9
Opening Leads, Shooting and High-level Drama

Before moving on to a 27-board session of quiz hands, I'll cover three final topics. One is that of opening leads, and how much the form of the game should affect your choice. Secondly, you may have heard of the expression 'shooting', which basically means trying to catch up when your game is not exactly sailing along. I have fairly strong opinions on whether and how this course should be pursued, which I'll share with you. Finally, there is the matter of tactics, which is how to proceed when you're not entirely sure whether your side should be playing or defending on a particular deal.

Opening Leads

In teams and rubber bridge, the foremost objective is to try and defeat the contract, and you're not particularly concerned about giving up overtricks to declarer. In a pairs game, an extra trick takes on greater significance as it might be the difference between a good result and a relatively poor one. The question is whether to stick with or abandon the time-honored recommendations of fourth-best and leading from strength rather than weakness.

From Robert Ewen and Mike Lawrence to the more recent efforts of David Bird and Taf Anthias, there have been many books written on opening leads. I'm going to confine myself to some deals from actual play to explore whether opening leads at matchpoints should be business as usual or if a slight adjustment in thought processes might be required.

Our first look has you on opening lead after this bidding sequence:

West (you)	North	East	South
	pass	pass	1NT[1]
all pass			

1. 12-14.

Your hand consists of:

♠ Q 9 8 3   ♡ 8 7 4 3   ◇ A 10 3   ♣ J 10

With two four-card majors, you'll be leading one of them, but the question is do you go on the attack with a spade or be somewhat more cautious with a heart? If you decide to lead a heart, standard practice is to lead the highest or second-highest with a four-card holding that does not contain an honor.

What if I were to tell you that an initial spade lead would give declarer an extra trick in that suit whereas a heart lead would not? You might be somewhat upset if you had opted to start with a spade. But then I'd go on to tell you that you'll still be far better off in the end than the heart leaders. How can that be? Let's look at how the play would likely go once we see all four hands:

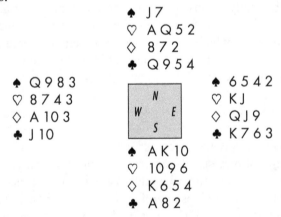

```
              ♠ J 7
              ♡ A Q 5 2
              ◇ 8 7 2
              ♣ Q 9 5 4
♠ Q 9 8 3            ♠ 6 5 4 2
♡ 8 7 4 3      N     ♡ K J
◇ A 10 3     W   E   ◇ Q J 9
♣ J 10         S     ♣ K 7 6 3
              ♠ A K 10
              ♡ 10 9 6
              ◇ K 6 5 4
              ♣ A 8 2
```

On a spade lead, declarer wins in hand. Of his three seven-card fits, he has the most spots in hearts, so he'll run the ♡10, losing to your partner's jack. Back comes a spade, and South wins again to lead a heart to the queen and king. East now shifts to the ◇Q, trapping declarer's king, and after the second round of the suit, will then play a third round of spades. Declarer will get three spades, the two rounded aces, and maybe another trick in hearts or clubs, but that's it. He will go down one or two.

Now let's see what happens if West leads a high heart. Declarer will know immediately that both the king and jack are in the East hand, so he'll disdain the finesse and rise with the ace. Not unexpectedly, an honor drops; he will now play ace and another club, setting up three tricks in that suit since you have the J10 doubleton. When all is said and done, he'll score three clubs, two or three hearts and two spades, making his contract easily.

The scores on the board are indicative of an even split between the spade and heart leads:

East-West	+110	1 pair
	+100	2 pairs
	+50	4 pairs
	−90	3 pairs
	−120	4 pairs
	−150	1 pair

With one exception, the contract was the same across the field, a notrump partscore by North-South. It made eight times, and went down the other six. That means there were just as many, if not a few more, players who led a heart rather than a spade.

My feeling is that when you're defending a partscore contract, especially against notrump, there is room in partner's hand for some high cards in your long suit. That being the case, 'fourth-best from longest and strongest' will generally turn out to be a productive lead. This brings us to our next example, with RHO having opened a strong notrump followed by three passes:

♠ A 3   ♡ K 9 8 2   ◇ Q 9 6 5 4   ♣ Q 5

Should you lead a diamond or a heart? The diamonds are longer, the hearts slightly better. Some players tend to lead a major against a notrump contract as RHO has not opened a major and LHO hasn't used Stayman. Here, with the opponents not having tried for game, there is room in partner's hand for at least 7 HCP and possibly more. This is what he in fact held:

♠ 10 9 4 2   ♡ Q 6 5   ◇ K 10 6   ♣ K J 4

A diamond lead sets up four tricks in the suit, while a heart is good for declarer, as he now has a second trick. Yes, it was fortunate that partner's ten-spot was in diamonds, when he could have had the same card in the heart suit. That said, if he has no ten-spot in either red suit, a diamond would still be the better lead. The results here are:

East-West	+300	1 pair	-90	4 pairs
	+200	4 pairs	-110	1 pair
	+130	1 pair	-120	1 pair
	+100	5 pairs		

The +200 scores would have been the result of a diamond lead, whereas the -90s and -120 would have been a heart lead. The +100s could have been either lead, although are more likely to have been a diamond.

Some hands will offer a choice of three leads, not just two. For our next exhibit, the auction has gone:

West (you)	North	East	South
		pass	1NT
all pass			

♠ J 6   ♡ K Q 3   ◇ A 10 7 6   ♣ J 8 4 3

Your strongest holding is in hearts, but the two longest suits are diamonds and clubs. With a better spot in the major, a heart might conceivably be your lead, but it's too much of a shot in the dark with what you actually have. A diamond might allow South to score an undeserved trick, whereas a club might also be productive and a bit safer in not giving anything away. So what turns out to be the best start?

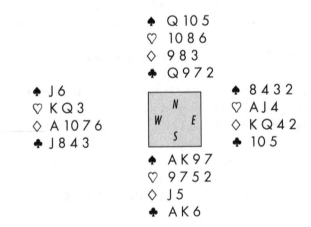

A diamond lead beats the contract quickly, as the defense will start by cashing four tricks in the suit. If West wins the final round of the suit, he will likely switch to the ♡K, as dummy has good holdings in the black suits. Likewise, if East takes the fourth diamond, he will also probably lead from his strength (hearts) rather than his weakness. The defenders will then score three more tricks in that suit.

A heart lead would likely have achieved the same result, as the defense could take the first three tricks and then switch to diamonds. However, that would be much easier for East to do than it might be for West.

A club lead turns out to be a disaster, as South will be able to pick up the suit and take the first eight tricks in the black suits. The traveler reveals:

East-West	+100	7 pairs
	−90	3 pairs
	−120	6 pairs

The -120s had to be the result of a club lead. As for the -90s and +100s, we'd surmise that West led a red suit and the defense either took the first seven tricks or allowed declarer to gain the lead.

This doesn't mean you should always be tracking out your long suit as the opening lead, however. Let's say the auction has gone 1NT on your right followed by three passes. What is your lead on the next three hands?

♠ Q J 3   ♡ A 10 5   ◇ 9 7 5   ♣ A 7 4 3
♠ Q J 3   ♡ A 10 5   ◇ A 7 5   ♣ 9 7 4 3
♠ Q J 3   ♡ A 10 5   ◇ 9 7 5   ♣ 9 7 4 3

On the first hand, a club is a good opening salvo. If it doesn't work out, there will be time to switch to a major suit once you regain the lead. With you holding 11 HCP, trying to hit partner with a major-suit lead will have its share of misses.

The second hand is more of a guess. You have the same point-count, but the clubs are pretty feeble, so the ♠Q lead might turn out better for your side.

On the third hand, partner rates to have about 10 points, so a major-suit lead is considerably more attractive, and I suspect the ♠Q would be the choice of many players.

When the opponents bid game, the choice of leads becomes much tougher as you have to decide whether to try and beat the contract. Sometimes you can make the attempt without much risk, but there are other hands where you might be giving up extra overtricks to declarer.

We'll start with this hand as our jumping-off point, with two different auctions. You are sitting West:

West	North	East	South
			1NT
pass	3NT	all pass	

♠ 10 5 4   ♡ K J 10 7   ◇ 5   ♣ 10 8 7 5 4

There are only two serious candidates here, each of the rounded suits. A club isn't overly enterprising, although it could be a safer lead. The ♡J, meanwhile, could be more productive in terms of getting immediate tricks and since there is room in partner's hand for about 8-10 points, it is probably a slight favorite over a club, both in terms of defeating the contract and winning more tricks even if you don't beat their game. However, it's a different matter if the bidding has gone:

West	North	East	South
			1NT
pass	2♣	pass	2♠
pass	3NT	all pass	

Since North hasn't raised opener's major to game, it was a heart fit he was looking for and he'll have four of them. This reduces the probability of a heart lead being successful and you should now look to your five-card suit, trying to prevent additional overtricks.

What about the situation where you have a long suit with some high cards but no outside entry? Should you be going for the gusto or trying to find a safer lead? Here is a pair of hands to consider when the auction has gone 1NT – 3NT:

♠ K 10 9 5 2   ♡ 9 5 2   ◇ 9 8 7 3   ♣ 7
♠ 8 6 3   ♡ J 10 8   ◇ Q 7 5 4 2   ♣ 8 6

In the first case, yes, a spade lead might cost a trick, but it is an unbid major and LHO has not made a Stayman inquiry. Any other suit would be a guess that could work out just as badly, so you might as well lead the ♠10.

On the second hand, the long suit doesn't have quite as much body. Either opponent could have diamond length, and the prospects of establishing long-suit winners are remote. Beside, you have an alternative lead that could be effective, that being the ♡J.

At times, you'll have to weigh your desire to beat the enemy contract against making a lead that won't give declarer any freebies. As our final example, you hold as North:

♠J 107   ♡65   ◇K 9 2   ♣K 9 7 6 4

What would you lead against each of these auctions?

West	East
1NT	2◇*
2♡	3NT
pass	

West	East
1NT	2◇*
2♡	3NT
4♡	pass

Against 3NT the choice is between the black suits, a fourth-best club or the ♠J. The club spots are just good enough to consider leading that suit, and you may have an entry with the ◇K. If the contract is 4♡, though, the minor-suit foray loses some of its allure as you might be giving up a trick that you won't be able to get back. The ♠J would combine safety with some opportunity to set up a winner for your side, and a trump lead too is likely to be fairly safe. The complete deal is:

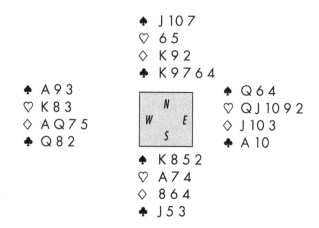

As I mentioned in Chapter 7, in a transfer auction it is often right for opener to correct to the 5-3 major-suit fit even with 4-3-3-3 distribution. Here, a club lead is the best shot to defeat 3NT as the ♣A cannot be held up. Although the Deep Finesse analysis software says 3NT can be made, that can only be accomplished if West plays for the ◇K to be offside and runs the hearts, causing North some discard problems. However, at pairs every declarer will knock out the ♡A and then finesse in diamonds, as there will be two overtricks available if that succeeds. If North leads the ♠J against the notrump game, declarer gets home by a whisker as he can win the ace and drive out the ♡A. Even on a diamond shift and another round of spades from North now, West's nine-spot will prevent the opponents from taking more than one trick in the suit.

Meanwhile, a club lead will allow a 4♡ contract to make while the ♠J will beat it if North-South defend accurately.

Shooting

'Shooting' is an expression that you might have heard in the course of your time at the bridge table. Simply put, it means going against the field in your choice of bid or line of play. Usually, this is because you don't feel you're doing well and and you are trying to catch up by stirring the pot.

I have sometimes been a practitioner of shooting, but I try and keep these parameters in mind when I do:

- The time to shoot is when you're having a decent game but not one that you expect to win with at your current pace. For example, say you are three-quarters of the way through a session and you estimate that you're at about 56-57%. A respectable showing, to be sure, but you'll probably need several tops or near-tops to get you to a winning score.

  You should *not* be shooting when you have a game below 50% and would need a miracle to win. It's just not your day, so play your normal game for the rest of the session and don't try anything outrageous. Indulging in shooting in these circumstances will often leave a sour taste in the opponents' mouths. Moreover, if your heroics backfire and one of the pairs who gained a nice result from you ends up winning the event, you won't have earned any fans amongst the other contending pairs who did not benefit from your largesse.

- If you elect to indulge in shooting, you may have a chance if your actions are slightly unusual but with a grain of logic in them. By contrast, if you're doing stuff that is wildly anti-percentage you are in all likelihood doomed to failure and, once again, may be creating an abundance of hard feelings at the table.

With those words of advice in mind, let's move on to a few specific examples. You've been dealt this hand as East:

♠ J ♡ K 7 6 5 2 ◊ K Q 9 7 ♣ 10 9 3

The bidding has started out with:

West	North	East	South
1♣	pass	1♡	pass
2NT	pass	?	

Standard operating procedure for East would be to check back for three-card support in his major, intending to bid 4♡ if opener shows it.

If you were striving for a different and possibly better result, the way to do it would be to forego the major-suit game entirely and simply raise to 3NT. Since the partnership has a combined point total of 27-28 HCP, playing the hand in notrump could result in the same number of tricks as a heart contract would.

What is the outcome of the respective game contracts? The layout is:

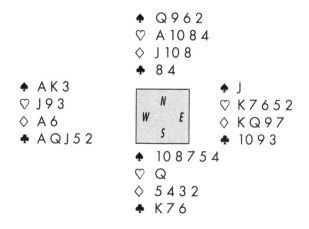

Indeed there is a 5-3 heart fit, but with the suit breaking 4-1, three tricks will have to be lost in 4♡. What about 3NT? North's lead is almost certain to be a spade, and dummy's jack holds the trick. Declarer then finesses successfully in clubs, picking up that suit for five tricks, after which he leads up to dummy's ♡K, winning twelve tricks in all for a super result.

Our next hand is one where opener can shoot mildly or wildly. As West, you hold:

♠ Q 9 6   ♡ Q 9 5   ◇ 10   ♣ A K 10 8 5 3

The auction has begun with:

West	North	East	South
		pass	pass
1♣	pass	2NT	pass
?			

A significant majority of players would retreat to 3♣ on these cards, ending the auction. However, some players might look at the hand in this way:

- I have a source of tricks with my excellent six-card club suit;
- The opponents are probably going to lead a major, and I have honors in both suits;
- So why don't I leave the contract in notrump rather than play it in clubs?

This is a prime example of an intelligent but not outlandish shoot. The result that awaits those who stand their ground in notrump is:

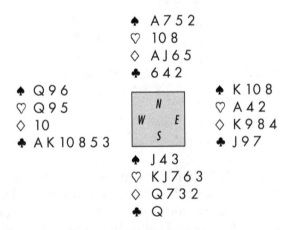

```
                    ♠ A 7 5 2
                    ♡ 10 8
                    ◇ A J 6 5
                    ♣ 6 4 2
     ♠ Q 9 6                        ♠ K 10 8
     ♡ Q 9 5           N            ♡ A 4 2
     ◇ 10          W       E        ◇ K 9 8 4
     ♣ A K 10 8 5 3      S          ♣ J 9 7
                    ♠ J 4 3
                    ♡ K J 7 6 3
                    ◇ Q 7 3 2
                    ♣ Q
```

South will lead a heart and if declarer puts up the queen, he will tally up at least nine tricks with a fair chance at a tenth. Even on a diamond lead, East's spot cards along with dummy's ten-spot are good enough for a second stopper.

The previous two shooting decisions were of the mild variety. North was on much shakier ground with his choice on this hand:

♠ A 10 7 6 4 3   ♡ K 10   ◇ 7 5   ♣ 10 8 4

The auction went:

West	North	East	South
			2NT
pass	3♡*	pass	3♠
pass	3NT	all pass	

Granted, he would have ended up in spades if opener had three of them, but the fact remains that he was offering 3NT as a contract. It would take Kx or better in spades in partner's hand for that to be right, otherwise it would be difficult to establish his six-card suit and it might wither on the vine. He came up smelling like a rose, however, as the four hands were:

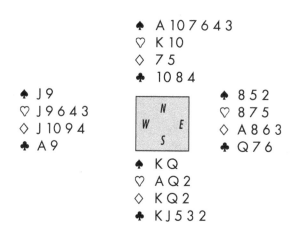

```
                    ♠ A 10 7 6 4 3
                    ♡ K 10
                    ◇ 7 5
                    ♣ 10 8 4
  ♠ J 9                              ♠ 8 5 2
  ♡ J 9 6 4 3         N              ♡ 8 7 5
  ◇ J 10 9 4      W       E          ◇ A 8 6 3
  ♣ A 9               S              ♣ Q 7 6
                    ♠ K Q
                    ♡ A Q 2
                    ◇ K Q 2
                    ♣ K J 5 3 2
```

As you can see, everything was nicely positioned for the declaring side in notrump. Opener had the doubleton ♠KQ, the ♡K was an entry, and both the ◇A and ♣Q were onside.

We'll have a few more examples of this type in the quiz, but in the meantime let's move on to another topic.

Tactics

Some people have a tendency to equate tactics with shooting, but they're quite difference in their nature. Shooting is when a player takes an action that would have some advocates but not have majority approval, in the hope that it will be the right one on this particular deal. In making a tactical bid, a player is not deliberately going against the field, but is taking his action because he really has no idea whom the deal belongs to, or the proper level he should venture to. He therefore takes a guess himself or makes a bid that forces the opponents to guess.

Many tactical situations revolve around whether to go high or low on the bid you're going to make. Can you afford to take the 'scenic route', as a friend of mine once described it, or should you be getting to where you intend to be right away? You'll need to anticipate what might happen with each of the choices before you.

Our first hand, with you in the West chair and the opponents vulnerable is:

♠ Q J 5 3   ♡ 5   ◇ A 7 6 4   ♣ 10 8 7 6

You are third to speak, after:

West	North	East	South
		1♠	2◇
?			

Since you don't have quite enough in high cards for a 3◇ cuebid, showing a limit raise or better, the choices here are between a robust 2♠ and a leap to game in opener's major. There are two good reasons for you to take the four-level plunge, in my opinion. They are:

- Your hand could be worth up to four tricks for partner, those being the ◇A, the ♠Q and two heart ruffs. That could well be enough to bring him up to ten tricks.
- Where are all the hearts on this hand? If North has length in the suit and was about to bid it, 4♠ by you would make it highly inconvenient for him to mention them. The other possibility is that hearts are opener's second suit, in which case your shortness and four-card trump support will be useful holdings.

Whatever your rationale is, the jump to game works like a charm this time, as this is the quartet of hands:

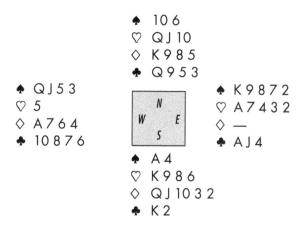

```
                    ♠ 10 6
                    ♡ Q J 10
                    ◇ K 9 8 5
                    ♣ Q 9 5 3
♠ Q J 5 3          ┌─────────┐          ♠ K 9 8 7 2
♡ 5                │    N    │          ♡ A 7 4 3 2
◇ A 7 6 4          │ W     E │          ◇ —
♣ 10 8 7 6         │    S    │          ♣ A J 4
                   └─────────┘
                    ♠ A 4
                    ♡ K 9 8 6
                    ◇ Q J 10 3 2
                    ♣ K 2
```

Although opener has a void in the opponents' suit and 5-5 in the majors, his spot cards in the long suits are nothing to write home about and you might only have three spades, so it's not clear he would have tried for game over 2♠.

Although the best defense for North-South is to start with ace and another trump, the ◇Q will probably be the actual lead, after which declarer can embark on a merry cross-ruff. Even on two rounds of trumps he gets to ruff two hearts and pitch a club away on the ◇A. All he'll lose is a spade, a heart and a club.

North-South have a nine-card diamond fit but the colors are wrong for North to bid at the five-level and 5◇ doubled would not be a happy contract on the lead of West's singleton heart.

For our second example, you are South with your side vulnerable, with this hand:

♠K Q 8 ♡J 8 5 ◇K Q 10 9 8 7 ♣7

This has been the auction so far:

West	North	East	South
pass	1♠	3♣	?

There are three choices for responder here, all of them having blemishes. One is to cuebid 4♣, which is a bit shy on points and leaves the good diamond suit unshown. Another is to jump to 4♠, which you certainly expect to make, but there might be a slam your way. You may get a chance to show the diamonds if the auction continues with West bidding 5♣. If North passes that, you can then bid 5◇. But what if he doubles? Should you respect his decision or bid on?

The final course of action is to delay the spade support for the time being and bid 3◊. If West doesn't go crazy in the bidding, your side will be well-placed, although a jump to 5♣ will give you a problem. Again, you're in no-man's-land if North doubles, but at least you'll know he doesn't have a diamond fit.

A slower approach with 3◊ has another way of paying off, as we'll see upon viewing all the hands:

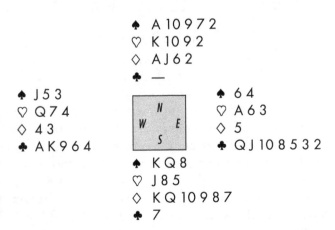

```
                  ♠ A 10 9 7 2
                  ♡ K 10 9 2
                  ◊ A J 6 2
                  ♣ —
  ♠ J 5 3                          ♠ 6 4
  ♡ Q 7 4          N               ♡ A 6 3
  ◊ 4 3        W       E           ◊ 5
  ♣ A K 9 6 4      S               ♣ Q J 10 8 5 3 2
                  ♠ K Q 8
                  ♡ J 8 5
                  ◊ K Q 10 9 8 7
                  ♣ 7
```

West's bid is going to be 5♣ regardless of the action you take. However, if you have bid the diamonds, opener will probably now just shrug his shoulders and jump to 6◊. While his point-count is minimal, he has great trump support and a void in the opponents' suit. You can make 6◊, and even if East-West take the 7♣ sacrifice they aren't going to score well as it goes for 1100 and not many pairs will reach the slam in your direction.

Who Knows? High-level Decisions and Freak Hands

Earlier in this book, we discussed auctions where one pair was clearly sacrificing against what they thought was a making contract by the opponents. In this section, we'll be looking at cases where it is not clear who the deal belongs to, and each side will be bidding with some hope and expectation of making their contract.

There's an air of uncertainty on this type of deal. Sometimes both sides will be able to make game their way. That's somewhat rare, happening less than one time in a hundred based on 864 deals that I've gone through in the process of collecting examples for this book. That's not the whole story, however, as there are instances where one side's contract may take a specific lead to defeat it. Alternatively, the cards may lie in such a way that the 'sacrifice' turns out to be a make and the side that figures the deal belongs to them finds out that it doesn't. Here is a case in point:

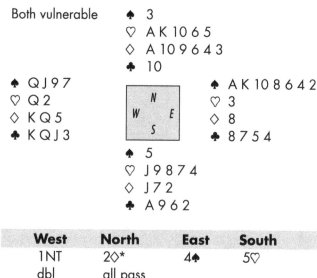

Both vulnerable

North
♠ 3
♡ A K 10 6 5
♢ A 10 9 6 4 3
♣ 10

West
♠ Q J 9 7
♡ Q 2
♢ K Q 5
♣ K Q J 3

East
♠ A K 10 8 6 4 2
♡ 3
♢ 8
♣ 8 7 5 4

South
♠ 5
♡ J 9 8 7 4
♢ J 7 2
♣ A 9 6 2

West	North	East	South
1NT	2♢*	4♠	5♡
dbl	all pass		

Aside from North, whose bid of 2♢ shows the red suits, each of the other three players has a decision to make at some point of the auction.

East's 4♠ is to play, and his assumption is that the deal belongs to his side with partner having shown 15-17 HCP and a balanced hand. South's expectation is that the opponents' contract will usually be a make since they appear to have a double fit in spades and clubs. His bid of 5♡ is a two-way shot. At the very least, it will be a very cheap sacrifice in their excellent fit, down one at the very worst. At the same time, the contract might even scrape home.

The irony of this deal is that 4♠ can be defeated on a heart to the ace and a club back, whereupon North gets a ruff. However, North-South reap a handsome profit from their decision to 'save'. It turns out that 5♡ will make their way since by finessing in diamonds against the strong notrumper, they'll be able to hold the losers in that suit to one. So it happens that the side with the majority of high-card points is the one that is in sacrifice mode, which is far from obvious to them.

Because responder jumped to a major-suit game after partner opened 1NT, this is deemed to be a forcing situation when the opponents bid 5♡. North-South therefore cannot be allowed to play undoubled, so the choice for East-West is to bid on or double the opponents' contract. At this point, East-West are doomed to a poor matchpoints result even if they bid on to 5♠, as that contract will be doubled and defeated. On the face of it, you would think that opener has no business doubling 5♡, since he has a good fit for partner's spades and very little defense aside from the ◊KQ. He could bid on himself, or at least pass to express a neutral opinion, in which case East will bid 5♠. However, there is a contingent of players (including experts) who feel that West's double here shows nothing other than two quick losers in the enemy suit. That might have been what opener was trying to show and possibly, although East-West were a regular partnership, they didn't have a firm agreement for this type of situation.

The main features of volatile deals that could belong to either side are:

- Excellent trump fits of 10-11 cards
- Both sides have a fit in two suits, and/or....
- One or more hands contain a void, which is a 'wild card' that may dramatically affect the trick-taking potential.

Those of you who have played any type of organized bridge have likely gone to a bar or restaurant after the game and talked over the more interesting deals from the session. On the following one, two of the pairs could scarcely believe each other's result. It all came about from which black suit East opened at the one-level.

Both vulnerable

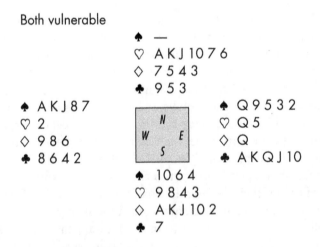

```
                ♠ —
                ♡ A K J 10 7 6
                ◊ 7 5 4 3
                ♣ 9 5 3
♠ A K J 8 7                        ♠ Q 9 5 3 2
♡ 2              N                 ♡ Q 5
◊ 9 8 6      W       E             ◊ Q
♣ 8 6 4 2        S                 ♣ A K Q J 10
                ♠ 10 6 4
                ♡ 9 8 4 3
                ◊ A K J 10 2
                ♣ 7
```

At player A's table, the auction went:

West	North	East	South
		1♠	pass
4♠	all pass		

South and North each have 8 HCP, and taking direct action is not really feasible with either hand.

At player B's table, the bidding was vastly different:

West	North	East	South
		1♣	1◇
1♠	3♡	4◇	4♡
4♠	5◇	5♠	6◇
pass	pass	dbl	all pass

Nowadays, most players open the higher-ranking suit if they are 5-5 in the blacks. Once upon a time, however, the general consensus was that if opener had minimum values he should open 1♣ and then bid spades twice, not having to increase the level if responder bids a red suit. There are still people who feel that way, and our East was one of them.

The result of this seemingly minor difference in the choice of opening bid was that the auction quickly zoomed into the stratosphere. South was able to get his diamond suit in at the one-level, and over West's 1♠, North made a fit-showing jump to 3♡, showing nine or more cards in the red suits. East, with outstanding support for partner's major, then cuebid 4◇ and both sides eventually went to the five-level in their double fit.

When South bid 6◇, West passed. Because of his club fit, he didn't have much in the way of defense but did not want to bid 6♠ ahead of partner, who could easily be planning to double 6◇. As an aside, responder will likely have a heart control since he appears to be willing to entertain a 6♠ bid from partner. Diamonds are not so much of a worry as opener has advertised a control in that suit when he bid 4◇.

If the form of the game were teams, East would surely bid 6♠, knowing the opponents have a massive heart-diamond fit and not being able to afford the price-tag if their contract happens to make. At pairs, though, he didn't expect a six-level contract to make and their contract may also be going down.

As always on hands of this type, a void such as the one North has in spades is a wild card that has a noticeable effect on the result. It's one of those rare occasions where game makes one way and slam the other. Moreover, despite having 24 HCP to the opponents' 16, it will be East-West who need to be in sacrifice mode. Yes, there are some clues from the bidding, but it's hard to tell for sure.

Next up is a deal which features several voids, but how lively the auction is going to be will depend on West's choice of opening bid:

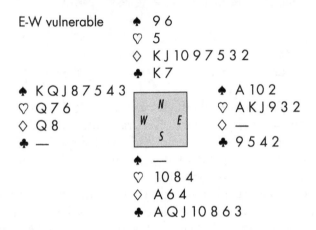

E-W vulnerable
```
                 ♠ 9 6
                 ♡ 5
                 ◇ K J 10 9 7 5 3 2
                 ♣ K 7
♠ K Q J 8 7 5 4 3              ♠ A 10 2
♡ Q 7 6                        ♡ A K J 9 3 2
◇ Q 8                          ◇ —
♣ —                            ♣ 9 5 4 2
                 ♠ —
                 ♡ 10 8 4
                 ◇ A 6 4
                 ♣ A Q J 10 8 6 3
```

West deals and is surely going to bid some number of spades, the question being whether to open 1♠ or 4♠. Some players don't much like preempting with an outside void, especially when holding the master suit, and would go with 1♠, which allows West to preempt in diamonds. East is now seriously thinking of at least a small slam, while South is quite willing to bid on vigorously in diamonds, as it will be a cheap sacrifice and even have an outside chance of making. As you can see, the defense will probably only take a couple of tricks against a diamond contract. The fly in the ointment, however, is that East-West can make a grand slam in spades, although bidding it might be too tall an order.

The auction might be somewhat tamer if West opens 4♠. North is pretty much shut out of the bidding now as he has good distribution but his hand is somewhat meager in high cards. East will think about slam but there could be two quick losers in the club suit. If he passes, South will enter the fray with 5♣, but East is still hard pressed to do anything more than bid 5♠ at this point.

Vulnerability conditions may dictate a player's course of action, as witness our next example. As South, you hold:

♠ K 6 2 ♡ 6 4 ◇ A K 9 ♣ K J 10 9 6

The auction has gone:

West	North	East	South
			1♣
1♡	3◇*	3♡	?

North's 3◊ is a fit-showing jump, promising length and values in both minor suits.

What do you think the trick-taking potential is for each side? Do you bid on if neither side is vulnerable? How about if both sides are vulnerable?

Using Total Tricks as our guide, we can expect a ten-card fit in clubs for North-South, while East-West will likely have nine or ten hearts between them. As a result, there will be 19 or 20 total tricks available in all in each side's best fit.

If your side is not vulnerable, the odds favor bidding on in clubs at match-points, to whatever level you need to. You might be allowed to play in 4♣, and even if West bids on to 4♡, you should take the push to the five-level. You may not be able to defeat their game, and don't expect to go down more than one in 5♣. Even if the opponents double, going -100 will still yield a better result than selling out to 3♡ in the first place.

If both sides are vulnerable, the scenario changes dramatically, and bidding 4♣ is not a good idea. Now when the opponents bid 4♡, even if that contract is making, 5♣ doubled will be too expensive. Your -200 will be a poor score compared to the -140/-170 you would have if you hadn't gone any further.

The entire deal is:

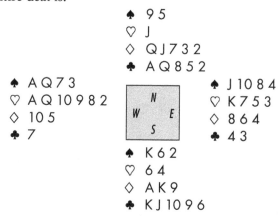

```
              ♠ 9 5
              ♡ J
              ◇ Q J 7 3 2
              ♣ A Q 8 5 2
♠ A Q 7 3                    ♠ J 10 8 4
♡ A Q 10 9 8 2      N        ♡ K 7 5 3
◇ 10 5          W       E    ◇ 8 6 4
♣ 7                 S        ♣ 4 3
              ♠ K 6 2
              ♡ 6 4
              ◇ A K 9
              ♣ K J 10 9 6
```

As is typical with deals where each side has lots of trumps and a double fit, the possibilities are endless. East-West can make ten tricks in hearts (or spades). Meanwhile, 5♣ by North-South can be defeated, but to get the job done West has to underlead his ♡A so partner can return a spade. Otherwise, declarer can draw trumps and pitch two of his spades on the long diamonds for eleven tricks.

QUIZ

1. You are sitting East, vulnerable against non-vulnerable opponents. You're looking at:

♠Q7 ♡J9762 ◇KJ43 ♣K3

Your side has remained silent as the opponents weren't too ambitious in their bidding:

West	North	East	South
	1♣	pass	1♠
pass	1NT	pass	2♣
all pass			

What is your opening lead?

2. As North with your side vulnerable, you have:

♠K965 ♡A982 ◇AK9 ♣97

Partner opens 1♣. What is your response in each of these situations?

a) You're in the first or second round of the event.

b) You're about two-thirds of the way through and feel as if you might need a good board.

3. For this one you are South, vulnerable against non-vulnerable opponents. You have these cards:

♠Q762 ♡9 ◇A10842 ♣K74

The bidding has started tamely enough:

West	North	East	South
pass	2♠	3♡	?

You have a nice fit in partner's major, but they likely have a good fit as well. What is your bid?

4. You're West, with North the dealer and neither side vulnerable:

♠ J 9 8 6   ♡ 10 4   ◇ K Q 10 8   ♣ K 8 7

You're on lead against a notrump game, the opponents having got there via this auction:

West	North	East	South
	1♣	1♡	pass
1NT	2♣	pass	3NT
all pass			

What do you place face-up on the table?

5. On this new deal, you occupy the West seat with South the dealer and both sides vulnerable. As you tally up your points, you're finally able to open the bidding:

♠ K Q 10 9   ♡ A J 10   ◇ Q J 10   ♣ Q 9 8

West	North	East	South
			pass
1NT	pass	2NT	pass
?			

Do you stop here or do you move onward and upward?

6. You're North now with East the dealer and your side vulnerable. You've picked up this mundane collection:

♠ A J 7   ♡ K 9 7 4   ◇ 6 2   ♣ K 7 5 4

Alas, you're shut out of the bidding as the auction goes:

West	North	East	South
1♠	pass	2NT*	pass
4♠	all pass		

What do you fancy as your lead?

7. With neither side vulnerable, you're looking at this rather impressive hand as South:

♠— ♡Q 10 9 7 4 3 ◇A K J 10 ♣A Q 9

The bidding has gone:

West	North	East	South
			1♡
pass	3♣*	3♠	?

Partner's 3♣ was a Bergen raise, showing 6-9 points and at least four-card support. That is good news, but what now after East has come in with 3♠?

8. Last chance for glory. You are West for this one, and North-South are vulnerable as you pick up:

♠7 ♡Q 10 7 2 ◇K J 9 8 7 2 ♣8 7

There follows a far from peaceful auction:

West	North	East	South
	pass	1♣	4♠
pass	pass	5♣	pass
pass	5♠	pass	pass
?			

So here we are. Do you pass, double or bid on in partner's suit?

1.   E-W vulnerable

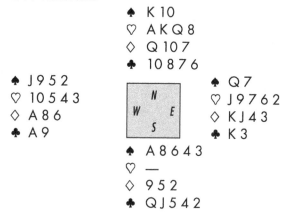

<pre>
                              ♠ K 10
                              ♡ A K Q 8
                              ◇ Q 10 7
                              ♣ 10 8 7 6
       ♠ J 9 5 2   ♠ Q 7
       ♡ 10 5 4 3   N   ♡ J 9 7 6 2
       ◇ A 8 6   W   E   ◇ K J 4 3
       ♣ A 9   S   ♣ K 3
                              ♠ A 8 6 4 3
                              ♡ —
                              ◇ 9 5 2
                              ♣ Q J 5 4 2
</pre>

West	North	East	South
	1♣	pass	1♠
pass	1NT	pass	2♣
all pass			

East is on lead with a choice between the red suits. What he knows from the bidding is that dummy probably has a singleton or void in one of them, as he's taken his side out of the highest-paying contract to a lowly minor suit. North has indicated a balanced minimum hand with his rebid. If he has a second suit, it will be hearts since he hasn't opened 1◇ in the first place.

When the opponents are in a partscore contract, your side will have close to half the points and because of that, an attacking lead will often bear fruit. Here, a diamond lead will result in the maximum number of the tricks for the defense, as you will collect an immediate three winners plus another two in the trump suit

A heart lead, though, will not fare as well. Declarer will gratefully pitch all three diamonds on his ♡AKQ and wind up losing just the ace and king of clubs, making five.

2.   N-S vulnerable

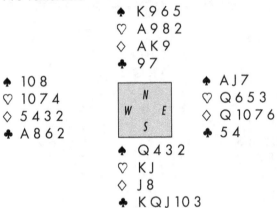

♠ K 9 6 5
♡ A 9 8 2
◇ A K 9
♣ 9 7

♠ 10 8
♡ 10 7 4
◇ 5 4 3 2
♣ A 8 6 2

♠ A J 7
♡ Q 6 5 3
◇ Q 10 7 6
♣ 5 4

♠ Q 4 3 2
♡ K J
◇ J 8
♣ K Q J 10 3

Normal auction	
North	**South**
	1♣
1♡	1♠
4♠	pass

'Shooting' auction	
North	**South**
	1♣
3NT	pass

The auction on the left has responder bidding his majors up the line, and getting to his side's 4-4 spade fit once partner rebids in that major.

If you are in need of a top board to improve your chances of winning, one way of trying for it is to ignore the major suits altogether and bid 3NT, ostensibly showing 13-15 points and denying major-suit length. With a double stopper in the unbid minor, you are gambling that notrump will have the same number of tricks as either major suit.

You're right this time, but it could have easily been the wrong decision. For example, if South has ♠QJ32 and ♣KQ1043 instead, a notrump contract is considerably worse than 4♠.

3. N-S vulnerable

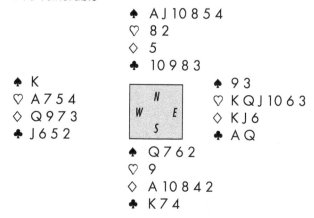

	♠ A J 10 8 5 4	
	♡ 8 2	
	◇ 5	
	♣ 10 9 8 3	
♠ K		♠ 9 3
♡ A 7 5 4	N	♡ K Q J 10 6 3
◇ Q 9 7 3	W E	◇ K J 6
♣ J 6 5 2	S	♣ A Q
	♠ Q 7 6 2	
	♡ 9	
	◇ A 10 8 4 2	
	♣ K 7 4	

West	North	East	South
pass	2♠	3♡	3♠
4♡	pass	pass	4♠
pass	pass	dbl	all pass

Hey, I only collect these deals and report the bidding that actually occurred. North really did open 2♠ on that broken suit at adverse colors.

East's 3♡ overcall is natural. South realized that 4♠ was a possible make for his side, but that if he went there immediately, his LHO had ample trump support and was likely to bid 5♡. Hence his decision to 'walk the dog' with 3♠ and then bid on after West raised partner to 4♡, trying to appear forlorn and reluctant.

Perhaps West should have smelled a rat and continued to the five-level in hearts, but he passed and then East, with quite a few potential losers and what appeared to be good defensive prospects, doubled. He found out to his chagrin that 4♠ made, losing only a heart and two clubs. Meanwhile, 5♡ would have been a good save, as the defense gets two pointed aces, a diamond ruff and an eventual club for -500. That's if the opponents find a double, which is a stretch for either member of the North-South partnership.

4.   Neither vulnerable

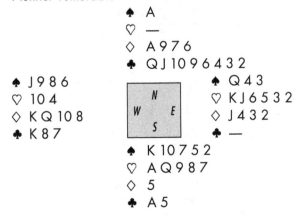

```
                        ♠ A
                        ♡ —
                        ◇ A 9 7 6
                        ♣ Q J 10 9 6 4 3 2
    ♠ J 9 8 6                          ♠ Q 4 3
    ♡ 10 4              N              ♡ K J 6 5 3 2
    ◇ K Q 10 8      W       E          ◇ J 4 3 2
    ♣ K 8 7              S              ♣ —
                        ♠ K 10 7 5 2
                        ♡ A Q 9 8 7
                        ◇ 5
                        ♣ A 5
```

West	North	East	South
	1♣	1♡	pass
1NT	2♣	pass	3NT
all pass			

Granted, opener showed an unbalanced hand with extra club length, but then again he didn't jump to 3♣ so he doesn't have a ton of extras point-wise.

South's jump to 3NT after his initial pass can only mean one thing: he was hoping for a re-opening double from partner because he has length and strength in the heart suit.

If West recognizes the signals from the auction, he should know this is not the time to be leading partner's suit, especially since he has a viable alternative with his good diamond holding. Leading a top diamond will hold them to nine tricks as he'll get in with the ♣K to cash three more tricks in that suit. On a heart lead, declarer will make the contract with one or two overtricks.

5. Both vulnerable

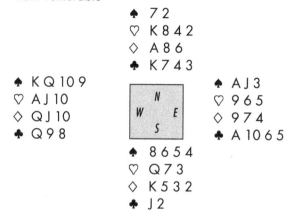

♠ 7 2
♡ K 8 4 2
♢ A 8 6
♣ K 7 4 3

♠ K Q 10 9
♡ A J 10
♢ Q J 10
♣ Q 9 8

♠ A J 3
♡ 9 6 5
♢ 9 7 4
♣ A 10 6 5

♠ 8 6 5 4
♡ Q 7 3
♢ K 5 3 2
♣ J 2

West	North	East	South
			pass
1NT	pass	2NT	pass
?			

One of my favorite partners (my wife) once told me that when partner invited in notrump and she had a hand right in the middle of her range, she would accept if she had fewer than three cards below the eight in rank.

Well, this hand is 'only' 15 HCP, but *all* the spot cards are tens, nines and eights. Will that feature of the hand suffice to accept and bid game?

If you are in the early stages of the event or are rolling along nicely, you'll be going slightly against the field of point-counters if you do make the commitment. That said, it looks to be quite a juicy assortment of cards and I wouldn't fault opener if he went for the jackpot. If his score requires a boost in the form of a great result, this would be the perfect time to try for it.

If North leads either rounded suit, that makes life easier for declarer. But he can develop tricks on his own, with the club suit being his focus. He can pass the ♣9 to South's jack and then repeat the finesse on the next round of the suit, ending up with three club winners to go with four spades and two or three more tricks in diamonds and hearts.

6. E-W vulnerable

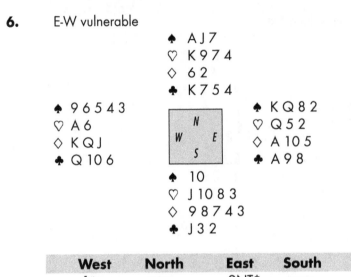

♠ A J 7
♡ K 9 7 4
◇ 6 2
♣ K 7 5 4

♠ 9 6 5 4 3
♡ A 6
◇ K Q J
♣ Q 10 6

♠ K Q 8 2
♡ Q 5 2
◇ A 10 5
♣ A 9 8

♠ 10
♡ J 10 8 3
◇ 9 8 7 4 3
♣ J 3 2

West	North	East	South
1♠	pass	2NT*	pass
4♠	all pass		

Here you're on lead after responder has shown a game-forcing raise and opener has jumped to 4♠, showing a minimum hand with no shortness.

Coming up with the right answer on this deal is a matter of simply doing your math. Even if the opponents are rock-bottom for their bids and have a combined point-count of 25 or 26, your 11 points only leaves room in partner's hand for 3 or 4, if that. With that information at your disposal, this is no time to be getting aggressive with your lead. Since you have the potential for a second winner in the trump suit, the ◇6 from your worthless doubleton is likely to be the least costly of your four options.

You aren't going to be defeating their contract here regardless of what you lead, but the diamond should hold declarer to ten tricks. Once he has drawn trumps, he will have to play on the rounded suits himself and whichever one he gives you a trick in, you will just play the suit back and wait to eventually take your other king.

As you can see, a heart or club lead will be futile and declarer will make his game with an overtrick. Compare the first quiz deal, where the opponents were in a partscore and partner was a favorite to hold at least some high cards; that definitely isn't going to be the case here and the opening leader has to curb his ambitions to a certain extent.

7.   Neither vulnerable

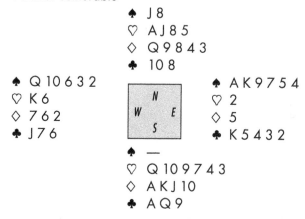

	♠ J 8	
	♡ A J 8 5	
	◇ Q 9 8 4 3	
	♣ 10 8	

♠ Q 10 6 3 2   ♠ A K 9 7 5 4
♡ K 6   ♡ 2
◇ 7 6 2   ◇ 5
♣ J 7 6   ♣ K 5 4 3 2

	♠ —	
	♡ Q 10 9 7 4 3	
	◇ A K J 10	
	♣ A Q 9	

West	North	East	South
			1♡
pass	3♣¹	3♠	4◇
4♠	5◇	5♠	6♡
all pass			

1. Bergen raise.

There are some auctions where you don't want to be too revealing about your distribution, but on this deal you have several good reasons for introducing the diamond suit. Even though responder has a maximum of 9 HCP, if his values are in the right places you may have a slam your way. When the opponents are in possession of the highest-ranked suit and are likely to keep on bidding, you want to involve North in the process and have him assess his red-suit holdings. Also, a 4◇ continuation definitively confirms the deal belongs to your side and, if East-West don't go quietly, one of you will have to double or bid on.

If opener shows his distribution, North-South will reach the promised land as responder will confirm the double fit by bidding 5◇ after West bids 4♠. Regardless of whether East bids 5♠ or passes, South has enough information to bid the slam. West is not going to take the 6♠ sacrifice as he has a potential trick with the ♡K, and East may also pass and try to beat the slam rather than be a hero.

If opener keeps woodenly bidding the hearts, the opponents will do the same with their spade fit and South can't do much other than double 5♠, not knowing whether 6♡ will have a play.

8.   N-S vulnerable

	♠ K 10 9 3
	♡ 6 4 3
	◇ A Q 10 3
	♣ 9 6

♠ 7		♠ —
♡ Q 10 7 2	N	♡ K 9 8 5
◇ K J 9 8 7 2	W E	◇ 6 5
♣ 8 7	S	♣ A K Q J 5 4 2

	♠ A Q J 8 6 5 4 2
	♡ A J
	◇ 4
	♣ 10 3

West	North	East	South
	pass	1♣	4♠
pass	pass	5♣	pass
pass	5♠	all pass	

After partner's initial pass, South can assume there is no chance for slam and he therefore goes directly to 4♠ over RHO's opening bid.

East's 5♣ has two ways to pay off for his side. West could have enough values for that contract to make, but even if it goes down, the opponents might be cold for their game.

West is under the spotlight when 5♠ comes back around to him, with three plausible choices. He can double, assuming the deal belongs to his side, bid 6♣ if he thinks 5♠ their way is a make, or pass. Bidding on is something not many people would do at matchpoints when partner has opened the bidding and then taken further action at the five-level, so it comes down to pass or double.

West has one key piece of information to guide him. After having bid 5♣, East failed to double when North pushed on to 5♠. That suggests his action was based primarily on offensive values rather than quick tricks on defense. Therefore, East-West are not going to beat 5♠ a lot, if at all.

Against the final contract, the defense takes two clubs and switches to a heart. Declarer will then have to guess whether to finesse in diamonds to get rid of his heart loser, or assume that opener has the king of that suit. If no one has doubled, he might well play a diamond to the ace, ruff a diamond, go back to dummy in the trump suit and trump a third diamond, hoping the king will fall.

If West has doubled, nothing really justifies that other than holding a red-suit king, and South might be inclined to go with the straight finesse, which is the path to success on this deal.

10
Final Quiz

The final chapter will consist of twenty-seven quiz hands, as if you were playing in a one-session pairs game (although since these are deals taken from real life, the rotation of vulnerability from board to board won't mirror an actual game). You'll have a variety of challenges to face, most of them in bidding but some in defense and declarer play as well.

You're assumed to be playing 2/1 with 15-17 notrump as your system. If the opponents interfere over your 1NT opening, negative doubles are in effect. In some of the problems, we'll give you some additional bells and whistles for your convention card.

Depending on table counts, most pairs games consist of rounds of two or three boards. For this chapters, let's assume nine rounds of three boards each, and I will present the problems in groups of three. On each board you will be South, and you'll be asked to decide on a bid and/or play. Then I will discuss that group of hands, after which you'll move on to the next round. When you see the entire deal, you'll often find out that several players will have had a choice of bids during the auction phase.

So here we go.

Round 1
Board 1 Both vulnerable.

♠ 10 8 5 ♡ Q 5 4 3 ◇ A K 9 6 4 ♣ Q

West	North	East	South
	1♡	1♠	?

Which of the following options do you prefer?

    a) A simple 2◇?
    b) A fit-showing jump to 3◇?
    c) A 4♣ splinter raise?
    d) 4♡?
    e) A 2♠ cuebid?

Board 2   Neither vulnerable.

♠ A K J 7 6 4   ♡ K 3   ◇ Q J   ♣ 6 5 2

Your side has a free run, as the bidding goes:

West	North	East	South
		pass	1♠
pass	2◇	pass	2♠
pass	3♣	pass	3NT
pass	4NT	pass	?

Partner's 4NT was quantitative, inviting slam. Do you pass or go on? If the latter, what is your bid?

Board 3   Now you get to play a hand. After a straight 1NT – 3NT auction, West leads the ♡3 (fourth best):

> ♠ K 7 4
> ♡ A 8
> ◇ J 10 6 3 2
> ♣ Q 10 6
>
> ▬▬▬▬
>
> ♠ A J 2
> ♡ K 10 9 2
> ◇ A 7
> ♣ K 7 5 3

You play low from dummy and take RHO's jack with your king. What's your plan for getting to nine or more tricks?

Round 1 Discussion

Board 1

Both vulnerable

```
                      ♠ A
                      ♡ A K 10 9 8 6 2
                      ◇ 3 2
                      ♣ 10 7 3
♠ Q 7 4 3                              ♠ K J 9 6 2
♡ J 7              ┌─────────┐         ♡ —
◇ 10 7 5          │    N    │         ◇ Q J 8
♣ J 9 8 2         │ W     E │         ♣ A K 6 5 4
                  │    S    │
                  └─────────┘
                      ♠ 10 8 5
                      ♡ Q 5 4 3
                      ◇ A K 9 6 4
                      ♣ Q
```

West	North	East	South
pass	1♡	1♠	3◇
pass	3♠	pass	4♣
pass	4NT	pass	5♣
pass	6♡	all pass	

East might have gone with a Michaels cuebid of 2♡, but most players will not take that action with medium-strength hands. The prevailing wisdom is that Michaels should be used when the overcaller is 'mini' (less than 12 HCP) or 'maxi' (close to game-forcing). Moreover, the hand is playable in diamonds if partner has length in that suit.

South's hand is much too good for a distributional raise to 4♡, with a side suit headed by the ace-king along with shortness in clubs. Yet a 2◇ bid is vulnerable to LHO vigorously raising spades, in which case you might not be able to communicate all the features of your hand to opener. It comes down, then, to a 2♠ cuebid, a fit-showing jump of 3◇ or a splinter raise of 4♣. I think the quality of the diamond suit takes precedence for now over the club short-ness. However, the cuebid is also a viable option, since the hand contains both offensive values and defensive tricks. Fit-showing jumps have a wider range point-wise and don't have to be this rich in high cards.

Opener is minimum in high cards, and as we've mentioned earlier, you don't generally want to go looking for marginal games or slams at pairs. However, if the bidding has revealed some attractive distributional features, it can't hurt to look if you aren't jeopardizing a plus. Here, opener knows that his side has an eleven-card fit and that partner has at least five good diamonds, and he himself has both first- and second-round control in spades.

Since he is always going to bid at least game, he might as well try a 3♠ cuebid along the way and see if that gets any kind of reaction from South.

For responder, that is just what the doctor ordered as he can now launch into RKCB with 4NT. Partner shows 0 or 3 keycards with 5♦ (presumably three) and the slam is duly reached. Technically, in RKCB auctions where the reply is 1/4 or 0/3 and the asker signs off, the other player is expected to keep going with the greater number of keycards.

Board 2

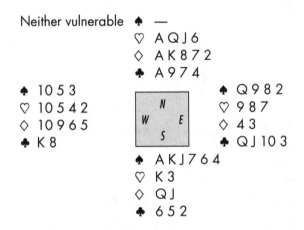

Neither vulnerable

North:
- ♠ —
- ♡ A Q J 6
- ◇ A K 8 7 2
- ♣ A 9 7 4

West:
- ♠ 10 5 3
- ♡ 10 5 4 2
- ◇ 10 9 6 5
- ♣ K 8

East:
- ♠ Q 9 8 2
- ♡ 9 8 7
- ◇ 4 3
- ♣ Q J 10 3

South:
- ♠ A K J 7 6 4
- ♡ K 3
- ◇ Q J
- ♣ 6 5 2

West	North	East	South
		pass	1♠
pass	2◇	pass	2♠
pass	3♣	pass	3NT
pass	4NT	pass	6NT
all pass			

On his second turn, North introduces clubs as his second suit because opener hasn't mentioned hearts but may have club length to go with his spades. A few players might take a 3◇ preference on the South cards, but most are apt to bid 3NT at this juncture.

From North's point of view, he does not force to slam as he has a void in partner's major, and there is no eight-card fit in sight. But with 18 HCP, he has enough to invite with a quantitative 4NT. This is not RKCB, as no fit has been agreed and partner's last bid was in notrump.

Opener doesn't have much extra with his 14 HCP, but he should go on to slam. The reason is that North is certain to have five or more diamonds, and the QJ doubleton in partner's suit is a great holding. At this point, he could offer a choice of slams with 6◇ or just bid to the highest-paying contract of

6NT. The form of scoring dictates the latter action. Here, 6NT has twelve winners off the top with five diamonds, four hearts and three black suit tricks.

There's probably not a whole lot of difference in how the bidding would go at teams, as responder would be leery about the potential misfit despite his wealth of high cards. At matchpoints, North-South will go for the highest-paying contract, but even at IMPs, they might play the contract in notrump rather than the minor suit, giving declarer the opportunity to test other suits in case the diamond split is foul.

Board 3

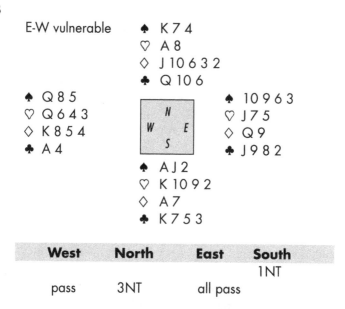

E-W vulnerable

North: ♠ K 7 4 ♡ A 8 ◇ J 10 6 3 2 ♣ Q 10 6

West: ♠ Q 8 5 ♡ Q 6 4 3 ◇ K 8 5 4 ♣ A 4

East: ♠ 10 9 6 3 ♡ J 7 5 ◇ Q 9 ♣ J 9 8 2

South: ♠ A J 2 ♡ K 10 9 2 ◇ A 7 ♣ K 7 5 3

West	North	East	South
			1NT
pass	3NT	all pass	

You play low from dummy since the heart lead guarantees you three tricks in that suit. That gets you up to seven eventual winners: three hearts, two spades, a club and a diamond. The suit that offers the best shot at two more is diamonds. How should you go about playing that suit?

If they divide 3-3, it won't matter what you do as they'll all come tumbling down on the third round. What if you get the more likely split of 4-2? You can still prevail if the player with the short diamonds has an honor. First lay down the ace and then play a low diamond from each hand. East wins the queen and continues hearts, which is taken with dummy's ace. Now comes the ◇J, forcing the king. West cashes a heart but South now has nine tricks in the form of three each in hearts and diamonds, two in spades and an eventual club.

You would expect nine tricks in 3NT to be an average score, as it is a normal contract. However, such is not the case, as the results are:

North-South	+430	1 pair
	+400	5 pairs
	–50	4 pairs
	–150	1 pair

You might find this a bit surprising, but there were some declarers who only took the 3-3 split in the diamond suit into account. They didn't look further into the hand and realize that the contract is also makeable against a 4-2 break with a doubleton honor in the short hand. Although 3NT is a normal contract that was reached at every table, some declarers went down because they didn't play the diamond suit to best advantage, so +400 was a decent score.

Round 2

Board 4 You've been dealt this mundane collection, with neither side vulnerable:

♠ K J 6 5 ♡ K 8 7 5 ♢ 7 2 ♣ A 6 5

The story thus far has been:

West	North	East	South
1♢	pass	1NT	?

Do you pass or venture a takeout double?

Board 5 With the opponents vulnerable, you are looking at this hand:

♠ J 10 8 ♡ K Q ♢ A J 10 5 ♣ A J 4 2

This question consists of two parts. The auction has gone:

West	North	East	South
			1NT
pass	2♢*	2♠	pass
pass	dbl	pass	?

Partner's double is value-showing rather than straight penalty. You can expect him to have somewhere between 7 and 9 points. With less than that, responder would have passed and with more, he would have bid game. Are you going to sit for the double? If not, what action do you take?

We'll now assume that you've gone for the gusto by leaving the double in, hoping for +200 or better against the vulnerable opponents. Your lead was the ♡K and this is the dummy that greeted you:

Dummy
♠ 4 3
♡ 10 6 3
◇ K 9 6 3
♣ K 10 7 5

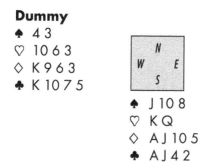

♠ J 10 8
♡ K Q
◇ A J 10 5
♣ A J 4 2

It's a bit of a downer, as dummy has the minor-suit kings sitting over your aces. Partner encourages on the first round of hearts. How should you continue the defense?

Board 6   How confident have you been with your decisions so far? Of course, you're not going to have any breathers as you've been dealt these cards:

♠ Q 10 9 6 4 2   ♡ J 9 6   ◇ 8 4   ♣ A 4

Partner has spared you the temptation of opening a weak two-bid:

West	North	East	South
	1NT	pass	2♡*
pass	2♠	pass	?

Are you content to settle in a partscore or do you think the hand is worth a game try?

Round 2 Discussion

Board 4

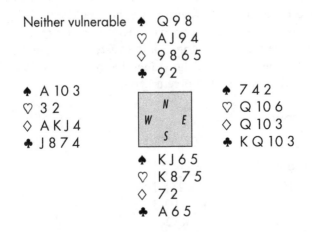

Neither vulnerable

North
- ♠ Q 9 8
- ♡ A J 9 4
- ◇ 9 8 6 5
- ♣ 9 2

West
- ♠ A 10 3
- ♡ 3 2
- ◇ A K J 4
- ♣ J 8 7 4

East
- ♠ 7 4 2
- ♡ Q 10 6
- ◇ Q 10 3
- ♣ K Q 10 3

South
- ♠ K J 6 5
- ♡ K 8 7 5
- ◇ 7 2
- ♣ A 6 5

West	North	East	South
1◇	pass	1NT	dbl
pass	2♡	pass	pass
3♣	all pass		

South has a rather motley 11-count, but the takeout double is justified by his having 4-4 in the major suits and his side being non-vulnerable. Also, defending 1NT is seldom a good result in a pairs game.

If South had passed, opener would have left the contract in notrump, the highest-paying spot for his side. After the double, an immediate 2♣ bid is an option as he knows the opponents have an eight-card or better fit in hearts. Here he passes, reserving his decision for later. When North bids hearts and responder fails to double, West then competes with his other minor and 3♣ becomes the final contract.

Let's check out the fate of the three contracts. East's 1NT probably gets a spade lead from South and once declarer takes his ace, he'll go after the club suit for extra tricks. The defenders will score three spades, two hearts and the ace of clubs, as E-W will stagger home with seven tricks and +90. Meanwhile, 2♡ by North will also make on the nose as he'll lose a spade, two diamonds, a club and a heart.

Against 3♣ by West, North likely tables the ♡A on the first trick and shifts to a spade when he sees dummy. The defense will then collect two tricks in each major and the ♣A. So both 2NT and 3♣ would be down one. The results on this board, not unexpectedly, are all over the place. When the South hand made the light takeout double, his side went plus, either declaring hearts or defeating the enemy contract. Otherwise, East-West typically ended up in 1NT or a club partscore, making each time.

Board 5

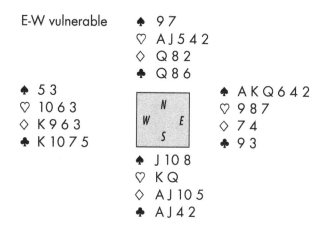

	West	North	East	South
				1NT
	pass	2◇*	2♠	pass
	pass	dbl	pass	?

East's 2♠ is somewhat risky at unfavorable colors, but with his suit being so good he is not expecting to get doubled and certainly would like partner to lead spades. Responder's double merely says he has invitational values rather than the very weak hand he might have had for his transfer bid. Since he is 'under' the overcaller, North's action is more takeout than penalty, and he could have either one or two cards in the enemy suit. Any of these hands would qualify:

♠A7 ♡109542 ◇KJ2 ♣865
♠97 ♡AJ542 ◇Q82 ♣Q86
♠7 ♡A10542 ◇J975 ♣K106

If responder is in possession of the first hand, your side will score very well defending the opponents' 2♠ contract. With the last example, you'll own the majority of the high-card points, but they will have a nine-card fit and it will be touch-and-go to manage enough tricks to beat them. The middle hand is what North actually had, where your expectation will be a one- or two-trick set.

Opener doesn't have a sure trump trick, but knows his side has East-West outgunned in high cards and they are vulnerable, so he passes in the hope of getting +200 or better. If the colors were different and the opponents were not vulnerable, he'd be more inclined to head towards a minor-suit contract.

This deal is all about making it easy for partner. South leads the ♡K, which wins the first trick. He should then cash *both* minor-suit aces and only then continue with the ♡Q. North at this point should know partner has a doubleton heart (since he hasn't pulled the double to 3♡). He therefore overtakes with the ace, cashes the jack and then plays a fourth round of hearts. South will ruff if declarer discards, and if East ruffs high, that builds a trump trick for his J10x. The defense just manages to score a one-trick set.

As you can see from this and other deals in this book, matchpoints is not for the faint of heart. At pairs and with the opponents vulnerable, North-South were willing to risk the contract making a fraction of the time as there was a good chance for +200 or better and a likely top. At teams, it's unlikely the auction would have gone the same way.

Board 6

N-S vulnerable

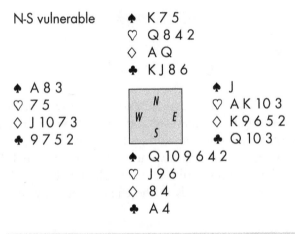

	♠ K 7 5	
	♡ Q 8 4 2	
	◇ A Q	
	♣ K J 8 6	

♠ A 8 3		♠ J
♡ 7 5		♡ A K 10 3
◇ J 10 7 3		◇ K 9 6 5 2
♣ 9 7 5 2		♣ Q 10 3

	♠ Q 10 9 6 4 2	
	♡ J 9 6	
	◇ 8 4	
	♣ A 4	

West	North	East	South
	1NT	pass	2♡*
pass	2♠	pass	?

East has a decent enough hand but passes because of the vulnerability and because his side was using Cappelletti as their defense to a 1NT opening. He would have had to treat his hand as a diamond one-suiter and his suit was not all that robust. If they had been playing DONT, he could have bid 2◇ to show that minor and a higher-ranking suit.

At any rate, South transfers to spades and then needs to decide whether to pass or invite. As you'll recall from an earlier chapter, this is a basic application of the 4-point principle. He has an eight-loser hand and, even with the expected four 'dream cards' from partner, that will leave his side a trick short of game. As it turns out, an invitational raise to 3♠ would result in a minus as the defense cashes two hearts followed by a heart ruff and a diamond shift, holding declarer to eight tricks.

This is an excellent illustration of the difference between matchpoints and teams. At the latter form of the game, South might have invited because at teams, even a game that is in the 35-40% range is worth bidding if your side is vulnerable. But at pairs, any time you go minus it won't be a good result as the field will likely settle in partscore.

Round 3

Board 7 This time you have a better hand with both sides vulnerable:

♠ A K 10 9 2   ♡ A 5   ◇ A 4 2   ♣ Q 9 6

You are first to speak. Would you open 1♠ or 1NT?

If you open 1♠, the auction will then go:

West	North	East	South
			1♠
2◇	2♠	pass	?

Do you pass, bid game or try for game? If you were to look for game, how would you do it?

Finally, let's say your side reaches a 4♠ contract on the ◇K lead. When dummy comes down, you see:

♠ Q J 8
♡ J 9 8 6 4
◇ 10 3
♣ K 10 3
―――――
♠ A K 10 9 2
♡ A 5
◇ A 4 2
♣ Q 9 6

What line of play do you take to try and bring the contract home?

Board 8   With both sides vulnerable, the quality of your hand has severely diminished for this one:

♠ 7   ♡ 9 7 2   ◇ A 8 5 4   ♣ J 9 6 5 2

Partner opens 1♠. With this 5-count that includes an ace, do you respond?

Board 9   Now for a deal that takes an unexpected turn in the bidding. The opponents are vulnerable and you hold:

♠ Q J 8 2   ♡ A J 5 3   ◇ 6 2   ♣ K 8 7

The auction has proceeded:

West	North	East	South
1◇	pass	1NT	dbl
all pass			

Your partner doesn't seem to realize your double was for takeout and has left it in. Or does he know what he's doing? And what is your lead?

Round 3 Discussion

Board 7

Both vulnerable

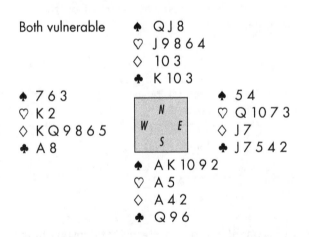

	♠ Q J 8
	♡ J 9 8 6 4
	◇ 10 3
	♣ K 10 3

♠ 7 6 3   ♠ 5 4
♡ K 2   ♡ Q 10 7 3
◇ K Q 9 8 6 5   ◇ J 7
♣ A 8   ♣ J 7 5 4 2

♠ A K 10 9 2
♡ A 5
◇ A 4 2
♣ Q 9 6

West	North	East	South
			1♠
2◇	2♠	pass	3♣
Pass	4♠	all pass	

With 17 HCP and a five-card suit, South judges his hand to be too strong for a 1NT opening and starts out with 1♠. After LHO overcalls and partner raises, he then makes a help-suit game try with 3♣, as the queen of that suit is his only 'soft' high card. North has a minimum hand for his 2♠ bid, but that doesn't matter as his black-suit holdings are excellent and he should carry on to game. West leads the ◊K against 4♠.

Aside from a certain loser in the heart suit, declarer has some work to do in each of the minors. He can ruff a diamond loser, and should make certain to use a high spade as it's entirely possible the overcall was made on a six-card suit. After that is done, he needs to hold the clubs to one loser. For his bid, West will likely have the ♣A. But the play of the diamond and trump suits will reveal nine of his cards, with only four left in hearts and clubs. That makes it more likely for the ♣J to be in the East hand.

Bidding and making game will be a near-top, as there are two possible divergences in the auction for the rest of the field. If South opens 1NT, responder will place the contract in 2♡ regardless of what his RHO does. And even if the bidding does start as shown above, North with his threadbare hand might decline the game try.

Board 8

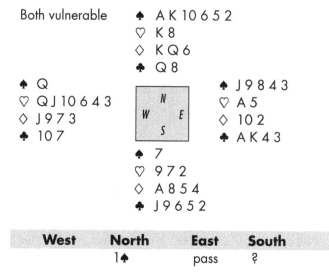

Both vulnerable	♠ A K 10 6 5 2
	♡ K 8
	◊ K Q 6
	♣ Q 8

♠ Q   ♠ J 9 8 4 3
♡ Q J 10 6 4 3   ♡ A 5
◊ J 9 7 3   ◊ 10 2
♣ 10 7   ♣ A K 4 3

            ♠ 7
            ♡ 9 7 2
            ◊ A 8 5 4
            ♣ J 9 6 5 2

West	North	East	South
	1♠	pass	?

The general feeling amongst experts is that if responder has 5 points that include an ace, he should dredge up a bid when partner opens. I'm mostly on board with that sentiment, but when the hand completely lacks support for either major, I lean towards a pass.

What is the field likely to do with this hand? My guess is that a majority of players would respond, but the split would be around 60-40 between the options of bidding and passing. So it boils down to whatever your gut feeling is. Whatever your decision is, it won't end up being an awful result.

If South responds 1NT, opener as you can see will jump to 3♠. East at this point might double for penalty. He will cash two high clubs plus the ♡A, and then play a third round of clubs. Partner will ruff with the ♠Q to promote extra trump tricks, and the contract will be down at least two.

If South passes, West is close to being able to balance with 2♡ in passout seat, but with no ace or king he'll reluctantly hold his tongue.

Board 9

E-W vulnerable

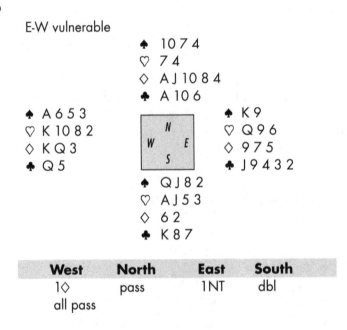

```
                    ♠ 10 7 4
                    ♡ 7 4
                    ♢ A J 10 8 4
                    ♣ A 10 6
  ♠ A 6 5 3                        ♠ K 9
  ♡ K 10 8 2         N            ♡ Q 9 6
  ♢ K Q 3       W         E       ♢ 9 7 5
  ♣ Q 5             S            ♣ J 9 4 3 2
                    ♠ Q J 8 2
                    ♡ A J 5 3
                    ♢ 6 2
                    ♣ K 8 7
```

West	North	East	South
1♢	pass	1NT	dbl
all pass			

This is another deal where South has both majors but a hand in the range of 10-11 points. Once again, the vulnerability is in his favor, so he goes with a takeout double.

Both of my expert consultants, Andy and Keith, like to say, 'Please take out my takeout doubles'. North would normally do so, especially if his hand were weak. The fact that he has left in the double of 1NT would seem to indicate:

- He has a respectable number of points and figures the contract can be defeated, and...
- His long suit is diamonds.

There are two reasonable leads for South to make. In practice, either a spade or a diamond will defeat the contract handily. A diamond is best, as North can establish four tricks in the suit with the ♣A as an entry. If the lead is a spade, South has to go up on the first round of clubs and shift to a diamond at that point.

Garnering a significant plus against 1NT doubled won't be a common occurrence. In fact, only a few Souths competed at their turn, and East-West got to play 1NT, sometimes getting a heart lead which improved the chances of making it.

Round 4

Board 10 You now find yourself on play. With your side vulnerable, you've picked up:

♠ A Q 8 5 3   ♡ J 8   ◇ J 6 4   ♣ K Q 9

There has been an initial flurry of bidding that quickly subsided:

West	North	East	South
1♣	pass	1◇	1♠
pass	2♠	all pass	

The lead from West is the ◇K and partner tables this dummy:

♠ 9 7 2
♡ 10 7 6 4
◇ A 9 2
♣ A 8 6

♠ A Q 8 5 3
♡ J 8
◇ J 6 4
♣ K Q 9

Do you think the contract is makeable? And what rates to be the best line of play?

Board 11 You're on play again for our next deal. Your hand consists of:

♠ K 4   ♡ K Q 2   ◇ A Q 8 2   ♣ Q J 10 7

The auction has gone:

West	North	East	South
2♡	pass	pass	2NT
pass	3♣	pass	3◇
pass	3NT	all pass	

When you're in balancing chair, the range for the notrump bids depends on the level. You should add roughly 3 HCP for each level. A 1NT bid in passout seat is normally agreed upon as 11-14. When the opponents have got in your face with a weak two-bid, South's 2NT bid here would be 14 to 17. Having regaled you with that piece of information, let's look at what dummy has to offer:

♠ A Q 9 3
♡ 8 5
◇ K J 6
♣ A 9 8 6

♠ K 4
♡ K Q 2
◇ A Q 8 2
♣ Q J 10 7

The lead is the ♡7 as East puts up the ten. There could be a lot of tricks to be had if the ♣K is sitting nicely. What is your line of play?

Board 12 With the opponents vulnerable you have:

♠ 5 4 3   ♡ A   ◇ Q 10 7 4 2   ♣ Q 6 5 4

West	North	East	South
			pass
pass	1◇	dbl	?

What is your choice of level in advertising diamond support?

Round 4 Discussion

Board 10

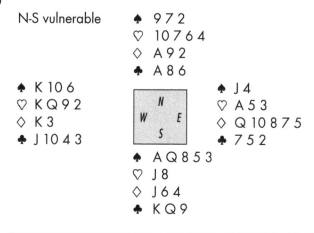

N-S vulnerable

North:
♠ 9 7 2
♡ 10 7 6 4
◇ A 9 2
♣ A 8 6

West:
♠ K 10 6
♡ K Q 9 2
◇ K 3
♣ J 10 4 3

East:
♠ J 4
♡ A 5 3
◇ Q 10 8 7 5
♣ 7 5 2

South:
♠ A Q 8 5 3
♡ J 8
◇ J 6 4
♣ K Q 9

West	North	East	South
1♣	pass	1◇	1♠
pass	2♠	all pass	

If you gave the East hand to a group of people, you'd likely receive votes for both 1◇ and 1NT as the response. Bidding 1◇ allows a pass if partner rebids 1♡ and a reluctant 1NT if he continues with 1♠. On the flip side, 1NT makes it difficult for South to compete in a major suit if he is so inclined.

West has the option of bidding 1NT at his second turn. Since partner has responded and opener's action would be at the one-level, it would be his normal rebid showing a minimum balanced hand. Since West has an aceless twelve-count, he elects to pass and that is also reasonable.

Sometimes the most innocuous deals can produce a terrible result. Upon getting the ◇K lead, declarer took the ace and finessed in spades. West won and played another diamond, getting his ruff as partner played the ten-spot, suit preference for the higher-ranking side suit. West cashed his ♡K and played another one to the ace, whereupon East played a fourth round of diamonds and no matter what declarer played, another trump had to be lost.

Let's take this step by step for South. Although you generally want to play for overtricks in a pairs game, sometimes the evidence from the bidding and the lead can serve as a warning sign. The opening lead appears to be a doubleton. West can't have all the top heart honors as he hasn't led one; that being the case, he doesn't have the values for his bid unless he has the ♠K. Also, to have enough points to respond, East has to have one heart honor. It is futile, then, to try for extra tricks as all it will accomplish is possibly going down. Upon winning the first trick, declarer should just play ace and another spade. If West's king were doubleton, he would lose just the one trump trick.

As it is, he'll lose a second spade but not a third. He can reach dummy with the ♣A later to play a diamond towards his jack. All he'll lose is two spades, two hearts and the ◇Q, making eight tricks on the nose.

Board 11

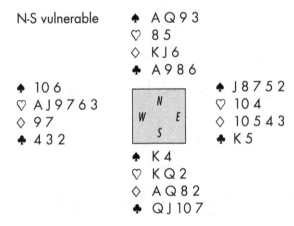

```
                                    ♠ A Q 9 3
     N-S vulnerable                 ♡ 8 5
                                    ◇ K J 6
                                    ♣ A 9 8 6
     ♠ 10 6                                        ♠ J 8 7 5 2
     ♡ A J 9 7 6 3          N                      ♡ 10 4
     ◇ 9 7              W       E                   ◇ 10 5 4 3
     ♣ 4 3 2                S                       ♣ K 5
                                    ♠ K 4
                                    ♡ K Q 2
                                    ◇ A Q 8 2
                                    ♣ Q J 10 7
```

West	North	East	South
2♡	pass	pass	2NT
pass	3♣	pass	3◇
pass	3NT	all pass	

North's 3♣ was Stayman, asking for a four-card major, which South denied. Personally, I would have doubled for takeout initially on the North cards, but he felt that the hand wasn't quite robust enough.

West leads the ♡6 as East puts up the ten. Making the contract is not going to be a problem as declarer has a heart, three spades, four diamonds and a club off the top. Moreover, if the ♣K is in West's hand, then he can take a finesse in the suit and win the first twelve tricks. It's quite possible that West has the ♣K for his 2♡ opening, but equally likely that he has nothing other than six hearts to the AJ. However, this is not an either-or hand where you risk the club finesse or settle for nine tricks. What you *can* do to guarantee at least one overtrick, and possibly two, is duck the first round of hearts entirely. East will continue a heart; West clears the suit with the ace and another as you win the third round. Now you can take the club finesse without any risk, as East is certain to be out of hearts.

This is a typical risk-reward scenario that is quite common in pairs games. By winning the first heart and playing on clubs, the reward is twelve tricks but the risk is down two. If you cash nine tricks, there is no risk but a minimal reward. Finally, if you duck the first heart and play an honor on the second round, it's a happy medium as you again have no risk but the reward is either ten or eleven tricks.

Board 12

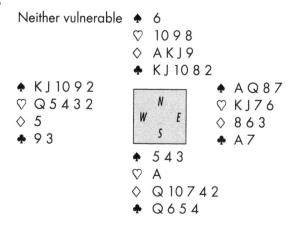

Neither vulnerable
```
                        ♠ 6
                        ♡ 10 9 8
                        ◇ A K J 9
                        ♣ K J 10 8 2

 ♠ K J 10 9 2                              ♠ A Q 8 7
 ♡ Q 5 4 3 2          N                    ♡ K J 7 6
 ◇ 5               W     E                 ◇ 8 6 3
 ♣ 9 3                   S                 ♣ A 7

                        ♠ 5 4 3
                        ♡ A
                        ◇ Q 10 7 4 2
                        ♣ Q 6 5 4
```

West	North	East	South
			pass
pass	1◇	dbl	4◇
4♠	5◇	dbl	pass
5♡	pass	5♠	all pass

This is a dynamic deal, to say the least. The best opening salvo with the North hand is an issue that still has not been fully resolved, even among top-level players. Most of them, however, would open 1◇ rather than 1♣ to allow themselves a convenient rebid over a major-suit response.

Now let's move on to East's double. Even though he has only two clubs, more people than not would take that action nowadays because the hand has excellent support for the majors and full opening values. If partner bids clubs, you'll just have to live with it; if he has no major-suit length, he'll probably have five or more clubs.

Over to South, and the question of how vigorously he should support diamonds. On a side note, a partnership needs to discuss whether inverted minor-suit raises are on or off when the opponents double or overcall. Some pairs also elect to use a convention called 'flip-flop', whereby 2NT by responder over a double is the preemptive raise and a jump to 3◇ would be a hand like this. A simple raise to 2◇ after the interference is normally the basic 6-9 HCP, whereas a jump to 4◇ is also preemptive, but more so than the jump to the three-level.

Of our group of three, Andy raised to 2♦, Keith bid 3♦ and I went all the way to 4♦ with the extreme major-suit shortness. That suggests there would be not be much of a consensus even among a larger group of people.

Over 4♦, West with his 5-5 in the majors bids spades, the higher ranking (and better) of the two suits. Not vulnerable, opener realizes that East-West will probably make their contract. The question for him is whether to mention his second suit, which may be helpful to the opponents, or keep it under wraps and just bid 5♦.

East doubles as he has good defense outside spades and a balanced hand, but partner's hand is totally offensive in nature and he removes to 5♡. The doubler, with a better spade holding, converts back to that major.

North knows by this point that the opponents have a two-suited fit in the majors, and his side might not have all that many tricks to take when partner has made a preemptive raise. As for South, he will probably elect to defend once the opponents have been pushed to the five-level, since he has an ace, but he too might not double.

The curious aspect of this deal is that North-South were in sacrifice mode when they bid on to 5♦, but that contract turns out to make. East-West might have been bidding on in the major suits with some expectation of being successful in their contract, but actually they were the pair that was saving. The reality is sometimes different from the assumption, which can easily happen on high-level deals where each side has a double fit.

This deal is also an illustration of how coming in with a 'ballpark' hand rather than waiting for ideal distribution to compete is sometimes necessary for a pair to get its just due.

Round 5

Board 13 Vulnerable against not, you've picked up:

♠ Q 6 5 4 3 ♡ K J 10 4 2 ♦ K J 3 ♣ —

The auction has got high rather quickly:

West	North	East	South
	1NT	4♣	dbl
pass	4♡	pass	?

Partner's 1NT was 15-17. Your double of East's 4♣ was negative, showing both majors. Over North's 4♡, is a slam try in order or is it best to pass? If you make a move, what should it be?

Board 14 For your next challenge, your side is vulnerable and you have:

♠ A 10 7 6 4   ♡ 9   ◇ Q 10 7   ♣ A K J 7

You dealt, and the bidding so far has been:

West	North	East	South
			1♠
pass	2◇	pass	3♣
pass	3♠	pass	?

First of all, what do you think of the 3♣ rebid? Do you agree with it or would you have raised partner's diamonds immediately?

At this point, with partner having subsequently raised your major and shown at least mild slam interest, do you cooperate or just bid 4♠?

Board 15 Neither side is vulnerable and you are the owner of these cards:

♠ A Q J 10   ♡ 5   ◇ K 7 6 5 3   ♣ 9 5 4

You have two choices to make on this auction:

West	North	East	South
pass	1♡	2◇	?

This is a three-part question:

a) Do you make a negative double or pass for the time being, not making an immediate commitment towards defending or playing the hand?

b) If you pass, opener will come back in with a double. Do you convert it for penalties or bid the major? If the latter, how many spades would you be inclined to bid?

c) Finally, if you elect to defend 2◇ doubled, what is your lead?

Round 5 Discussion

Board 13

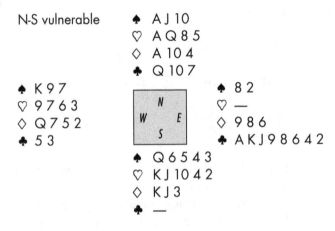

N-S vulnerable

	♠ A J 10
	♡ A Q 8 5
	◊ A 10 4
	♣ Q 10 7

♠ K 9 7		♠ 8 2
♡ 9 7 6 3		♡ —
◊ Q 7 5 2		◊ 9 8 6
♣ 5 3		♣ A K J 9 8 6 4 2

	♠ Q 6 5 4 3
	♡ K J 10 4 2
	◊ K J 3
	♣ —

West	North	East	South
	1NT	4♣	dbl
pass	4♡	pass	5♣
pass	5◊	pass	6♡
all pass			

The decision responder faces after partner bids 4♡ over the negative double is whether to try for slam. Can North have enough for it to have a play? And will your side be safe at the five-level if opener rejects a slam try?

According to the 4-point principle, slam could be decent if partner doesn't have too much wastage in the enemy suit. If you give him the ♠AK, the ♡A and the ◊A, you want to be in 6♡. However, if you make his four 'dream cards' the aces of your three suits and the ♡Q, there could be a problem in the spade suit as you would expect foul splits with East having eight or more clubs. In most cases, the five-level will probably be safe, so that is not a huge issue.

Whatever you do, you should not just bid slam as you need quite a lot from partner. Nor would a straight keycard ask do the trick as opener might have the ♣A, a card that would be useless for your purposes. The only sensible try is 5♣, cuebidding your void in the enemy suit. What you'd really like to get out of partner is a return cuebid of 5◊, at which point you can make the choice between going and stopping. Partner does indeed co-operate with 5◊, so you now take the plunge and bid the slam.

In 6♡, the lead will be a top club and the 4-0 trump split is an annoyance but it can be overcome. Declarer ruffs and plays one of the high hearts from table, getting the bad news. Now he finesses in spades and might as well run the queen as he pretty much needs that suit to be 3-2. Once the first two rounds of spades hold, he can finish drawing trumps and wind up taking at least twelve tricks. The only remaining issue now is whether to take the diamond finesse for thirteen winners. If you elect to do so, it will have to be prior to drawing the rest of the trumps as otherwise you risk going down. Since you may well be in the minority in getting to slam, you should be content with making it as your score is going to be well above average.

The scores on the deal are:

North-South	+1430	3 pairs
	+1100	1 pair
	+800	2 pairs
	+710	3 pairs
	+680	3 pairs
	+660	1 pair

You'll notice several things by looking at the results. Not many South players went looking for slam, and that is a common theme at matchpoints where you don't want to be in a high-level contract that is at best a toss-up to make. The pairs who were in 6♡ or 6♠ did not venture a diamond finesse and made exactly twelve tricks. Also, a few Easts bid 5♣ either immediately or after the opponents bid their major-suit game. At teams, -800 would not be too much of a hit with the opponents cold for eleven to thirteen tricks. However, at pairs it's going to be a wretched score, losing out to the E-W pairs whose opponents stop in game. Finally, the North-South pairs that play game in a major *do* need to bring in the diamond suit without losing a trick to get at least a few matchpoints.

Board 14

N-S vulnerable

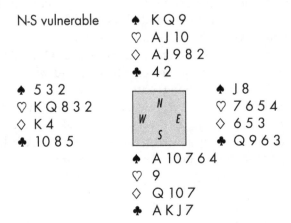

North hand:
♠ K Q 9
♡ A J 10
◇ A J 9 8 2
♣ 4 2

West hand:
♠ 5 3 2
♡ K Q 8 3 2
◇ K 4
♣ 10 8 5

East hand:
♠ J 8
♡ 7 6 5 4
◇ 6 5 3
♣ Q 9 6 3

South hand:
♠ A 10 7 6 4
♡ 9
◇ Q 10 7
♣ A K J 7

Auction 1

North	South
	1♠
2◇	3♣
3♠	4♣
4NT	5♡
6♠	pass

Auction 2

North	South
	1♠
2◇	3◇
3♠	4♣
4NT	5♡
6♠	pass

In the auction on the left, the diamond fit is never fully uncovered as responder supported partner's major after he rebid the four-card club suit. Now 4◇ by South is more likely to be read as a cuebid than diamond support. South's trumps are nothing to write home about but he has the queen of partner's minor and controls in both rounded suits. At this point, North will have to take over as he won't be getting any further cooperation from partner.

The answer to 'Should opener raise diamonds instead of bidding clubs at his second turn?' is 'Yes'. The only time North is going to have four clubs is if he has five or more diamonds, as he would have responded 2♣ with 4-4 in the minors. Responder has a much easier time of it in the auction on the right when partner cuebids 4♣ after supporting diamonds. He knows there is a double fit and might even be wondering if his side have a grand slam their way.

Even in a club pairs game, a majority of 2/1 partnerships would bid the slam as opener soon becomes aware of the double fit and has controls in both unbid suits, while responder has the trump quality.

Board 15

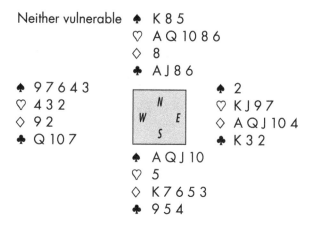

Neither vulnerable

North hand:
♠ K 8 5
♡ A Q 10 8 6
◇ 8
♣ A J 8 6

West hand:
♠ 9 7 6 4 3
♡ 4 3 2
◇ 9 2
♣ Q 10 7

East hand:
♠ 2
♡ K J 9 7
◇ A Q J 10 4
♣ K 3 2

South hand:
♠ A Q J 10
♡ 5
◇ K 7 6 5 3
♣ 9 5 4

West	North	East	South
pass	1♡	2◇	pass
pass	dbl	all pass	

Although some players might have gone with a negative double on the South cards, it will only bear fruit if partner can bid spades. The doubler should have two possible resting spots and with a total misfit for hearts and three small clubs, he doesn't have the type of hand that can play in either rounded suit. Because of that, our responder passes for now, whereupon North re-opens with a double. South finds himself at the crossroads, with the option of bidding spades or leaving the double in. Bidding 2♠ is not a serious contender as opener will likely pass and +140 or +170 won't be a fabulous result when your expectation against 2◇ doubled would be +300 or better. If he chooses to bid the major, responder should invite game by jumping to 3♠.

At the table, South decided with his shortness in partner's major to get whatever he could against 2◇ doubled.

Most players would automatically lead the singleton heart, since it is partner's suit, but there is a reasonable alternative in the form of a top spade. The objective in going that route would be to try and force declarer to ruff, bringing him down to fewer trumps than you have.

Most books on defense mention that you shouldn't lead from an unsupported ace, but opener should have length in spades because he has made a takeout double and the chances of him owning the king of that suit are pretty good.

Most of the field will be leading partner's suit on this hand, so going with a spade lead is a form of 'shooting'. However, as I mentioned in an earlier chapter, such actions are never complete rolls of the dice but will have an element of logic to them.

In this case, a top spade and continuation is easily the best start, as declarer will have to ruff and essentially play the clubs and hearts out of his own hand. Provided North leads a trump on one of the occasions he gets in, all East can manage is four diamonds and one or two other tricks. On a heart lead, South will get one or two ruffs, but the contract will fare much better as declarer will simply play low on the second round of hearts.

The results for this hand are quite illuminating:

North-South	+500	1 pair
	+420	1 pair
	+300	4 pairs
	+140	1 pair
	+100	3 pairs
	−50	2 pairs
	−100	1 pair

The pair that scored +500 may well have led spades. There are several +300s, where South upon getting his heart ruff and noticing there were five small spades on board likely switched gears and played that suit. The +100s occurred when the defense went a heart to the ace, heart ruff, club to the ace and another ruff. This made it easy for declarer once he finally gained the lead as he was able to draw trumps, South being down to just three of them.

Two North-South pairs landed in a spade contract, one of them reaching game. A diamond was almost certainly the lead, after which South can play a club to dummy's eight-spot to bring in that suit for one loser.

You'll notice that East-West went plus three times. That would only happen if South made a negative double and opener bid clubs, whereupon responder tried 3NT with inadequate spot cards in the enemy suit.

Round 6

Board 16 Both vulnerable, you're in the South chair with this rather nondescript collection:

♠ K 8 7 ♡ 9 5 2 ◇ J 6 2 ♣ Q J 8 7

The auction gets underway with:

West	North	East	South
		pass	pass
1♣	dbl	pass/rdbl	?

What do you bid if East passes? Is your choice any different if he redoubles?

Board 17 Neither vulnerable this time, as you hold:

♠ A J 8 ♡ A 10 8 7 3 ◇ Q 8 2 ♣ J 7

The opponents have looked for game and then come to a halt via:

West	North	East	South
1♣	pass	1♡	pass
1♠	pass	2NT	all pass

East-West are playing weak notrumps, for what it's worth. What is your opening lead?

Board 18 Both sides vulnerable for this one, as you're looking at a halfway respectable hand:

♠ 10 8 2 ♡ K 5 4 3 ◇ K Q 7 6 ♣ K 9

Partner has shown signs of life for your side and you need to choose the path you're going to take:

West	North	East	South
1♠	2♣	pass	?

What appeals to you the most on these cards?

Round 6 Discussion
Board 16

Both vulnerable

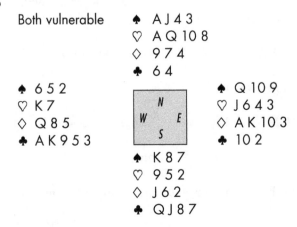

```
              ♠ A J 4 3
              ♡ A Q 10 8
              ◇ 9 7 4
              ♣ 6 4
♠ 6 5 2              N              ♠ Q 10 9
♡ K 7           W       E          ♡ J 6 4 3
◇ Q 8 5             S              ◇ A K 10 3
♣ A K 9 5 3                        ♣ 10 2
              ♠ K 8 7
              ♡ 9 5 2
              ◇ J 6 2
              ♣ Q J 8 7
```

West	North	East	South
		pass	pass
1♣	dbl	redbl	pass
pass	1♡	1NT	all pass

North's double is threadbare point-wise, but all his high cards are in his long suits so I believe a lot of players would take the same action. If East passes, South might bid 1NT; technically that is 8-10 HCP, but he has 7 HCP and what looks like a double stopper in their suit.

After the redouble, however, South should realize that partner has made a light takeout double and his side could be in trouble. As always in pairs, your objective is to go plus or take the smallest possible minus. If South were to bid 1NT under these circumstances, that is the one contract that is absolutely going to be doubled. He should therefore pass, leaving it to North to choose a port in the storm.

When the doubler retreats to 1♡, we can see by looking at all four hands that it can be defeated, but East's spot cards in the suit aren't so hot. He might well bid 1NT and let the opponents off the hook.

With diamonds 3-3, 1NT by East will make seven or eight tricks. If North-South were to play the same contract, East would double and on a club lead the best declarer can do is five tricks for -500.

Results:

North-South	–90	1 pair	–200	2 pairs
	–120	3 pairs	–340	1 pair
	–150	2 pairs	–500	1 pair
	–170	1 pair		

As you can see, slightly over half the time East-West declared a notrump partscore, making anywhere from seven to nine tricks. Four times North doubled 1♣ and ended up anywhere from -200 to -500 (the -340 happened when South passed the redouble and so did North).

Board 17

Neither vulnerable

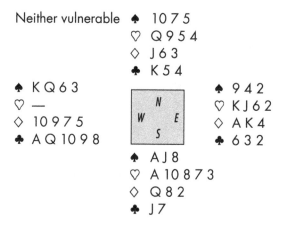

♠ 10 7 5
♡ Q 9 5 4
◇ J 6 3
♣ K 5 4

♠ K Q 6 3
♡ —
◇ 10 9 7 5
♣ A Q 10 9 8

♠ 9 4 2
♡ K J 6 2
◇ A K 4
♣ 6 3 2

♠ A J 8
♡ A 10 8 7 3
◇ Q 8 2
♣ J 7

West	North	East	South
1♣	pass	1♡	pass
1♠	pass	2NT	all pass

Although diamonds is the unbid suit, there is a fair amount of evidence that points to a heart as the best opening lead, even with RHO having bid the suit.

Consider what dummy is going to have. His hand is minimum, since he has passed 2NT. In addition, he can't have balanced distribution since he didn't open a weak notrump. So he is going to be short in one of the red suits. Which one? If he had three-card heart support, you might have seen a raise out of him. So by process of elimination, he will have shortness in hearts.

On a heart lead, declarer has no chance in his 2NT contract. After taking North's queen with his king, he'll then finesse in clubs. North wins and plays back the ♡9, whereupon the defense takes four more tricks in that suit plus the ♠A for down one. On a diamond lead, declarer has enough time to get to eight tricks if he plays the black suits in the correct order.

There will be no unanimity amongst the field on the opening lead for this deal. Diamonds is the unbid suit, although one in which declarer will probably have a stopper. Hearts is South's longest and best suit. Some players might shoot out the ♣J, figuring that is where partner's length is. The 'fourth best' adage is as old as the hills, but still remarkably effective, particularly against notrump contracts.

Board 18

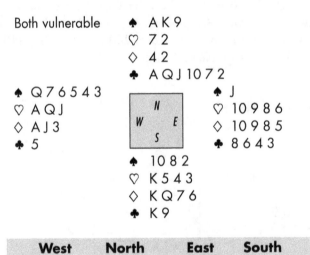

Both vulnerable

	♠ A K 9	
	♡ 7 2	
	◇ 4 2	
	♣ A Q J 10 7 2	
♠ Q 7 6 5 4 3		♠ J
♡ A Q J		♡ 10 9 8 6
◇ A J 3		◇ 10 9 8 5
♣ 5		♣ 8 6 4 3
	♠ 10 8 2	
	♡ K 5 4 3	
	◇ K Q 7 6	
	♣ K 9	

West	North	East	South
1♠	2♣	pass	2♠
pass	3NT	all pass	

South has a decent 11-count, but lacks a stopper in the enemy suit or a five-card suit of his own to bid. What to do, then? The most sensible course is to treat the doubleton king of partner's suit as adequate support, which it will be most of the time. For his vulnerable overcall, North will have either or both of a six-card suit or a very good hand pointwise.

The options would be a gentle boost to 3♣ or a 2♠ cuebid, showing a limit raise or better. As it turns out, North may venture 3NT over the single raise and would bid it confidently if partner were to cuebid.

A few Souths might pass the two-level overcall without three-card support or a high card in the enemy suit, but whenever he shows the faintest signs of life, North-South will reach the notrump game for an above-average score. In fact, ten tricks are available regardless of the lead as declarer can negotiate six clubs, three spades (with the singleton jack dropping on his left) and a diamond. That result would be a near-top.

Round 7

Board 19 On this occasion, you are vulnerable against not:

♠ A Q 6 5   ♡ K J 9 8 3   ◇ 10 8   ♣ 5 3

Your side has slowly climbed upwards:

West	North	East	South
	1◇	pass	1♡
pass	2♣	pass	2NT
pass	3♡	pass	?

Is that all she wrote or should you continue on?

Board 20 You are holding this collection after three passes with your side vulnerable:

♠ —   ♡ Q 9 6 2   ◇ A J 10 8 4   ♣ K Q 7 3

You've got a decent hand, but with extreme shortness in the master suit, spades. Do you open the bidding or pass?

Board 21 For your next decision, you are vulnerable against not with a dreary-looking hand:

♠ 10 5 4   ♡ A 6 3   ◇ K 7 3   ♣ 8 7 5 3

The auction has been:

West	North	East	South
3♡	dbl	pass	?

Oh, joy, a takeout double from partner. Do you have any bright ideas about what to do?

Round 7 Discussion

Board 19

```
         N-S vulnerable     ♠ 7
                            ♡ A Q 5
                            ◇ K Q 9 7 2
                            ♣ K J 10 8
    ♠ K 9 8 4                          ♠ J 10 3 2
    ♡ 10 7 4          N                ♡ 6 2
    ◇ A 5 3       W        E           ◇ J 6 4
    ♣ A 9 7           S                ♣ Q 6 4 2
                            ♠ A Q 6 5
                            ♡ K J 9 8 3
                            ◇ 10 8
                            ♣ 5 3
```

West	North	East	South
	1◇	pass	1♡
pass	2♣	pass	2NT
pass	3♡	pass	4♡
all pass			

This is an auction where the two players sometimes are not on the same wavelength due to a lack of discussion. The general rule for regular partnerships is that when one of them invites game with 2NT, it says, 'Give it up or place us in a minor suit'. Therefore, when opener doesn't repeat one of his suits or pass 2NT, his bid is forcing. There are other reasons why 3♡ should be forward-going. North cannot be sure whether there is an eight-card fit in partner's major. Also, if he had minimum values without the ◇K, he would only have a two-bid hand and might have gone with the three-card raise at his previous turn. His delayed raise, then, is accepting the game try and offering partner a choice between 3NT and 4♡.

Against 4♡, West might lead either a trump or a spade. Declarer will have options in the play, either to ruff his spade losers or set up minor-suit tricks by playing on diamonds. There are no adverse splits, so he will be able to come to ten tricks one way or another.

Results:

North-South				
+650	2 pairs		+170	1 pair
+620	1 pair		+140	1 pair
+600	2 pairs		+90	1 pair
+230	1 pair		−100	2 pairs
+200	2 pairs		−200	1 pair

As you can see with the 200s and 230s, five North-South pairs languished in a partscore, usually making with overtricks. You don't want to be on shaky ground with invitational auctions of this type, and if a bad result happens, you should be hashing it out with partner so that it doesn't occur a second time.

Board 20

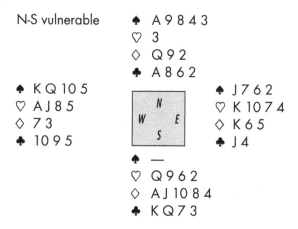

N-S vulnerable

```
                 ♠ A 9 8 4 3
                 ♡ 3
                 ◇ Q 9 2
                 ♣ A 8 6 2
♠ K Q 10 5                      ♠ J 7 6 2
♡ A J 8 5          N            ♡ K 10 7 4
◇ 7 3          W       E        ◇ K 6 5
♣ 10 9 5           S            ♣ J 4
                 ♠ —
                 ♡ Q 9 6 2
                 ◇ A J 10 8 4
                 ♣ K Q 7 3
```

West	North	East	South
pass	pass	pass	1◇
pass	1♠	pass	2♣
pass	3♣	all pass	

You may have heard of the Pearson points rule for whether to open in fourth seat. You're supposed to tally up the high-card points and the number of spades, and if the total is 15 or more, you open. With less than that, you should pass.

It's a useful guideline to follow, especially on balanced hands. However, South has good values and three potential trump suits. He would open in a heartbeat if he were in any other position. He also has potential tricks on defense. Yes, the opponents might have a spade fit, but if they do, the suit will be breaking poorly for them.

As you can see here, East-West do have eight-card fits in both majors but neither of them will play very well. Meanwhile, North-South have fits in the minor suits and could make up to eleven tricks their way. The bidders in fourth seat will get a decent result, while the Souths who pass the hand out won't fare very well.

Board 21

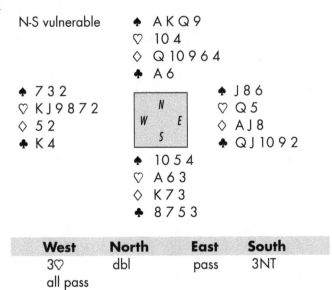

N-S vulnerable

♠ A K Q 9
♡ 10 4
♢ Q 10 9 6 4
♣ A 6

♠ 7 3 2
♡ K J 9 8 7 2
♢ 5 2
♣ K 4

♠ J 8 6
♡ Q 5
♢ A J 8
♣ Q J 10 9 2

♠ 10 5 4
♡ A 6 3
♢ K 7 3
♣ 8 7 5 3

West	North	East	South
3♡	dbl	pass	3NT
all pass			

After West's wildly undisciplined 3♡ opening, North doesn't have much choice but to double. It's not perfect, but what else is there? With 15 HCP, he can't afford to pass and hope for a balancing action from partner that may never come. There is more than adequate support for the pointed suits, even if the hand lacks a third club. The takeout double keeps several contracts in the picture, as we shall see.

When the deal was played, South bid 4♣ which became the final contract and went down three when the smoke had cleared. He was not happy with partner's action, but the fact is that 4♣ just can't be right as four of a minor is never going to fetch you a lot of matchpoints. Now I grant you that no bid is that attractive, but at least either pass or 3NT carries a more lucrative reward if it succeeds.

Declarer can make 3NT by playing East for the ♢J. He also shouldn't assume that West's bid is based on a seven-card suit as it might only be six. Double-dummy, 3NT can be beaten if East switches to a *low* club upon being allowed to hold the first trick, but the chances of that happening are remote.

If South elects to try for a good score by assuming that no game will make and passing 3♡ doubled, that will also pay off for his side. The defense will be able to take three spades and one trick in each of the other suits for down two.

The other feasible action is to bid 3♠ over the double, which is likely to be a seven-card fit and does not risk the four-level. It's not quite so hair-raising as either 3NT or leaving in partner's double Indeed, 3♠ would become the final contract as North doesn't have the tickets to go any further, and it will likely come home with nine tricks.

On some occasions, very light preempts will turn out well, but you'll note in this case that if West had passed, the North-South pair would likely have ground to a halt in a notrump or diamond partscore.

Round 8

Board 22 You're vulnerable against not holding these cards:

♠ Q J 8 6 2 ♡ A Q 5 2 ◇ 9 ♣ K J 3

The auction has gone:

West	North	East	South
	1◇	3♣	?

A good hand, but what is the best way of describing it?

Board 23 Both sides are vulnerable for this hand:

♠ J ♡ Q 10 9 8 7 4 2 ◇ J 10 9 6 5 ♣ —

You're not thrilled with the way this auction has gone so far:

West	North	East	South
2NT	3♣	pass	?

Do you look for greener pastures in the heart suit? Or grit your teeth and pass?

Board 24 Both sides are vulnerable and you have these cards:

♠ K 10 7 5 4 3 ♡ Q 5 3 ◇ Q 2 ♣ A 3

The bidding goes:

West	North	East	South
	1◇	pass	1♠
pass	3♠	pass	?

You certainly have enough for game. Do you feel there might be a slam your way? How would you proceed?

Round 8 Discussion

Board 22

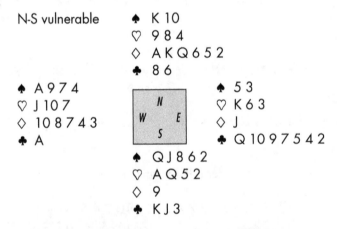

N-S vulnerable

♠ K 10
♡ 9 8 4
◇ A K Q 6 5 2
♣ 8 6

♠ A 9 7 4
♡ J 10 7
◇ 10 8 7 4 3
♣ A

♠ 5 3
♡ K 6 3
◇ J
♣ Q 10 9 7 5 4 2

♠ Q J 8 6 2
♡ A Q 5 2
◇ 9
♣ K J 3

West	North	East	South
	1◇	3♣	dbl
pass	3◇	pass	3NT
all pass			

If you bid 3♠ after East's preempt, everything will be hunky-dory if partner has three-card support. If he doesn't, though, he won't be able to bid 3NT as you have the club stoppers. He'll likely repeat his diamonds as that is your shortness.

The negative double caters to a heart fit and will still get you to spades if North has four of them. If he has three, it's quite possible that 3NT might still be the best contract for your side. It's the most flexible action, keeping notrump as a second arrow in your quiver if partner can't bid either major suit.

Yes, 4♠ could make on this layout, but it's not a gimme by any means. Meanwhile, declarer has no difficulty in scoring ten or eleven tricks in notrump, especially if the lead happens to be the ♣A. There will be some pairs in notrump, but perhaps more in either 4♠ or some number of diamonds.

Board 23

Both vulnerable

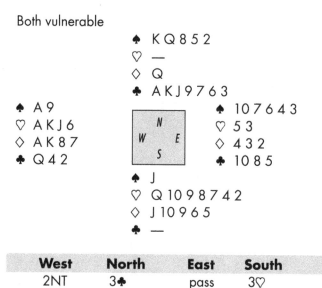

	♠ K Q 8 5 2	
	♡ —	
	◇ Q	
	♣ A K J 9 7 6 3	
♠ A 9		♠ 10 7 6 4 3
♡ A K J 6		♡ 5 3
◇ A K 8 7		◇ 4 3 2
♣ Q 4 2		♣ 10 8 5
	♠ J	
	♡ Q 10 9 8 7 4 2	
	◇ J 10 9 6 5	
	♣ —	

West	North	East	South
2NT	3♣	pass	3♡
dbl	3♠	dbl	all pass

South received a bitter lesson on this deal about the inadvisability of rescue missions. Of the four suits in the deck, opener is least prepared to double clubs or spades, although he might choose to do so anyway. In any event, 3♣ by North is the best contract by a mile and even if West doubles, East might interpret it as more takeout than penalty and remove to 3♠.

Bidding 3♡ on the South hand is a textbook case of masterminding. Partner has entered the fray vulnerable over West's 2NT opening, so shouldn't he have a long and very good suit to do that? Meanwhile your own suit is missing the ace, king and jack, and could be North's singleton or void. Your side is probably headed for a minus, but East hasn't taken a bid and you don't know what the strong hand is going to do. You might as well pass for now, and maybe reconsider if the opponents do double and it comes back around to you.

As you can see, 3♣ would hardly be a disaster and might even make. Both 3♡ and 3♠ are hopeless contracts, with results of -500 or much worse.

The Souths who left partner in 3♠ and didn't go into panic mode got the best results, while those who tried to improve the contract fared the worst.

Board 24

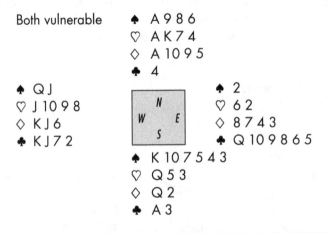

Both vulnerable

North hand:
♠ A 9 8 6
♡ A K 7 4
◇ A 10 9 5
♣ 4

West hand:
♠ Q J
♡ J 10 9 8
◇ K J 6
♣ K J 7 2

East hand:
♠ 2
♡ 6 2
◇ 8 7 4 3
♣ Q 10 9 8 6 5

South hand:
♠ K 10 7 5 4 3
♡ Q 5 3
◇ Q 2
♣ A 3

West	North	East	South
	1◇	pass	1♠
pass	3♠	pass	4♣
pass	4NT	pass	5♠
pass	6♠	all pass	

While opener might feel that 3♠ on his second turn might not be enough, the values are not quite there for either a jump to game opposite what might be a four-card suit or a splinter raise of 4♣.

While his ♡Q is a nebulous value (at least in his eyes), South has a six-card suit, an outside ace and the queen of the suit partner has opened. He is worth the one try with a 4♣ cuebid, after which opener takes over and launches into a keycard inquiry. Since he knows his side has a ten-card fit, South treats his extra length as the equivalent of having the queen of trumps and answers 5♠ rather than 5♡. North could make a further ask with 5NT, but even if partner shows the ◇K, he cannot be sure of thirteen tricks in a spade contract, so he contents himself with 6♠.

The lead from West will be the ♡J and once declarer draws trumps and ruffs his club loser, he will take all the tricks as West cannot hold on to both the fourth heart and the ◇K.

Note that for responder it isn't strictly a matter of deciding whether to go for slam. With space available below the game-level, he can offer up one encouraging bid, after which opener is in a better position to count tricks and take it from there. I would guess that around two-thirds of the South players in a club game would just bid 4♠ rather than cuebid. The pairs that reach slam will earn themselves a very good result.

Round 9

Board 25 You are vulnerable against not, and this is what you've been dealt:

♠K95 ♡A76 ◇K3 ♣Q10653

There's been some action prior to your first turn:

West	North	East	South
1NT	2♡	pass	?

West's 1NT opening was 15-17, and partner's 2♡ overcall was natural. What do you have to say?

Board 26 We come to a new deal with your side vulnerable against not. You're back to your usual standard of cardholding, with:

♠Q3 ♡86542 ◇32 ♣K932

Partner deals and opens the bidding with 1♠. Should you respond or not?

Board 27 Both sides are vulnerable for the final board, and you've been dealt this:

♠A65 ♡A1062 ◇5 ♣AJ942

Your side has a free run for a change, with the auction going:

West	North	East	South
	pass	pass	1♣
pass	1NT	pass	?

Back to clubs or stay in notrump?

Round 9 Discussion

Board 25

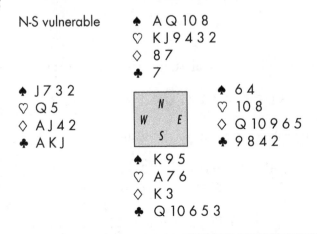

N-S vulnerable

```
              ♠ A Q 10 8
              ♡ K J 9 4 3 2
              ◇ 8 7
              ♣ 7
♠ J 7 3 2                      ♠ 6 4
♡ Q 5            N             ♡ 10 8
◇ A J 4 2    W       E         ◇ Q 10 9 6 5
♣ A K J          S             ♣ 9 8 4 2
              ♠ K 9 5
              ♡ A 7 6
              ◇ K 3
              ♣ Q 10 6 5 3
```

West	North	East	South
1NT	2♡	pass	2NT*
pass	4♡	all pass	

When the opening bid has been in a suit and partner overcalls, you always have the cuebid to promise a limit raise or better. There is no suit to cuebid when they've opened 1NT, so a lot of partnerships use 2NT as a power raise with near-opening values, as opposed to 3♡, which is based on more distribution and fewer points. South's 2NT bid is therefore analogous to the cuebid action that your side would have available in a suit auction.

Knowing that partner will have eleven or more points and support, North decides his 4-6 in the majors is enough to bid game. While the ♣Q is a wasted card and the ◇K won't take a trick, the major suits behave well enough for 4♡ to make.

Some pairs will languish in a partscore as they're not in the habit of bidding game when a strong notrump has been opened against them. However, if partner generally has good cards for his vulnerable overcalls, you won't be risking a minus by inviting.

Board 26

N-S vulnerable

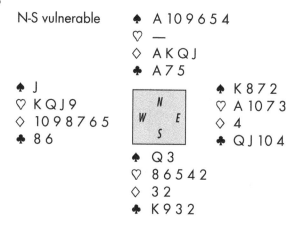

♠ A 10 9 6 5 4
♡ —
◇ A K Q J
♣ A 7 5

♠ J
♡ K Q J 9
◇ 10 9 8 7 6 5
♣ 8 6

♠ K 8 7 2
♡ A 10 7 3
◇ 4
♣ Q J 10 4

♠ Q 3
♡ 8 6 5 4 2
◇ 3 2
♣ K 9 3 2

West	North	East	South
	1♠	pass	1NT*
pass	3◇	pass	3♠
pass	4♠	all pass	

This is the second installment of whether to respond to a one-level opening bid with 5 HCP. On the board from the third round, responder had an ace but shortness in both majors. The outlook is slightly better for South here. The queen of partner's suit will be a useful card, and the ♣K might also be a trick. South at least has a doubleton in spades, and length in the other major if opener happens to bid that suit. Taking all this into account, he elects to bid a forcing notrump.

North jumps to 3◇ and now responder takes a preference to 3♠, which can often be made on a doubleton and in no way guarantees three-card support. How much length partner has doesn't matter to opener, as he has a six-card suit, and carries on to game in spades. East has no reason to lead anything but the ♣Q. Declarer will then play on the trump suit and cruise home with eleven tricks, his only losers being a spade and a club.

There likely won't be much in this board when you look at the results. A few pairs might not reach game, but most Souths will dredge up a response and then it will be a piece of cake.

Board 27

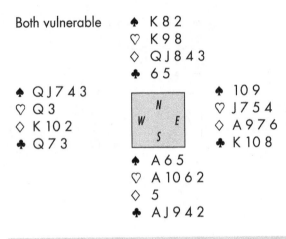

Both vulnerable

```
                    ♠ K 8 2
                    ♡ K 9 8
                    ♢ Q J 8 4 3
                    ♣ 6 5
  ♠ Q J 7 4 3                      ♠ 10 9
  ♡ Q 3             N              ♡ J 7 5 4
  ♢ K 10 2       W     E           ♢ A 9 7 6
  ♣ Q 7 3           S              ♣ K 10 8
                    ♠ A 6 5
                    ♡ A 10 6 2
                    ♢ 5
                    ♣ A J 9 4 2
```

West	North	East	South
	pass	pass	1♣
pass	1NT	all pass	

Responding 1◊ would have been an option for North, but with both major-suit kings, he decides to respond 1NT.

If your singleton were in a major suit, you would likely want to skedaddle out of 1NT and into a minor. With the actual hand, though, notrump could easily be the right place to be. A major-suit lead would not concern you, and since partner hasn't raised clubs, he probably has length in diamonds. Also, notrump is the highest-paying contract, so you elect to pass.

East's best suit is diamonds and he might well lead them, but a heart or even the ♠109 doubleton are options as well, since neither major suit has been bid. Any red-suit lead turns out to be good for declarer, as a diamond will be into his five-card suit and a heart will end up giving him four tricks just in that suit alone. When North plays on clubs, he'll find out they are sitting favorably and he can bring that suit in for four winners as well.

While 2♣ by South also makes without much problem, he could lose up to four tricks, and +110 is the best-case scenario; meanwhile notrump makes anywhere from +120 all the way up to +180.